CHILD
OF MINE

CHILD OF MINE

WRITERS

TALK ABOUT

THE FIRST YEAR

OF MOTHERHOOD

EDITED BY

CHRISTINA BAKER KLINE

HYPERION

NEW YORK

Library of Congress Cataloging-in-Publication Data

Child of mine : writers talk about the first year of motherhood / edited by
   Christina Baker Kline.
       p.   cm.
     ISBN 0-7868-6233-5
     1. Motherhood—United States.   2. Childbirth—United States.
   3. Mother and infant—United States.   4. Mothers—United States—
   Biography.   I. Kline, Christina Baker, 1964–   .
   HQ759.C554   1997
   306.874'3—dc21   96-46325
                                                           CIP

Book Designed by Holly McNeeley

FIRST EDITION

10   9   8   7   6   5   4   3   2   1

FOR HAYDEN AND WILLIAM

It is only because I . . . had a baby that I discovered
    this place
where voices do not expect to be heard,
trees routinely falling in forests
where no one comes to listen—except the other like
    voices,
trapped in the same circumstance of motherhood.

NINA BARRETT, *The Playgroup*

CONTENTS

Acknowledgments

Child of Mine was conceived over lunch with my agent, mentor, and friend, Beth Vesel, on a spring day in 1995 when my son, Hayden, was six months old and hers, Liam, was four months old. My sister, Cynthia Baker, a new mother herself, was of invaluable assistance in developing the proposal and reading manuscripts. Cathi Hanauer gave generously of her time and wisdom. Leslie Wells, my editor, guided the book with an expert hand.

I would like to thank Nina Barrett, Andrea Chapin, Casey Fuetsch, Marita Golden, Katie Greenebaum, Kim Holman, Elizabeth Oness, Judith Pascoe, Natalie Pearson, Luisa Perkins, Tory Perry, Ariadne Platero, Caroline Press, Deborah Rogers, Jessica Sabat, Tracy Chutorian Semler, Susan Squire, and Rebecca Walker for their valuable input.

My husband, David Kline, is the unseen partner in my labor. His encouragement and advice are manifest in the book. Tina Baker and Carole Kline, my mother and mother-in-law, contributed their seasoned perspectives. My neighborhood new mothers' group stimulated ideas and provided communal support. Rabbiea Barran, with grace and good humor, made this project possible by taking care of Hayden and his brother, William (born *in medias res*), while I stole away to work.

Finally, I would like to thank the contributors themselves, many of whom took risks in the candor with which they told their stories. "I worry about what my son will think when he reads this," one writer said. "But I have to believe it's better to tell the truth, in all its complication, than to perpetuate a myth. Someday, I think, he'll be better for knowing."

CHILD
OF MINE

INTRODUCTION

CHRISTINA BAKER KLINE

It is three o'clock on a crisp October morning in Manhattan, and everything is quiet. In the glow from the streetlights I can see my six-week-old son in his bassinet, his tiny form moving slightly as he breathes, and I watch him carefully for a minute to make sure he's asleep. It's been another one of those nights. Twice already since his eleven o'clock "bedtime"—my husband and I call it that to delude ourselves into thinking there's a difference between day and night—he's woken crying to be fed, and twice I've nursed him to sleep in the rocking chair by the window.

Now, leaning back and closing my eyes, I try to relax. "Come to bed," my husband murmurs, but it's no use; I'm wide awake. I may be on the baby's schedule, but I'm nowhere near as adaptable as he is. I lean over to the bedside table and turn on the small lamp, then reach for one of the books stacked up in a pile like research for a term paper: *What to Expect the First Year, Bringing Up*

Mommy, Your Baby and Child, Diary of a Baby, Mothering Heights. I've already read most of them (especially the sections that pertain to my baby's age and stage), and, for all the help they've been in different ways, none is exactly what I'm looking for.

I open the novel I was reading before my son was born—one without a single baby in it—but it fails to hold my attention. Though I'd like to say otherwise, I have little interest, at the moment, in reading about anything other than what I'm going through. But I'm tired of the self-help manuals for new mommies, the how-to guides, the chirpy and reductive parenting magazines. Standing at the window, I look across the street at the rows of apartment windows and imagine another sleepless mother holding a baby in a dimly lit room. How many of us are there, I wonder, each in her own home, perhaps far from family, without ready access to other mothers who might provide a sense of community? How many of us are wondering how we'll ever make sense of this experience on our own?

As I think about the woman with her baby, I realize how much I want to know what women in my situation are thinking and feeling. I want to hear about their ambivalence, longings, discoveries, joys, and fears, and gauge them against my own. Most of all, I want to get a sense of how other mothers have forged a path through the sometimes perilous wilderness of their own trepidations and doubts and the opinions and beliefs of others, from experts to their own families. With a craving as urgent as my longing for chocolate in the early stages of pregnancy, I want to hear the voices of other new mothers, telling me I'm not crazy—or alone. Talking to me.

———

No one could have told me, when I found out I was pregnant for the first time, how overwhelming, exhilarating, and lonely becoming a mother would be. I thought I would handle it the way I had handled other momentous events in my life, like planning my wedding or finding a job: I would read everything I could get my hands on about the subject, make lists, and talk to everyone I knew to find out how *they* had done it. It took me months to realize that this strategy, while practical, wasn't going to be enough. The lists I devised in my head—sign up for Lamaze and baby-safety classes, buy a crib and receiving blankets and diapers, paint the spare room—gave me a sense of control, but control wasn't necessarily what I needed. What I needed was confirmation that my experience was as complex and profound and terrifying as it was beginning to seem.

When I gave birth, I felt as if I had been granted entrance into a private "Mothers Only" club of people just like me—and, at the same time, that I had never been more alone in my life. I found that much of the literature available to new mothers presents parenting as a how-to chore, a connect-the-dots task that is pragmatic, rational, task-oriented, and forward-progressing. These books and magazines create a standard reality, an objective benchmark by which mothers can assess their skills and their progress. They tell you what is "normal"—what to expect each month of the countdown to birth, and then how your baby should look and act as she grows. The issues are clear-cut, and the message is plain: Don't panic, motherhood is manageable if you follow these simple rules. As a new mother, it was comforting to hear this, but I kept wanting to read between the lines. Anne Lamott's *Operating Instructions: A Journal of My Son's First Year* was one of the few first-person accounts I found that acknowledged what the writer Judith Schwartz calls the "map of ambivalence" every mother carries. Lamott's quirky, idiosyncratic recounting of her experience as a single mother of a colicky baby left me hungry for more first-person accounts.

While many aspects of motherhood are universal, the core of each woman's experience is highly, resolutely individual—and therefore deeply personal. For this reason, there is a limit to how much help new mothers can be to each other. We are all so invested in our own particular choices; we are so susceptible to admonishment and fearful of being perceived as inadequate. The new mothers I talked to provided me with companionship and camaraderie, but rarely revealed what they really felt about what they were going through. Neither, I admit, did I. We could not seem to articulate in person what we might have said on paper. When we gathered over coffee or in playgroups, we talked about our babies' stages, their health, the food they ate, programs at the Y, our own weight and fitness, breast-feeding, working, and child-care. We danced around the scary issues, our fears about our children's development, our anxiety about our own stagnation (or workaholism), our suspicion that other mothers were more confident, more organized, more efficient, more productive than we were. Certainly, with babies crawling around demanding food and toys and attention, we rarely had a moment for sustained discussion. But I think we were also afraid that by admitting our own vulnerabilities and ambivalence we would be exposing too much, opening ourselves up to judgment or, worse, condemnation.

Judgment comes from the most unexpected places: an old woman in the grocery store, scolding me for taking my baby out without a hat; an acquaintance who tells me that my seven-month-old son looks like "a football player, not an intellectual"; my mother, whose well-intentioned worrying stirs up anxieties that keep me awake at night. My mother brings the assumptions of a different generation as well as the child-rearing techniques she used on me to any discussion. When, at four months, my son began rejecting my breast in favor of the bottle, my mother, a breast-feeding revolutionary from the Sixties, refused to condone the possibility that I might wean him. She believed that my baby would be stunted for life, disengaged and detached, without this vital connection. I tried for weeks to make it work, prolonging the agony for myself and for my baby because I wanted to appease my mother and other breast-feeding advocates who scowled openly when they saw an infant with a bottle on the street. I wanted to do it right. I often wished I had other voices to listen to. What were my peers thinking? How did other new mothers feel about this?

To a large extent, many of us feel that we can't talk about the parts of our mothering experiences that touch us most deeply. Without a clear sense of direction, it is easy to get lost in the maze of expectations, spoken and unspoken, others have of you. Fearing that we are abnormal, demented, or weird, it is easier for many of us to remain silent about our deepest fears and darkest thoughts, and even to deny that we have them.

"Perhaps we share stories in much the same spirit that explorers share maps," says Gloria Steinem in *Revolution from Within,* "hoping to speed each other's journey, but knowing the journey we make will be our own." As a new mother, I have been struck not only by how much I want to hear the truth about other women's mothering experiences, but by how few such stories are available on the bookshelves. This scarcity of resources underscored the isolation that I—and, I found, other new mothers—felt during the weeks and months after childbirth. So I asked a diverse group of women from around the country to write personal narratives on a specific aspect of new motherhood that interests them, from preconception to the end of the first year.

These narratives, as I imagined them, would explore the powerful physical, intellectual, and emotional experiences that women go through as mothers—the complex realities and real-life details of mothering. I wanted women to reveal through writing those things they couldn't or wouldn't say out loud, to delve into and interpret what they were really feeling—and to put those thoughts and feelings out there for the rest of us to mull over, argue, or identify with. In providing a forum for many voices, many realities, many conflicting ideas and experiences, I hoped to dispel the notion that certain feelings about becoming a mother are appropriate, and others are not. Ambivalence, or a highly personal and complicated response to the totemic notion of "motherhood," colors nearly every conversation I've had with new mothers, but it remains a taboo subject for serious discussion. In asking women to write subjectively about how they live and what is significant to them about becoming mothers, I was asking them to set sail from a safe harbor into uncharted territory.

Having a baby can be terrifying and isolating, especially as extended families living in the same town become a thing of the past. *Child of Mine* is about reconstructing that community, with all its wisdom, compassion, and support, for new mothers today. The narratives comprise a diverse array of voices—enriching and contradicting and echoing each other, and offering different perspectives on the same issues. They range from intensely personal stories to those that are more overtly philosophical or political. Some are practical; others theoretical; some optimistic and others cautionary. Though they vary greatly in style and content, the essays share several basic qualities: Rooted in personal detail, they are thoughtful, thought-provoking, probing, analytical—and accessible. Together, as they farm the emotional terrain of new motherhood, they expand upon the definition of the term "motherhood" and examine what mothering means in the world today.

Having a baby is different for everyone. Because this book contains the stories of many women—from a poverty-stricken mother in rural Vermont to an accomplished career woman in New York to a single black journalist in Los Angeles to a stay-at-home mother in San Diego— each reader can find her place in it, and will discover the similarities of her experience with women outwardly different from her. Noted fiction and nonfiction writers, as well as other women—lesser known, but with compelling stories to tell—submitted essays for consideration. Many came to me through word of mouth; two contributors even emerged from my neighborhood new mothers' group. All in all, these narratives reveal how becoming a mother changes a woman's life no matter who she is, where she lives, or how she identifies herself.

Though my objective was to include essays depicting a wide variety of backgrounds and experiences, the content of the pieces received ultimately determined the shape of the book. For a variety of reasons, some pieces I commissioned—on multiple births, having a child with disabilities, grief over losing a child, biracial issues, and lesbianism—never came to fruition. Or the subject shifted; women who originally intended to write on subjects such as body image, circumcision, and infertility found themselves moving on to other ideas. In "The Eternal Now," Alisa Kwitney sheds light on this strange fact of new motherhood: It is a constantly evolving state, and with each stage that passes, obsessions dissolve and re-form. Accordingly, though some writers do tackle "issues"—Jane Leavy on adoption and gender, Teri Robinson and Cathi Hanauer on breast-feeding, Meri Danquah on the legacy of abuse, for example—many others have chosen less well-defined topics.

It is important for the reader's experience that the pieces in this collection have literary and narrative power. To that end, I asked contributors to tackle, within the general confines of their chosen topics, the choices, dilemmas, sacrifices, self-doubt, and range of emotions that are embedded in their own mothering experiences. *What did no one tell you about becoming a mother that you would like to have known?* I asked them to consider. *What have you never admitted before, even to yourself? What issues have been difficult to talk about? How did having a baby change your life—before, during, and after the baby was born? What is exhilarating, shameful, joyous, despairing, fascinating, monotonous about being a mother?*

I asked contributors to explore intensely personal aspects of their lives. More than a few writers went through draft after draft, uncovering layers of emotion, shifting nuance and tone, before they felt they had accurately captured their experience. Many pieces evolved over the course of a year, as new mothers developed some perspective and their children grew. Some never came together. But for a number of writers, the intensity of the experience of reliving the first year was cathartic.

"I never imagined writing this piece would be such a difficult journey," one said. "I feel that I have come to terms with that time in my life. I can put it behind me now, and move on."

In asking tough questions—of themselves, their partners, their mothers, feminism, or society in general—contributors to this book redefine what it means to become a mother for a new generation of women. "I am known mainly for somewhat humorous writing, but I have no interest in glossing my first year of motherhood in that way," novelist Sarah Bird wrote in a letter indicating her interest in contributing to this book. "I hadn't considered writing about any of this until I was specifically asked to tell the truth, to break the silence, to admit the possibility that the equations of motherhood may not always balance out. I am grateful for the 'permission' to treat this as seriously as it deserves to be."

"If there is a secret to my writing," another contributor, Susan Cheever, remarked, "it is that I don't care about answers." The narratives in this book offer few conclusions or absolutes; instead, they reveal and explore complexities. Without glorifying or simplifying, these essays probe the subjective. From them emerges a multidimensional picture of motherhood today, with all its complications, stresses, and joys. Ultimately, this book will, I hope, become part of a new and vitally important conversation among women.

I. ANTICIPATION

LIFE WITHIN LIFE

NAOMI WOLF

I. Omens

We are in Italy, in a farmhouse outside Todi, a town made of stone the color of baked bread. We are visiting a house populated for a week with New York's disaffected: pale young people with dark sunglasses. The old sweet smell from the beds of lavender and thyme, and the bending olive trees, make a strange contrast with the lounging, bone-thin figures still sweaty from the plane trip.

A guest, a curator with the smooth blond hair and sharp features of her caste—a woman who has said nothing unusual in my hearing for three days—suddenly, apropos of nothing, leans over, looks with compassion into my eyes, and, still smoking, says with absolute conviction, "You're pregnant."

I resist this statement as a New Age shot in the dark. Nonesense; but nonetheless: Something is off. Was my cycle disturbed by travel? I wonder. By the rich food we've been eating, by the antibiotics I'm taking for a sore knee? My eyes in the mirror look like nothing I've ever seen before: yellowish and blurred, almost drunken. This must be what the guest sees; but surely it has been caused by too much red wine, by jet lag—by anything, I half-pray, but that thing.

Even as I wait, day by day, the question is always at the back of my consciousness. We sightsee, or nap in our high, white-plastered room, but I continually feel something indisputable: a sickness in my gut. It is a kind of nausea that is entirely new to me; it has a richness to it, as if I got sick to my stomach by overindulging in honey. If Midas touched a mountain of round, rich sweets, I feel as if that's what I would have in my belly.

As the days pass I feel an odd stirring of hope. I feel far away from the panic I imagined I'd feel in a situation like this, almost disloyal to myself while I begin to have stirrings of loyalty to something else. Every time I check to see and come back with no news, I experience in spite of myself a little thrill of joy.

II. Alien

At four and a quarter months I am due for a sonogram. I appear at the medical building that sprawls over a part of Virginia that only recently, my cabdriver tells me, was all apple orchards and dairy farms. Passed from one smiling white-coated woman to the next, I end up stripped to a gown, and lying under the cold hands of a technician. There are no windows anywhere. The technician, at once pert and professional, wipes a chilly gelatinous substance on my belly.

I am alone, and filled with trepidation at who or what I will encounter on the screen.

The technician moves the sensor over my abdomen

like a computer mouse. It feels odd to be, oneself, the informational field. On the black-and-white screen tumble gray-blue clouds, like the clouds of creation.

An oval emerges at length out of the chaos. "There you can see the top of the fetus's skull," the technician says without inflection. This is, after all, a routine part of her day, though to me it is the introduction of a lifetime. My heart starts to race.

She moves the mouse mysteriously over my abdomen, guided by some data that is unclear to me. "There you can see the back of its skull. Perfect," she remarks as colored digits and a measuring graph superimpose themselves over the image of this tiny chalice, the magic habitation of this creature's sensibility. "Right on track—just as big as it should be."

The skull vanishes, lost in the fog. "See that string of pearls?" she asks in her practiced voice. I squint at the screen. Out of the formlessness appears a sinuous x-ray serpent. It could be a strand of pearls, but the pearls of a fairy tale: a living, luminous thread. It shoots, undulating, through the darkness. I cannot recall ever seeing anything so beautiful. "See, each vertebra is there. Again, no visible defect."

Now the creature assembles itself against the mouse, manifesting its parts virtually with a will, as if it is battering against the membrane between us to make itself known to me. A hand appears, a forearm. The fist is utterly relaxed. There is nothing to grasp at yet. A foot, a footprint, white against the blackness; thin, ghostly shank, clumsy toes.

As I see that hand and that foot, something irrational happens; a lifetime's orientation toward women's rights over fetal rights lurches out of kilter. Some voice from the most primitive core of my brain—the voice of the species?—says: You must protect that little hand at all costs; no harm can come to it or its owner. That little human signature is now more important than you are.

The technician presses harder into what I would have guessed was some vital organ of mine; the creature— annoyed? playing?—shoots away from the sensor. We lose sight of it. "It's turning over," she says. "Somer-saulting." Then we find it again.

I scarcely breathe. Now it is reclining on its back, practically resting on its elbows, knees bent, in profile, like the stone gods in Mexico. Its face is in profile too, a perfect, eerie, conventional snub-nosed baby profile.

Then slowly, as if it is looking straight at me—as if to warn me not ever, ever to take for granted its familiar-ity—it turns its face forward. The sweet baby profile dissolves and reconfigures itself. The down all over my skin rises.

The eyes are not human eyes, but the overscale al-mond eye-shields that have characterized images of ma-levolent space invaders for forty years. The vast, sightless eyes, the flat skull-nose and delicate nostrils, the bulging brow, the thin cruel line of the mouth—this is the face; this is where the mythology about aliens must come from. And in a way it is not surprising. Now that we've lit up the dark regions of the world with electric-ity, the fairies have fled. In Malaysia, they say that the ghosts vanished after the electric lights came on. What place is left for us to populate with alien beings except the dimensions of the womb?

"Do all four-month fetuses look like E.T.?" I ask the technician in a voice that tries for lightness. I will have to love this child whether it comes out looking like E.T. or not.

She laughs. "Oh, sure. I should have told you ahead of time. They all look like that. We get so used to it we forget to mention it—but parents are often spooked when they see the face for the first time."

Wiped off, and dressed in my street clothes, I hail a cab. I leave the building holding a full-color printout of my baby, the photo taken in its reassuring baby profile. This must be the convention for these images—to hide the alien helmet discreetly from the camera's eye. The technician presented it to me already framed in a cheap plastic cube, suitable for hanging on my kitchen wall. It looks like a souvenir from Disneyland. The fetuses all look like that, I comfort myself. But I can make only the weakest of efforts to remember this baby's face as more conventional, less "other."

For, of course, it looks like an alien because it *is* an alien. Its true face is the one that turned the eyes of a whistling cosmos right at and through me. It is a baby in my belly but it is also a time-glider poised in inner space, ensouled already. Or to become ensouled, perhaps, at some moment that I will be unaware of, as I am steaming broccoli or reading the morning paper. Emergent from God alone knows where, suspended on its journey that I can never fathom, of course it is an alien; of course it looks like that.

I hang the picture on the nail in the kitchen that holds the Maurice Sendak calendar—"Alligators All Around" is the scene for July. But I look at it from time to time and know that, while this is the guise it will assume so I can love it and take it through life, its first face is older, stranger, and something derived from far beyond my species. "Oh, look at its nose!" exclaims Yasmin, my upstairs neighbor. "Sweet, sweet little hands, all cuddled up!" I look, and I will cherish that nose and those hands. But I am not fooled. And I could swear that, when it looked at me, it conveyed this directly: Yes, I will be a baby eventually: small, helpless, and humanly lovable. But not yet.

III. Immersion

Hugely pregnant, I find myself one weekend at a shabby West Virginia resort, taking an aqua-aerobics class. We have made the trip because I need to feel babied myself for what could be the last time for a while. I straggle down the walkway beside the pool, balancing my belly carefully to guard against falling. The tile is slick under-foot.

All the other members of the class are elderly or mid-dle-aged women. Each one's body shows signs of lassi-tude and gravity. The only exception is the instructor, a young woman who is a fit five months pregnant. As she calls for questions before class begins, I slip into the pool and ask quietly what modifications I need to make, if any, given my eight months' pregnancy.

"Eight months!" she exclaims. Her voice echoes off the damp tile walls. The council of elders in the water turns toward us, their faces sympathetic and eager. "I'm tempted to ask you to get out of the water and show yourself to us! I'd like to see what I'm going to look like. Be sure to let me look you over when the class is done," she says. I slink down a little further in the water, which suddenly feels cool and makes my skin clammy.

"Do you know what it is?" bellows a woman from a corner of the pool to the instructor. "Not yet!" she yells back. All at once, the conversation bounces loudly from gray head to gray head.

"How much have you gained so far?" one calls out.

"Twenty pounds!" the instructor shouts.

"I had twins, I gained fifty!" another declares.

"Boy or girl?" asks a third.

"She's got a girl," asserts one more, "and she," the sybil says, pointing at my abdomen as I crouch underwater as if that could provide me with some privacy, "has got herself a boy."

"Really, how can you tell?" someone inquires.

"Well, because," says the sybil with what can only be called a squawk, "She's so *pointy!*"

As class gets underway, I struggle to move against the anger that has hardened in my chest. I seem to be in a frenzy in the water, trying to bend lower, leap higher, and do my submerged jumping jacks with more push against the resistance than any other members of the class. I thrash, I churn, I send myself flying through the waves. I feel that I am caught up in a paroxysm of physicality: I am asserting my own strength—my youth, my health—against the dreamlike sense of submersion that has begun to overwhelm me.

For all at once, the dreamy watery interior has become a nightmare. Looking up at the healthy instructor, five feet overhead, who is still more maiden than matron; and around at the gray heads and loosened bodies of the women in the water—women who have done their job and given the world their births—I realize I am with the latter now; it is as if this is a Dantesque allegory in which different levels have different meanings, and I have *slipped*. My sense of having an individual self melts away and I feel that I will, if I stay in this soft, lax water, become indistinct in the element of femaleness. Don't you know, the little waves seem to lap at me, that no woman is unique? Don't you know that this is your delusion? You are, they are, all liquid: the unbounded matrix out of which new life comes endlessly creeping.

My throat seems to close up, I feel so panicky. Out through the sliding-glass windows I can see the hard wintery world, the level I used to inhabit before I slipped into this luxurious swamp. That, I realize with a biting sense of nostalgia, is the world of reason, individuation, selfishness, the clash of ideas—the world occupied by, if not the rightful possession of, men. Down here is the slack, dreamy, physical mother-realm. My lust for the upper level, where I have lived all my life, is suddenly stronger than I can bear.

Flashing through my head, like the series of images people are said to witness before death, is a set of movie stills of what I want that is beyond me now:

I want to be addict-thin, smoking a black Gauloise, bending over a marble-topped table at an outdoor café in Les Halles. I want to be wearing a scarlet suit cut like a diamond. I want to be brushing ashes off my cuffs and arguing with a smart man, and winning.

I want to be speeding up the drop of Highway One in a car with the top down. I want the ocean wind to force itself against my face as I push the throttle down harder than the wind can blow.

I want to be packing my backpack at dawn, folding the three pieces of clothing that are my possessions, and opening the door on a desert road. I want to glance down at a lovely sleeping back and leave without saying goodbye.

Instead I am here, drowning, and knowing that what I am experiencing is the purest misogyny. This is it.

Just because I too am a woman does not mean I cannot experience this suffocating fear and hatred.

"You can do laps now around the pool," says the instructor, "and if someone is in your way, you can just go around them." I pass each swimmer in a burst of water and speed, running for my life, for *my* life.

IN SEARCH OF THE MATERNAL INSTINCT

ELISSA SCHAPPELL

Playing "house" as a child, I always wanted to be the baby, never the mommy, or the teenager—the baby, or the dog. Outside of Siamese cats I have never parented anything or anyone, not lovers, friends, or students. I have always been the kind of person other people take care of. So when I discovered the horrendous flu I had been nursing for two months was in fact pregnancy, I was both pleased and terrified. Mostly terrified, because at no time in my memory have I felt any maternal urges. I couldn't escape the idea that having a baby meant being tied down, it meant having to conform to society's expectations of what it meant to be a mother: June Cleaver with a baby on her hip dusting the house in sensible heels and a frilly apron, her wrists perfumed with pot roast, her eyes brimming with tears of boredom. Being a mother meant put away your playthings and play house *for real*. That meant balanced checkbooks, balanced meals, and a balanced personality. All very scary and uncharted territory for me, but I wanted to go there.

Needless to say, people were surprised when I announced I was pregnant. Upon hearing my news there was an uncomfortable silence, followed by congratulations and exultations of joy, but that silence reverberated in my head.

"Are you going to keep it?" someone inquired in gentle horror. Some joked, "Are you serious?" Others were more blatant: "Are you scared? Aren't you worried about your depression? Aren't you afraid of becoming like an Anne Sexton mom?" The answer to all these was, *You bet*.

In some abstract way I had at times thought of being a mother, but I wondered about how the extreme pain of labor would change me, and if I had a child wouldn't it surely put me through the brat water torture I put my parents through? I wondered about the existence of the maternal instinct when I read in the newspaper about a teenage mother leaving her hours-old baby wrapped up in a newspaper on the steps of a church. I wasn't horrified. I could imagine her fear, her terror of being solely responsible for a young life, and that worried me. Weren't we as humans wired with certain instincts that prevented us from snuffing out our race? Wasn't the maternal instinct, the instinct to protect and look after, built into all women? And if so, where were my maternal buttons?

If I trusted that at some point—say, when they handed my baby to me for the first time—the instinct would kick in and I would feel something other than dread, I wouldn't be so scared to be a mother. It was just that uncertainty of not knowing. No one knows what kind of parent they will be until they become one, and who knows how you change, how horrible and brutal you can become? I imagined one day just up and leaving my child as it sat in a filthy diaper smearing feces on the walls and howling like a rabid dog stuck in a trap. I was afraid that the child would eat me whole, swallow my life, and that I'd be nothing but what it fed off.

My other fear was that the instinct would kick in fast and furiously, and I'd become a brain-dead turbo-Mommy with a Kleenex tucked in my sleeve rattling on about nothing but constructive play and growth percentiles. I'd stop working and simply sit and gaze all day at my miraculous progeny. I'd lose my friends and start hanging out only with other mothers who snacked Cheerios out of tiny plastic bags, smelled faintly of baby vomit, and carried fat wallets stuffed with photos of startled-looking infants.

With one exception, none of my close friends had children. I felt like a pioneer, especially since this child would be the first grandchild born in the family on either side. The pressure was on. My comfortable status as the family bad girl was being compromised. I couldn't carry on the way I had. I didn't want to be one of those crazy alcoholic moms whose kids never dare bring friends home after school, but neither could I imagine being an earth mama who invited all the neighborhood tots over to do nature projects like making macaroni necklaces and Popsicle igloos.

I couldn't help measuring myself against my own mother, who assured me her pregnancy had been a breeze, birthing was a joy, and raising children (my sister Andrea and me) had been a marvelous adventure. I couldn't imagine driving all the carpools she drove, reading the millions of bedtime stories, chaperoning all

those field trips to terminally dull places like the Frank-
lin Mint, let alone baking all those damn brownies for
bake sales I forgot to tell her about until the night before.
I would be a very pale and bad imitation of her—if I
were lucky. You see, children instinctively like and trust
my mother. Not me; I have always been tongue-tied and
awkward with children, because I feel they see right
through me. Children know when you are lying to
them, not about obvious stuff like "The moon is made
of blue cheese," but more subtle and terrible things, like
"Of course mommy and daddy will never get a divorce"
and "There's no reason to be afraid of death." Children,
like horses and big dogs, sense when you are afraid of
them and rush in for the kill the minute they smell fear
on you.

It was rapidly becoming apparent that I would need a
miracle to bring this motherhood routine off. Where
were those maternal feelings I was counting on growing
inside me as our baby grew? And how was the baby
growing? Could it hear the Nina Simone records I
played for it? Along with the feeling of a pudgy fish
barrel-rolling in my belly, I wanted to feel the gentle
insistent pull of maternal affection. As I ran my hand
over my stomach, pressing the heel of a tiny foot with
my hand, I wanted to feel love, not wonder.

The third trimester began and I started to really
worry. I had hoped that some marvelous hormone
would be percolating through my system, but it wasn't
happening. I had hoped for the basketball-shaped stomach, the calm, serene smile and warm, pinky glow other
mothers had. Instead I was the Venus of Willendorf,
pregnant from the nose down, my skin so broken out I
resembled a cursed adolescent, which, coupled with the
fact that my hands were so swollen I had to remove my

wedding ring, made me look like a fat unwed teenager. I was miserable.

I hoped Lamaze class, and hanging out with other pregnant women, would jump-start my instinct. It quickly became clear that Rob, who had been reading all the current baby books, was going to be the teacher's pet—a fact that probably would have thrilled and re-lieved most women. It just heightened my feelings of inadequacy, and when the teacher assured me that "With Rob as your coach you'll have nothing to worry about!" I snapped, "Oh yeah, he's shaping up into mother of the year, a regular Mildred Pierce."

I couldn't help myself. I felt lousy that it was Rob who was eager to practice our breathing exercises at night. It was Rob who shoveled broccoli florets onto my plate and wanted to talk baby names. What made it worse was the fact that all the women in my class not only seemed overjoyed to be pregnant, but they knew what they were doing. They talked about the classical music they played for their in-utero infants, the kinds of prams they had purchased, and the high contrast mobile that would get your baby on the cognition fast track. They used French-sounding words like layette and bas-sinet with impunity.

Feeling low, I phoned my mother. After inquiring about my obscene water retention and recent craving for molasses cookies, she asked, "So how many times a day do you go into the nursery and just look at the baby's things?"

"All the time," I lied. I could feel my mother's loving approval beaming back at me from hundreds of miles away, and I felt guilty for lying to her, guilty for being emotionally deficient. I wanted to feel close to my mother, and I wanted to share my experience with her, but I wanted it to be the great experience she swore she had with me and my sister. I wanted her to tell me everything would be okay, but I didn't want to tell her the terrible truth. That with the exception of a tiny pair of red leopard-print shoes adorned with pompoms, which I kissed on occasion (which has as much to do with my love of shoes as anything), I felt no upsurge of affection for the crib, or the little clothes. They reminded me of doll clothes, and how I always wanted to play with stuffed animals instead of Barbies.

Perhaps I didn't have the instinct, but it seemed my body was built for birthing. I went into labor on my due date, and had a relatively easy (if there is such a thing) birthing experience. Rob, whom I had half-hoped would faint, or at least get woozy, was, as my Lamaze teacher predicted, an excellent coach. After the final push I felt the baby slip out and in a moment it was lying on my chest, and I was staring at my daughter. *Now*, I thought, *now, cry with joy*. But I didn't. I couldn't. It wasn't simply the surprise of seeing who it was that had been inside me, upside down and underwater, or that she was as purple and pointy as a crayon—it was the way my daughter looked at me, imprinting me in her brain. She seemed to look right into me, as if she knew me. It was the most terrifying and beautiful moment in my life, and it was gone like a soap bubble the minute my mind touched it.

Ensconced in my hospital room that evening and alone for the first time all day, I put her to my breast and she sucked hungrily, painfully. As she sucked I had the vertiginous sensation of being lofted up on the high end of a seesaw, then I felt as though I was falling through space, my heart racing. This feeling during nursing would stay with me for months. I felt diminished, claustrophobic, like my life was being drawn away. Could she sense how confused I felt—would my apprehension and stress make her colicky? She wrapped her hand around my finger tightly, and even though I knew it was only a reflex it seemed she was staking her claim, saying, You belong to me.

I tentatively unwrapped the swaddling which made her look like a sleepy caterpillar. I saw that her fingers were long like my mother's. She had my father's big toe, and my little sister's eyebrows. She looked just like pictures I'd seen of Rob as a newborn. She seemed to be put together of pieces of all the people I loved, so why did she seem so foreign to me? Did she really resemble them, or was I just trying to make her familiar?

I carefully placed her back in the bassinet and buzzed the nurse to come get her. I didn't trust myself to be alone with her. I felt guilty for sending her back, but as soon as she was gone I sank back in bed in relief and closed my eyes. I imagined Isadora sleeping in that fluorescently lit nursery under the watchful eye of nurses who could hear the tiniest cough and detect a heart murmur at a hundred paces, and knowing she was safe I fell into deep, dreamless sleep.

Rob was the first of the new fathers to arrive the next morning. He seemed so alive, vibrating the way the sun seems to when you stare at it too long. He was hard to look at.

"I went running for the first time in months," he crowed. "It was just amazing. I felt like I could lift a Volkswagen. I couldn't run fast enough. So, where is she?" His eyes darted around the room as if he half-suspected I'd stowed her under the bed or perhaps bedded her down in the sink.

"In the nursery," I said, feeling a little defensive.

"She's fine. They came and got her . . ." and before I could finish my sentence he was out the door. I could hear the eager squeak of his sneakers as he trotted off to retrieve her.

I felt stoppered, paralyzed with guilt. I had actually taken her back to the nursery after the morning feeding because I desperately wanted to shower. Alone in the room, I realized I didn't want Rob to hurry back. I was envious as I remembered how easily he had plucked Isadora from her bassinet yesterday when we first settled in my room. The confident way he hugged her in his arms, pressing her gently against his chest. As he held her I envisioned her heart tinier than my thumb, and his heart the size of his fist. He sat down in a chair with her in his arms and just gazed at her. "I have a daughter," he chuckled incredulously, his eyes sparkling with this new intimacy. And there in that room I witnessed my boyish husband metamorphosing into a father. He closed his eyes as if to savor the moment and in minutes he was asleep, with his daughter peacefully cradled in his arms. I lay there watching them with tears in my eyes. I was afraid to even hold her.

I insisted on carrying Isadora out of the hospital. After all, I was her mother. I wrapped both arms around her, clutching her to my chest. Flushed with endorphins, I felt fierce. I nearly shook with the anticipation that someone might try to tear her away from me, the adrenaline so thick I could choke on it. I might as well have been a snarling pit bull straining on its leash. Another mammalian instinct had shown itself the night before during the 2:00 A.M. feeding. After a few initial sucks Isadora started to cry. I didn't know what to do. She didn't want to nurse, and she wouldn't listen to my pleas of "Oh dear sweet baby girl please don't cry, please don't cry." Finally, instinctively, I started rocking her back and forth, back and forth the way I recalled seeing chimpanzee mothers rock their young in the zoo. I had no maternal instinct, but the animal instinct seemed alive in me. Perhaps I couldn't raise Isadora properly, but I could protect her should our neighborhood ever be overrun by wild dingoes.

At home a steady stream of family and friends poured in to gaze at Isadora and marvel at Rob's baby-handling skills. "How lucky you are to have such a great husband! He's such a wonderful father!" they proclaimed, as if they expected that when I brought Isadora home he might, like a giant angry hamster, try to eat her.

After two and a half months I discovered that I could differentiate between Isadora's "I'm-starving" cry and her "Hello-I'm-soaking-in-it" cry. I believed I knew which smiles were gas and which were for me. I realized I had been learning her language. I wanted to understand her, to know her. Away from the world of scolders and baby manuals, and in our own quiet way, we were bonding.

One gray winter afternoon several months later, Isadora was teething and was in an uncharacteristically cranky mood. I had a crushing headache and hadn't slept well the night before, so we were a very unhappy pair. My mother had suggested I massage Isadora's gums. So all day long I'd been rubbing her gums and letting her gnaw on my fingers, all to little avail. Feeling helpless, I put a Nina Simone CD on the stereo, one I'd listened to a lot while pregnant. I held Isadora in my arms, her chest against mine, one arm wrapped around my neck, her other held out to the side, her fist enfolded in my palm. I started to sway with her, not rocking, but danc-

ing. She held her head up, and for the first time all day
smiled back at me. I wondered if she remembered the
music from the womb. I spun slowly in a circle, and
dipped her. She laughed, and even though she'd
laughed before, this was the most beautiful and surprising sound I'd ever heard, like a butterfly giving a rasp-
berry. Her fingers squeezed my hand. We slow danced
for a long while. She rested her head on my shoulder
and sighed. Were the music and dancing just a distraction from her pain? Was it feeling close to me, sensing
how much I loved this music and loved sharing it with
her that calmed her? I tilted my head toward hers, feeling the warmth from the back of her neck on my throat.
The day's anxiety fled my body at her touch. I felt like
she belonged to me—like I was truly her mother. Felt
like this moment alone with her, each of us comforting
the other, was sacred.

I confess I'm still not crazy for other children. But I
can't explain how the weight of my daughter in my
arms calms me, sustains me, and sometimes makes me
deliriously happy. I'm not convinced that every woman
has a maternal instinct, but that we all are born with the
capacity to love and nurture. I can tell you that sometimes when I am out on the street without Isadora I feel
a sharp pang of loss that makes me stop and catch my
breath, and I wonder if that maybe isn't my maternal
instinct stretching its wings a bit. And though I still
stumble when I say, "I'm Isadora's mommy," it's not
because it doesn't feel right, but because I can't believe
my good fortune.

Waiting for Brendan

Judith Schwartz

Let me begin this story as it ends: I'm in the hospital and my newborn son is napping next to me. I find myself also floating on the edge of sleep, and as I half-doze I'm aware that this new face—this tiny face in all its infinite variation—is carving itself into my consciousness. It fills my internal mental screen as soon as I close my eyes. This little face, and the new little person it belongs to, is becoming not just familiar but intrinsic to me. Somewhere in some deep, nearly inaccessible part of myself, I am working at knowing him.

I feel a complete acceptance of this baby that, I'm sure, comes in part from how long I had to wait for him. My several-year saga in babymaking has been a big lesson in how little I could control. It began easily, effortlessly when, without articulating any kind of plan, we tossed aside the birth control and I immediately got pregnant. It then took a tragic turn when, despite watching everything I drank, ate, and breathed, I miscarried at ten weeks. Then we waited a year (not having a baby I knew I could control). And then I couldn't conceive. This was a story I couldn't make sense of, a plot where I couldn't adjust to the twists. I knew, theoretically at least, where this would lead, but that denouement—the birth of a baby—seemed increasingly out of reach.

The problem once we figured it out, was simple: My hormones weren't cooperating. Unfortunately, they decided not to cooperate in a way that didn't respond to medication. We knew I could conceive, but statistical probability does not a baby make. Month after month I was left to wonder why I kept coming up empty despite doing all the right things.

I was still struggling to get over that first loss, yet each month's disappointment compounded it. Getting pregnant meant not just having a baby but *undoing* the miscarriage. I'd see a pregnant woman and wonder what superior knowledge or talent had enabled her to achieve this extraordinary state. A large belly came to represent all that was lacking in me and in my life, the embodiment of all my failings. Those bellies, great with their monumental task, were everywhere, it seemed, just to spite me. I became so sensitive to others' reproductive status that I could tell when someone was pregnant merely by the way she settled onto a chair or tilted her head.

Those months of waiting wore on me, and on my husband, Tony. Our wish could only be fulfilled through our bodies, but my body wasn't doing its job. Longing for a baby wasn't so much a strain on our marriage as it was a constant presence, like a somber tune always playing in the background. There was a poignancy to our love that bordered on the melancholy, a richness but a sadness too.

Sex was both proving ground and refuge. I was depressed, but willed myself to see sex not as a chore but a realm where I could stretch out, feel pleasure, be whole. Take me, I would say to my unhappiness, take me but spare this wonderful love. Take anything, but this.

For far too long I felt on the wrong side of time. Those days I had not one but two times of month—the fertile time and the menstrual time—two poles of possibility and impossibility; illusion and disillusion; activity and stalemate. In health books for women this biological alternation is often described, brightly, as a cycle that's always beginning. In my experience it was less circular than a linear progression; it was more like a sine curve, undulating with the flux of mood, a trajectory moving into the temporal horizon and toward some theoretical vanishing point.

I had my own private chronology, with its own important dates and privately memorable markers: how long we'd been trying; how long since the miscarriage; how old the child would have been. Each season, each month, referred back to some memory of pain. No wonder I felt so *off*. Following the calendar wasn't an orderly task imposed by a doctor, like a prescription. Since apparently we were "fertile," the rules of medicine were less relevant than the rules of luck.

When it was my time of month we would make love a lot. That was a nice thing. In earlier months we pretended to ignore the biological imperative and would take to bed without needless commentary, loving each other with the ringing clarity of spontaneous desire. The potential intervention of fate only added an extra charge. But as time went on we could no longer hide behind the veneer of happy coincidence. We began to drop hints to each other about when might be a propitious moment, when to unhook the phone. Preoccupied, we became oblivious to the outward signs of domestic neglect: the dishes, and unpaid bills piling up around us. We would walk about the house, ostensibly tending to chores, passing each other and feigning disinterest even as the awareness of impending sex blanketed the room. The furtive glances and unspoken intentions gave us the sensation of having an affair. But, as married lovers, it was not the sex itself we wished to conceal, but the crude lack of subtlety in our shared dream.

After a while I came out of the depression. Time, I finally realized. It's only time that stands in the way—time until we find a fertility drug that works or until my cycle straightens out on its own. So maybe I won't win any awards for procreative efficiency. I could either resent every month of waiting or enjoy it, reveling in the time Tony and I had together. I began to live this new reality, to live in time as though I had only just discovered it. And within a few days of visiting a specialist who did no more than take my history, little Brendan was underway.

But that's my narrative, not Brendan's. The truth is, I knew early on that this baby transcended me. As soon as I began to feel this child growing within me, I realized it was time for me to let go of my anxieties, and my investment in this drama. This wasn't about me anymore. This was about something else, something much larger. And perhaps the learning I had done could connect me to that larger thing. I could let myself give in to the trust that I was beginning to feel, a trust that grew inside as a kind of parallel development to the baby. Getting pregnant had become such a preoccupation that I began to regard having a child as a personal challenge. But the birth of this child-to-be wouldn't be my triumph; it would be his own.

I do know that my extended prelude to pregnancy helped me through the labor. Whenever I felt myself heading toward the pain, I would remind myself: This baby is a gift. Labor may be scary and the contractions may hurt, but I just have to keep myself moving from one minute to the next. For it's the same truth I learned while waiting to conceive: All that stands between me and this baby is time.

I went into the birth well-read and well-schooled, expecting one of those infamous protracted first labors. What I got was a speeded-up version of my lesson in lack of control. First there was the usual: the contractions. How can you describe them? Inexorable. Excruciating. A kind of radiant pain. To me it felt that I was forced to keep running barefoot around the same track, about a third of which was paved with nails. I had my own mental tricks to rely on: Think of the baby. Think of how long it took to *get* here.

Then there was the *not* so usual. The nurse had been wandering out of the cramped examining room (the birthing rooms were filled up), leaving Tony to preside over some impressive high tech equipment and to watch me writhe as, once again, I'd round the bend. A boring, routine case, I could imagine her thinking. Until Tony called her back: Why did the monitor drop with each contraction? Out of nowhere, Dr. Warner and a resident appeared. Fetal distress, because the umbilical cord was constricting the baby's oxygen supply. My case was no longer routine.

Then the staff found me a room. They also found me an IV, an internal monitor, an oxygen mask, a narcotic (to take the "edge" off the contractions), and a surgical team ready to pounce at any minute to do an emergency cesarean. I was also ordered to stay in one position. This was a scenario we had not rehearsed. But I remained surprisingly calm. Why? Because I had no choice. All I could do was go around the endless track and confront the inevitable nails. Tony was left the task of worrying.

We were preparing ourselves for a long, difficult haul. But, miraculously, I dilated quickly, going from three to nine centimeters in about fifteen minutes. The room's atmosphere suddenly changed from anxious watchfulness to boisterous encouragement: Dr. Warner said it was time to push the baby out. I was so exhausted by that point that I swear I fell asleep between pushes. Count to ten, everybody yelled. My pushes felt like feeble grunts but they all cheered me on wildly nonetheless. And with a slight nudge of the forceps, Brendan was born. I'd like to say this was a grand, transforming moment, but all I felt was relief.

A day later, the theatrics of Brendan's arrival fades in significance; I can feel its impact diminish with each retelling. What's important is that everything turned out fine, and he's now dreaming peacefully by my bedside.

His is a shallow sleep, a sleep as delicate as his lovely skin; and as tenuous, I can't help but imagine, as his hold on this outer world. His face is wonderfully inventive and uncensored; I watch his expression change with startling rapidity. Over the last several hours he's had all sorts of new experiences—the chill glare of fluorescent lights, the sound of his father's voice, his first feeding at my breast—and I can see them all play across his features: Pursed lips turn into a grimace, which then fades into a rakish half-smile. It's as though he were running through the memory of his emergence into the world.

I watch this little other person, allow myself to enjoy his otherness. For Brendan is himself. He is not me. I have to let go of whatever dream of mine got mixed up in my wish for him while waiting. For the nine months of carrying him we were of one body, and I could live the fantasy that I could be completed by him. But not anymore. Not if we are each to grow, if we are each to continue the growth that began when he was indeed a part of me.

Despite Brendan's size he's alert and, so the nurses say, focuses unusually well for a newborn. And he's already a flirt, reserving his sweetest, wide-eyed look for his lady pediatrician. And as he works at suckling he occasionally pauses to make a funny panting sound which I could only describe as a series of rapid, exuberant sniffs. It's as if, in his pleasure, he can't quite keep up with his own breath, or that he's trying to say something the only way he knows how. I come to expect this rhythmic noise, which I find incredibly endearing. To me, it's almost like a musical motif—his very own theme song.

Let me end this story as it begins.

POKEGA, FROM THE HEART

MARCELLE CLEMENTS

Nipples. Bottles. Diapers. Wipes. Receiving blankets. Booties. Maybe six or so plain little undershirts. Onesies.

"What are onesies?" I asked. I was writing down the list of objects to take with me to Texas. My friend Nancy, who was also waiting to hear that her birth mother's labor had begun, had already packed. She and her husband were driving to Massachusetts and could bring whatever luggage they wanted in the trunk. But I was flying to San Antonio, and who knew what to bring for one's self? After all, there was no way to tell exactly when the baby would be born, how long the trip would last. The baby bag, though, carefully organized, wouldn't take up all that much room. I didn't want to bring anything excessive. I felt tremulous about bringing anything at all, in case it all went wrong and the birth mother changed her mind and—without dramatizing in the least—my life would be simply shot to hell for good. That's what I thought about while pack-

ing. Will she change her mind? Will the birth go well?
How will the baby be? Will she change her mind? Will
everything be all right? And: I can't even bear to think
about it not being all right.

"Ask the case worker at the agency if the hospital
will provide formula." Nancy spoke in a low, unin-
flected, and slightly constricted voice, because she knew
as well as I that this is a situation in which it isn't possible to relinquish yourself to your emotions and stay
sane. People are fond of talking of joy around the time
of a birth, but joy in this case is purely theoretical, con-
ditional, pending. Luckily, as prospective adoptive
mothers rather than "regular" mothers, Nancy and I had
no tradition of happy optimism to enforce, and we could
be frank with one another. In fact, I now realize, talking
with women who are "irregular" mothers was my first
experience of real freedom of thought around the subject
of children.

But then I got a call from the two nineteen-year-olds
who would henceforth be known as "my birth parents." Each of them in turn said, "I think you should
come," and then everything happened so fast and so intensely I didn't have to continue pondering the problems
of arrangements anymore. I took my packed bags down-
stairs, got in a taxi for the airport. In San Antonio, I
picked up a rented car equipped with car seat and, only
getting lost once or twice, got to the motel and checked
in. It was almost 3:00 A.M. by then. I hadn't even sat
down when the phone rang. "We're at the hospital,"
Steve said. "Come over right away." Considering my
nonexistent sense of direction, and the utterly deserted
nocturnal landscape, it is really astonishing that I managed to zap up the road, careen around the complex of
hospitals, and turn into the right parking lot in a flurry

of flying gravel. By the light of the EMERGENCY sign, I saw a good-looking kid standing there, wearing a baseball cap and smoking a cigarette, and it was Steve. "Not bad," he said. Five hours later, Angela gave birth and I was, if you will, a mother.

My son Luc, now a year and a month old, sometimes points his index finger at me and, in his most eloquent, emphatic tone, asks, "Mama?" Is that for me? I can't be too sure, since he also often says, with no less eloquence or emphasis, "Pokega!"

That's what I think about when people ask, "Is he yours?" As any adoptive mother has noticed, there are often persons who will refer to someone's "real" child, and never think twice of it if they haven't been taught all those fin-de-siècle adoption words which strike some people as so comical. *Birth mother. Biological family. Semi-open adoption.* Lately, perhaps because I've heard Luc's magisterial "Pokega" and "Mama" so often, I no longer internally flinch quite so hard when people will say, "Where was his 'real' mother from?" Perhaps I do still withdraw somewhat, but that seems reasonably self-protective to me.

Angela was more generous in granting me maternal rights. She had chosen me, after all, as his mother, just as I had chosen her. Indeed, she coached me, as much as possible. It was she, for instance, in the course of one of our frequent calls in the weeks before she gave birth to Luc, who first asked me whether I had gotten what I needed to bring to Texas.

"No," I admitted, somewhat sheepishly.

"Why not?" she asked.

"I don't know for sure," I said, thinking it was probably fear, just plain cowardice.

"Well, hey, you better get going," she said.

I've kept a few things, one or two of the little onesies, for instance. And, from the first day on, I took pictures of Luc, and of Angela and Steve, and some of all of us together, and of their family and friends, and their apartment building, and of Nikki, who has been our caseworker at the adoption agency, and of the judge and the courthouse. Am I his "real" mother? My guess is that I must feel mighty real to Luc, just as he cannot feel anything but real to me, as he blows raspberries and kisses, leans over the high chair and carefully drops tiny morsels of lunch overboard, or sings to himself in his crib when he's supposed to be napping, one plump leg draped over the side. He still often wears onesies, and I guess one of his realest attributes is the phenomenal amount of laundry he generates, especially now that he's up and about on his feet. Still unsteady, he toddles and waddles and staggers at top speed through the apartment, busy, busy, busy, emptying drawers whenever he gets enough of a head start, provoking the cat or being stalked by him, putting puzzle pieces almost in their place, and neatly segueing into hide and seek.

Hide and seek, in a way, is every adoptive family's game. Who does Luc look like? All of us, I imagine. Angela and Steve, and all the rest of his birth family, and also we who surround him now and whose facial expressions, mannerisms, tone of voice, and moods he so naturally mimics. In that sense, as in many others, we all share him still. Sometimes he reminds me very much of a photograph Angela gave me taken when she was twelve, which I am keeping for him.

I often find myself musing about Angela, wondering how she's doing, whether she's all right, whether her mother is being nice enough to her, whether she's still

eating all that unbelievable fried seafood they love in
Texas, whether her figure has gone back to normal since
the pregnancy, whether she's being more careful now
with birth control. Angela's twenty-first birthday was
last week.

Every once in a while, she telephones me. Maybe
they're moving and she wants to be sure I have her new
address, or just to talk. She gives me news of her friends,
and her family, and of her two-year-old. Sometimes I call
her. Often, I think of her and I don't allow myself to
call her. I don't want to have any relationship that will
become confusing for my son as he gets older. So following the agreement we both made with the adoption
agency, I mostly restrict myself to the photos I'm to send
once a month for six months, and then once a year for
five years.

But I've had the sense, all along, and Angela says she
does, too, that we will always feel connected to one another, in some warm and powerful way. I guess we'll
have this connection until one of us dies, and maybe
beyond as embodied in the life of this child who will
continue the world when we are gone.

In many ways, we make up our families as we go
along. Almost from the start, there is the favorite babysitter, the nursery school teacher, the best friend, or the
delightful creature yearned for as the best friend, the little boy across the hall who becomes our first crush.
Twenty, thirty, fifty years later, these people live in our
memories, many of them stilled in the perpetual smile of
youth, the eerie freeze-frame of loving memory. They
are the family of the heart, the real family, as poignantly
and affectionately remembered as the siblings and uncles
and second cousins who populated the world of our
childhood, if we were lucky. As time goes by, we add

to our family, but less and less as we grow older. We know, now, what the implications are. Do we want to become intimate with this stranger? Do we want to for-ever be bound? This is what makes so many decisions difficult, in adulthood, and none, perhaps, as complex and risky as adoption. Will we allow ourselves to love and be loved by this tiny genetic foreigner for whom we will be all of family?

Friends who are not familiar with the new world of adoption ask me if I'm not scared to keep Angela in my life. "What if she shows up at the door some day?" they ask.

Angela and I agree that there should be well-estab-lished boundaries. But adoptive children thirst to hear where they come from. My guess is that at some point during or after Luc's adolescence, the time will seem right for a meeting. I want him to know that he was desired, that his birth was a wonder, and that he was always the object of love and care. Surely, to give An-gela news of the child she gave birth to, to let her know that he's all right, and that he's loved, can only lessen the anxiety and fear and remorse.

Surely, he'll want to know some day that she wanted news of him, that she cared and wouldn't threaten whatever sense of identity he develops, that she'll be willing to be there for him when he needs her and not before.

And, let's be frank, what is the real fear my friends feel on my behalf? I think it's either that she will one day want him back, or that he will one day wish he were her son and not mine. But eventually, these things happen anyway. She'll have those feelings and he'll have those feelings and I'll have mine, and we will all three of us have to live with that. I'm betting my happiness on it and my child's. Sure, the stakes are high, but aren't they always? I don't owe him any less.

And don't I owe Angela anything, or myself? To me Angela is not a generic "birth mother." She has all the specificity of her humanity and our shared circumstances. Early in the morning of a specific, hazy spring day, she gave birth to Luc, who specifically weighed seven pounds, thirteen ounces. In the birthing room, she rested on a pillow they'd allowed her to bring from home. The pillowcase had a leopard-skin pattern. Steve was there, and a young cousin with bare feet and blond hair down to her hips. There was a friend Angela had met while they were both pregnant, who had relinquished a baby girl the preceding week. In the middle of the night, her mother and her sister arrived from another town. All through the night, there was not a single generic moment.

We all alternated spending time sitting next to Angela. In my hand her hand seemed small, her fingers thin and a little cold. Sometimes she closed her eyes and a half hour slipped away. There was time to talk but the night sped by with astounding rapidity. It was cool and the lights were low. Sometimes the room felt almost as if it were in motion, as if it were a train or a boat and we were all on a journey. The pace of the journey seemed regulated by a machine next to the bed that broadcast the sound of the baby's heart. The beating of the baby's heart became for me the counterpoint to every conversation in the room. I couldn't stop listening to it. It made every exchange seem resonant and intense.

It was all so odd, and yet I felt everything so viscerally. I knew this was a very strange thing I was living, but I felt hyperalert. Now that I think of it, I guess that sound, that heartbeat, let me know not only that he was alive, but that I was too. And that feeling—in case you're wondering whether I did the right thing—has never gone away.

And what did Angela feel? The mirror of my feelings, I think. Relief, excitement, fear, loss, hope.

He was born not long after dawn. She put him in my arms and I was holding him when he opened his eyes. She was moved by how thrilled I was.

I'd been told by the hordes of people who give one unsolicited advice in these circumstances exactly how I'd feel at that moment.

"As soon as you hold the baby, it's as if he were your biological child, there's no difference," is how one version goes.

"When you first hold the baby, you feel that he's a stranger. It takes some getting used to," is what other unsolicited advice-givers will tell you.

No. I didn't immediately feel euphoric, maternal, as if I'd been born for this and my whole life had led to this moment. Neither was I alienated, assailed by second thoughts, weirded out or freaked out.

I felt completely engaged and fascinated. How amazing it was to hold him. What an astonishing sight he was.

We had talked once or twice a week for most of her pregnancy. We got to know one another very, very well. I think I understand how she feels about giving up this baby. "I feel," she told me—and I think this was her greatest gift—"I feel as if it's less a loss than a new beginning, for all of us." And I think she understands how I feel about the miscarriages I had when I was trying to get pregnant. We know a lot, in other words, of one another's family fantasies. But also, I know she somehow manages to stay incredibly skinny, despite all that fried food. She knows I gave up smoking. I know she loves to swim. She knows I like to travel. I know the kind of books she likes and she knows the kind of music I like. In fact, while she was pregnant, I'd send her cassettes and she'd put Walkman earphones on her belly. The baby loved Mozart, how do you like that? And also Duke Ellington.

It was Angela's insistence that I come to Texas for the birth and I'm really glad I went, for me, and for her, and for Luc. Maybe he had a sense, right at the start, of this larger family, that there was not one but two sets of eyes, smiles, arms to hold him in a special motherly way. It was Angela who showed me how to feed him and burp him. I have photos of the first time we diapered him, on his first day of life. He is tiny and red in the middle of the frame of our two sets of hands. Some day he'll look at all these pictures taken in Texas and I hope what he'll see is there was nothing secretive or shameful about his beginnings, and that the first two women who were his family had come to be one another's family as well.

What I don't know is, when I brought him back to the motel from the hospital a few days later, did he then become in any way aware that now there was only one set of arms and eyes and smiles? We all did the best we could, that I know. So did he: The very first night, lying in the big bed next to me, he smiled. He really did, then closed his eyes and to the astonishment and disbelief of all my advisors, slept through the night.

Maybe all that one must surmount only enriches this version of motherhood and that's the meaning of the journey that begins in loss, veers toward life again in that moment when one signs a piece of paper creating a legal relationship with a child, and culminates when one is anxiously packing a bag for the trip to another woman's delivery.

Yet it seems as if the more adoption is common, the more it is criticized. In this era when "regular" parenthood is idealized more than any other institution—including marriage, religion, nationalism—why is this other profoundly compelling desire to raise a child so often seen as preposterous? Adoption is as old as biological parenthood. There has never been a time when there haven't been orphans raised by aunts, grandparents, strangers. There has never been a time when there haven't been mothers who ensure their children's welfare by placing them with another family. Yet the more adoption becomes accepted, overtly longed for, allowed to fill the great need of some, the more it appears to enrage others.

And it must be in this state of strange rage that viewers lend any credibility to the wicked, sadistic shadow plays evoked by the talk shows, those implausible melodramatic spectacles that get the highest ratings, in which every birth parent is either an extortionist or a victim, every adoptive parent an exploitative or an easily exploited subject, every child a forbidden prize.

One of the biggest changes, and what is perhaps most threatening to many people about modern adoption, is the lack of secrecy. What was once clandestine is now publicly disclosed; where there was shame there is now pride. It's increasingly unnecessary to base the present on an unacknowledged past, thereby condemning all parties to a false reality in perpetuum. Perhaps as these children grow, new traditions will begin falling into place, and packing that small bag to go to the other end of the country, or of the world, to pick up an infant who needs a parent will become as common and thrilling a romance as it should be. And it is a romance, an act of pure faith, a thrilling (albeit somewhat taxing) reality you feel you have created deliberately, with no imperative but the love you want to give and receive.

As for me, for a long time I couldn't bear to even consider the possibility that another woman could have been the one pulling into the dark hospital parking lot that night. I am not a superstitious person, nor a fatalist, really, but I do feel there was some natural dynamic, some break in the randomness, some right pattern that fell into place on this night, as if there was a fate or a will or a choice on all our parts, whichever you prefer—I don't care—that brought these particular people, and no other, together. There's only one Angela, one Steve, one Luc, one me. We are it. And at this moment there is certainly no doubt in my mind that I am the only creature who could or should have been the audience for Luc's pranks, the mediator in his relationship with the cat, the chief dispenser of hugs, kisses, and futile exhortations to enter the world of language by way of French and Cartesian thinking, the nevertheless attentive and grateful recipient of his Pokega and Mama declarations. It's terrible to contemplate anything else. But, fortunately, I don't have to: We already have a past together, even though the present now takes up all the available space. And that, in my view, is real family.

MOST RELUCTANTLY MOTHER

HELEN WINTERNITZ

I have a child now and some of the typical accoutrements of motherhood, a house and a husband and a schedule. This is an expectable enough state for many a woman, but one that for me is shocking when I muse on it, given my predilections and my past.

As a young girl I did play house, although it was an unusual variation of the age-old game. The setting was the muddy cow pond behind my home in the Connecticut countryside, and my playmates all were boys. We made houses not for dolls but for the frogs that lived in our ponds. Like primitive potters, we molded slabs of hard mud into walls and ceilings, building houses with large, frog-friendly doorways, buttressing the walls with sticks and carpeting the floors with field grasses. We would then catch a frog. Lifting a mud roof, we would carefully deposit the frog in its pondside domicile, retreat a distance and watch until it hopped back into the pond. To our disappointment, no frog ever returned to take up permanent residence.

I was as good at catching frogs as anyone in our small gang, my two brothers and three other boys who, living half a mile down our country road, were our nearest neighbors. I had no sisters. My parents treated me like any of the ubiquitous boys, allowing me to roam the woods, swamps, and streams, to pursue turtles, grass-hoppers, and foxes, to look for wild berries, hollow logs, caves, and any adventure that might be waiting in our sylvan world.

Unfettered by expectations of how a girl should act, I was a thoroughgoing tomboy, to use a label to which I object. I do not believe a girl who likes the wild should be characterized as a kind of boy. In my youth, I found it far stranger that any child would want to stay inside on a summer's day and play with dolls' petticoats, while pretending to be a mother. For me, such a future was unimaginable.

The worst present I received as a child was an extra-large doll from grandparents who did not understand my yen for the wild. The doll's head sprouted luxuriant nylon curls and its plastic face froze in an eternally be-atific smile. The doll was dressed in velvet and lace that would have made some other girl swoon. I was misera-ble. Most inappropriately girlish gifts could be tucked into dark corners and forgotten, but this big, stuffed doll was unhideable in the house. With the boys, I secretly carried the doll off into the woods. Thinking the doll a useless and even offensive object, best done away with, we skinned it and scattered its stuffing and other remains among the forgiving trees. I was spared from symbolic motherhood.

The boys and I were not barbarians, for we knew that a doll had no feelings, that it was merely a thing. Almost all living creatures, animals, we treated with respect, as if they were, in a rudimentary way, our real children.

Catfish and earthworms were exempt, at first. The boys and I went fishing with wood-pole rods, hooks baited with worms at the community swimming hole. The fish were smallish and we could jerk them up, writhing on the hook, and swing them onto land. In order to kill the fish as quickly as possible, to shorten their suffering, we would bash their primitive, bewhiskered heads with stones. One day, this scene for me suddenly turned gruesome: the desperately flailing fish, the smashed fish heads, the blood on the muddy stones. I never fished again. The moment had separated me from the boys. Instinctually, I was different. That my instincts one day would push me to having a baby would have astounded me back then, and for many years to come.

I remained very much in the male camp. Shepherded by my dutiful mother, I went to shop at the outset of each school year for a supply of dresses and a pair of respectable shoes. I hated those trips. Shopping and the rest of the domestic arts were uninteresting at best.

My mother was a housewife of the 1950s. She was a good mother first. She wrote delighting poems for our birthdays and waited for the time when she would have her own time to become a painter. She also was as brave as I would ever be. She was stricken by cancer, and I never heard her complain about the pain or the injustice of the disease. She died when I was thirteen. I was hysterical with grief for weeks, until I gradually gathered up all the toughness I had learned in the Connecticut woods and stopped crying, outwardly. I had to keep going and I did, with all of my own and my mother's gentleness locked up inside of me.

I traveled far from home and its confines. When I was twenty, I was off to Africa, where I lived and traveled intermittently for the next ten years, first as a teacher, then as a journalist. The time was the 1970s and no one questioned a woman traveling alone, working as a professional. I had plenty of desire for various men I encountered along the way, but no desire to marry. I had wild oats to sow in a wild place. The farther I ventured into the continent, into its mountains and deserts and fastness, the farther from the usual or expectable, the happier I was.

Early on, I climbed Mount Kilimanjaro. Having made the final ascent of the snow cone's 19,000 feet at night when the ice was firm and safe, I beheld dawn seeping, then flooding over the whole of the East African steppe, turning the world below from the color of pale smoke to glowing green. I lost my footing on the way down the cone, sliding on the ice, terrified at first and then joyous as I realized that no cliffs threatened my life and that I could guide myself with my mountain ax. I slalomed to the snowline without problem, except that I tore the backside out of my only pair of pants. I was intoxicated with my freedom.

Why would anybody give this up for settling down, getting caught in the bonds of family, in domestic details like worrying about pants or furniture? Children caught my attention from time to time, but not always happily. As I went, in one African country or another, children loved to shout "foreigner" at me in whatever language they spoke, curious and delighted and often collapsing in laughter at the sight of such strange white skin on a human being.

Children did seize my deeper emotions once, although horribly, when I witnessed a famine in the

Horn of Africa. The youngest victims were the most wretched. The eyes of the starving children were fixed in motionless stares as if they were watching something a thousand miles away. And, when they were dying, the light would slip noiselessly from their eyes, leaving blanks in their faces. The parched, cracked earth was littered with little corpses wrapped in rags. Hot breezes teased the rags into the air with a lively fluttering. I wrote furiously about these children, wanting impossibly to do better than the wind, to bring them back to life. I did not stay, though. I kept going.

From Africa, I went to the Middle East to write a book about living in a village on the West Bank. The Palestinians and Israelis then were fighting with stones and submachine guns for control of the tension-ridden land. To appease the Islamic fundamentalists who made up one faction in the village, I wore long skirts to conceal my body and scarves to cover my hair so that I came as close as possible to looking like an unusually fair Arab. The one impediment I could not overcome was the fact that I had no baby. The villagers learned quickly that I was thirty-seven years old, an age at which any woman there would have raised half a dozen children and be preparing for her next role as grandmother and domestic matriarch, her power measured by the strength of her progeny. Babies cooed and cried in every house, but I never went out of my way to hold one, thinking them unpleasant-looking, wrinkled creatures with nothing useful to say. I preferred, after the evening sun sank into the worn shoulders of the Judean Mountains, to sit up late with the village men, drinking coffee and talking about politics, culture, and their belief that everyone misunderstood their sufferings.

I, too, was misunderstood, suspected by some of being

a spy. Some of the fundamentalists tried to burn my hair and, when that failed to dislodge me, used the no-children argument with the village elders, who reluctantly asked me to leave. They could not explain away my childlessness.

As I adventured, I kept a suitably complicated, and sporadically tempestuous, relationship with a fellow journalist, who I knew would make a good father and husband if it came to that. I was the one not interested, too enamored of my work, entangled in the task of making books, edifices of words that mattered deeply to me. I moved to the political capital of the world, Washington, D.C., and immersed myself in writing books and teaching writing. Then, while reading students' pages, a task that prompted my mind to rebel and wander to less prosaic places, I tripped over an astounding idea, that of having a baby. I felt as if the idea had welled up from a spring that I had walked past in the woods but never stooped to examine, as was my wont with the actual springs of my childhood. I pushed away the idea, whose origin remained incomprehensible to me, but it came back as inexorably as the next batch of papers.

I was being tugged toward something that I could not box up in paragraphs, that I could not see, something below the level of my consciousness, something powerful and something I resisted. I knew I did not want to trade my freedom for motherhood, to suddenly become someone who planned weekly menus and shopped for items as dreary as diapers or everything else a baby needed, whatever that was. Booties? Jars of strained carrots? Rattles? Talcum powder? Bibs? Clothes? Tiny shoes for bronzing?

Consciously, I knew that if I wanted to procreate, I would have to act soon. My fortieth birthday had passed. Still, I believed babies off-putting, unattractive, and unnecessary. The global population was on the exponential increase. Did I need to add to the problem of too many people? Yet, the tug grew stronger; I was sliding toward motherhood more precipitously than that glissade down Kilimanjaro.

Intellectually, I can hazard guesses as to why I was making this inalterable decision, or, more accurately, why the decision was being made despite me. The universe is filled with creative forces that I do not understand and before which I am less than a mote. The universe, or its god force, gave birth to itself omnipotently. Who was I then, having been modeled with the physiology for having a baby, to stand up in my minuscule corner of the cosmic creation and say I would rather be climbing a mountain. I, too, was subject to earthly evolution, to the same impulse that made the first fishy blob of protoplasm crawl out of the primal ocean onto a harsh beach and take a breath of Precambrian air. Having a baby would mean forging a link in that chain of being, a connection with my ancestry from the ancient ocean as well as with those who will be my progeny.

Adding to the argument for motherhood was the desire, deeply buried to be sure, to re-create myself. This was not special to me, since all creatures have this lust. The lowly earthworm, with a neural agglomeration at its front end so primitive that it cannot be considered a brain, needs to reproduce, to pass on its genes to baby worms who will carry on the annelidan task of burrowing in the dark of the dirt. The Pacific salmon travels hundreds of miles, swimming up cataracts, braving the mesh of fishermen's nets and the quick claws of hungry bears, to return exhausted to its birthplace and breeding ground. That the salmon dies after its heroic effort to

spawn does not matter, for it has accomplished its purpose; it has passed on its genes and done its duty in the
cycle of voyage and birth. I was not different from the
worm or salmon, other than being more cerebral and
lacking the tenacity to tunnel underground or the ability
to ascend waterfalls.

I backstroked against the tug all the way, but I was
doomed. I began rationalizing. Perhaps, I thought, having a child might be all right once it was old enough
to appreciate frogs. Then we would have something in
common. After a few more years perhaps, I would be
able to read it the J.R.R. Tolkien triology about the fabu-
lous journeys of the hobbits, followed by other books
that I loved. Finally, exhausted from devising resistances
and searching for explanations, I capitulated to my emotions, my biology, my destiny. Whatever the odd mix
of psyche and intellect, it somehow had altered my outlook on becoming a mother.

Once I relented, my doubts diminished and then
evaporated. I actually wanted a baby. I also married the
journalist whom I had known so long, having stopped
fighting our love. By the age of forty-one, I was pregnant. I would travel the unfamiliar territory that lay
ahead, driven this time, not driving. I knew how to negotiate an icefield, a rain forest, or a civil war, but pregnancy was an unknown and uncontrollable state. In a
canoe, at least I had a paddle to steer. Pregnancy, for me,
was pure adventure.

What surprised me was that I knew this new course
was right, even though I did not enjoy being pregnant.
My waist thickened and my abdomen curved toward the
concave. I grew heavy and uncomfortable. People told
me I looked radiant and I snarled, insisting that they
were not looking at me but at some Norman Rockwell

stereotype of motherhood. Men offered to open doors for me and I snapped, telling them that my midriff might be large but that my arms remained strong.

At three months into the pregnancy, my husband and I had our first look, via sonogram, at the baby. Its heart was beating, but otherwise it was not a magnificent specimen of anything. It looked like a large, upside-down crayfish, not so different, I thought, from that primal sea creature of countless generations ago. Crayfish or no, though, I was astounded by its heartbeat. It was alive. My maternal instincts woke up. I would protect this thing in my belly. When it came time for an amniocentesis, I was terrified by the evilly long needle my obstetrician prepared to plunge into my rounded middle, terrified not for my own skin but for the baby curled just inside. My doctor, who was in previous careers both a mathematician in academia and fighter pilot in Vietnam, plunged in the needle with panache. He managed to extract the amniotic fluid for the routine testing without doing damage other than violating my instincts.

As the months went by, I continued to detest being pregnant and did what I could to act like my former self. With my writing students, I pretended I was getting fat. At the seven-month point, I took a spring vacation in New Hampshire, where, to prove I still had machismo, I took a quick, breath-stopping dive into a thawing mountain lake. Wearing long dresses that failed to conceal my pregnancy, I subjected an out-of-character image of myself to the cameras and questions of a book publicity tour. Back at home, I athletically swam laps in an Olympic-size pool.

The nadir of my pre-birth experience was the shopping. Near the end, I needed big clothes, but I hated the cutesy look of maternity clothes. I settled for wearing my husband's shirts and baggy shorts. We solved the baby equipment problem by simply taking a Consumer Reports book into the appropriate store with us, cornering a clerk, and pointing to whatever was most highly rated. Within minutes we had crib, car seat, and stroller, none of which we were psychologically ready to use. We set up the crib in an extra bedroom and it looked empty, out-of-place.

When the inevitable time arrived, my labor was particularly grueling, ending with my pilot-obstetrician yelling at me like a drill sergeant to push. It worked. The baby was born, and in the instant I laid eyes on him, wrinkled and ugly like the babies I always had ignored, I fell in love. He was red and warm and I held him on my breast. He was perfect.

My son opened a new continent for me, a territory of emotions as big and inviting and perilous as Africa. I comprehend now the bottomless beauty of a child's innocence and think back sometimes about the children of the famine, with more pain than ever. My love for my son extends automatically, reflexively to any child, allowing my feelings a large new freedom that I could never have foretold, allowing the lock off my gentleness.

Although I am the same no-lace woman, I gladly organize a simple wardrobe for my son. For his room, I painted, as my mother might have, watercolor landscapes of great blue mountain ranges that I am confident we both will climb, metaphorically and perhaps literally as well. I do not begrudge him the distraction he is from my work, the hours I spend on what I consider drudgery, washing and folding his clothes, mopping the floor after he has splashed it gleefully with whatever foods on his table strike his throwing fancy. The domestic tasks blotch the day, but still I do not mind. Impossible this would seem, given my history. But the equation is easy. The joys of wandering the intricate alleyways of a Syrian market or eating bluefish by the Black Sea are considerable, but not greater than those that my son provides me.

I wheel him in a stroller along a Washington sidewalk toward the woodsiest destination within range, and I laugh at the image I make: a new mother, engrossed with her baby, innocent of the world's harsh realities. "Wait a minute," I want to shout at the suited people hurrying past on the sidewalk. "Let me correct this picture. Babies are not my only interest. I have traveled up the Congo River, I have ducked bullets in the Middle East, I have written books about world politics, my mind is brimming with big thoughts." Instead, I smile to myself because these other feats are certainly no more significant than having a baby to sustain and to teach and be taught by. I roll him under the needles of a low-hanging pine branch and the tickling needles send him, and then me, off into a state of laughter. We sit down by an old oak tree and pat the moss growing on its bole. I have not had the pleasure of marveling at moss for a long time. Later, I catch a worm in the garden dirt and dangle it onto his palm. At first he is a little afraid, but when he feels the creature's snaky coolness, he smiles as if the whole world, backyard as well as the African outback, were a wonderment, and in the moment I believe him.

SPITTIN' IMAGE

RITA CIRESI

I'm from Connecticut; my husband is from California. We've never visited Oklahoma, but it's our favorite musical—especially the number in which Ado Annie, the Girl Who Can't Say No, finally decides to put a halt to her flirting and accepts Cowboy Will's marriage proposal with the coy line, "Supposing that we should have a third one?" and Will warns, "He better look a lot like me."

After Ado Annie swears, "Da spittin' image!" I always try to imagine actually *wanting* a child who would resemble me. Perhaps in the mythical middle of America—on the dry, flat plains once covered by clouds of red dust and populated by fresh-faced, ethnically indeterminate girls named Laurie and Annie, who flirt with cute cowboys in chaps and neckerchiefs called Curly and Will—such a thing might seem desirable. For in spite of her slightly Italianate name, Ado Annie cannot trace her family, as I can track mine, back to Naples and Sicily and, hey, maybe even North Africa? (How else do you explain all that olive skin and jet-black hair that pervades—and sometimes plagues—my family tree?) Annie knows she ain't a-goin' to be impregnated by a stud whose folks once might have lit the Sabbath candles in a thatched-roof hut in Poland—or is that Russia?—or, hell, Lithuania? and whose propensity toward blue eyes and blond hair probably can be attributed to a Cossack rape.

Famous American romantic duos—such as Ado Annie and Will, Bill and Hillary, and Barbie and Ken— look so alike I wonder if they don't all come from West Virginia, where cousins are purported to make whoopee on a regular basis. These classically cute, slightly incestuous-looking couples usually produce predictably charming offspring. Not so in our case. Neither my husband nor I is considered radically ugly, but we aren't conventionally beautiful either, and our looks clearly don't "match."

I've got nothing against my genes or my husband's, but I'm sure once they get mixed up, the result will be goofy stuff.

We were living in central Pennsylvania (appropriately surrounded by fecund acres of feed corn and lowing Holstein cows) when I get pregnant. When we hesitantly approach the contraception counter at Fay's Drug to buy a pregnancy test, we also buy, on impulse, five lottery tickets. When the stick turns pink (and our numbers fail to hit), we immediately start speculating on yet another wild shot at the jackpot: the chances of our baby winning any kind of beauty contest.

"Purty slim," I tell my husband.

He shrugs. "All babies are supposed to look like Winston Churchill."

"All WASP babies, maybe," I say glumly, sure ours will look like either Mussolini or Golda Meir.

"Do you suppose it'll have red hair?" my husband asks, knowing that once upon a time, we both had so much brass on our heads we were the butt of many a milkman joke. "What if it really does look like me?"

"Or *moi*," says I. "Even worse: What if it looks like both of us?"

We buy more lottery tickets and start saving for a nose job. For the baby, that is.

By now you will have guessed: In both our families, a good schnozz is not hard to find. To locate a magazine-pretty face—American-style—we might have to beat the bushes all the way back to Adam and Eve.

I descend—and I'm afraid, *look* like it—from a long line of ragpickers, cigar rollers, piano polishers, and spindle operators in the Smoothee Foundation Factory. I had foolish hopes that college would function as a sort of plastic surgery. For me to keep such a remarkable resemblance—after earning a B.A. and two graduate degrees—to a great-uncle who for fifty years stood on an assembly line attaching straps to bathing caps seems a dire fate indeed.

After I get pregnant, I stare for hours at the dozens of photographs of my solemn ancestors and the very few pictures that remain of the forebears on my husband's side. We don't know much about these people beyond their names, which sometimes are penned in spidery blue ink on the back. On my side, image after image of moon-faced Sicilian women in black buttoned shoes and lace dresses, and hawk-nosed men in spats and Panama hats. They sit stiffly posed on swings and cardboard moons and even unicycles, and the corner of each picture bears in elaborate silver script the name of these pre-Depression photo studios and their locations: Palermo, Trapani, Termini, Detroit, Baltimore, New York, New Haven. None of my relatives smile for the camera, as if determined not to give credence to the stereotype of happy-go-lucky Italians.

In the house in western Los Angeles where my husband grew up, I thumb through a yearbook published by the Bialystok *Landsmanschaft* that shows grainy photos of this pre-war ghetto: the butcher, the tailor, the matchmaker, the adolescent boy who had the words "Dirty Jew thief" cut into his forehead and cheeks because he stole a loaf of bread. Individual photos in the family album show smiling boys in knickers and sailor hats ready to visit the 1939 World's Fair; a girl in a drop-waist dress posed on a pony at Coney Island. Hard to believe—or all too easy to imagine—the fate of this happy little girl had her grandfather not emigrated at the turn of the century. Her pretty blond curls, ashes. The delicate locket around her neck melted for the gold.

"Look in mirror," says a Chinese woman in the office next to mine. "Pretty face, you get girl. Ugly face, boy."

"What if you suffer from perpetual lack of self-esteem?" I ask her.

"Maybe you get a bland-looking hermaphrodite," my secretary calls out.

The war between our genes, fought in a split-second blaze of glory as the sperm collided with the ovum, inevitably was a nasty thing, and I have nine long months to speculate on its various foul outcomes: male pattern baldness. Long-lobed ears that produce too much wax. Wrinkles that cross thick necks like multistrand chokers. Knock knees that creak when you walk up the stairs. Toes that curl more than your hair. Short waists. Withered elbows. Deep bruises beneath the eyes. Double chins. Triple chins. Low hairlines. Ridged fingernails. Hairy nostrils. Hairy legs and hairy chests. Hairy everything!

"At least we're both skinny," I tell my husband, conveniently forgetting for a moment that there were so many obese folks in our family that my sister and I once concocted an entertainment called "The Fat Relatives Game." This amusement ran along the lines of "Twenty Questions," and was played only in bed, out of earshot of our parents.

In the slow, serious voice used to simulate hypnosis, my sister intoned, "I am thinking of a fat relative." The field of fat relatives was wide and vastly populated, and it always took several questions before I could even attempt an accurate guess. First I had to determine whether the Fatty was male or female. Did he or she live in New Haven, East Haven, West Haven, or North Haven, or was it an out-of-town hefty, from Detroit or Baltimore or New York? What were his or her favorite foods to get fat on? Fried eggplant, fried dough, roasted peppers in oil, artichokes stuffed with bread crumbs and ground anchovies, braciole, manicotti, lasagne? Did he or she wear glasses? Did he or she have gray hair? Aha! Did he or she once fall through the webs of a lounge chair at Lighthouse Beach, on the sunny afternoon they announced over the loudspeaker that Marilyn Monroe had just committed suicide?

"Actually—I ought to tell you—you really should know—that a lot of people in my family were like—

kind of plump," I admit to my husband as we sit at Hoss's Steak House, where my plate reflects the awful bottomless pit of hunger and wild, disgusting cravings I will suffer from during my entire pregnancy and, alas, far beyond: an eight-ounce bloody steak, a baked potato with a big ball of butter, half a loaf of garlic bread and— still left over from my second trip to the all-you-can-eat salad bar—macaroni and peas and hard-boiled eggs, black olives and bacon bits, and enough sunflower seeds to feed a flock of parakeets for a year.

"Like who?" my husband says. "Who's plump?"

"They're all dead now."

I eat some more. A lot more. Then I ask, "What do people die of in your family?"

"Cancer. And yours?"

"Strokes and heart attacks."

He reaches across the table and scoops the butter out of my potato. I confiscate the steak sauce—the fine print on the label informs me it's loaded with preservatives.

Oh, what a meal! The baby burps and hiccups all night.

I sleep fitfully now. I dream of my mother's grim frown as she scrubbed the kitchen floor, the veins on my father's neck that throbbed like pudding on boil when he got angry, the wild look in my grandfather's eyes as he yanked the tails of our cats until they yowled in pain, the tears that ran down my grandmother's face when the top of the pepper shaker fell off and a cloud of black pepper fell onto her pasta. The thick, horsey locks of one of my sisters. The deep olive skin of my father, which often led people to mistake him for an Arab or a Greek. My uncle's long, thin legs as he rode a bike, round and round, on the blacktop in our backyard. Then the soft, genial grin of my godfather, the way he would lift me so high in the air I would rise above the picture of the Son of God that hung in my grandmother's front room, leading me to squeal, "Hello down there, Jesus!"

My pregnancy books—which are supposed to calm my fears, but do nothing more than fan the flames of my neurosis—demonstrate in monthly charts the progression of fetal growth, from a black speck of caviar to a squirmy tadpole, to a Jacques Cousteau frogman, to a translucent monkey sucking its thumb and strumming its penis like there's no tomorrow. Right around the Dr. Seuss's Star-Bellied Sneetch stage, I get an ultrasound, which makes me even more wigged out, not about the baby, but about my incredibly weak bladder, which feels poised to explode after drinking thirty-two ounces of liquid an hour before.

"Here we are," the technician announces, positioning the monitor on my stomach and turning the screen toward me to display a wide, almost evil face, spooky white against the black background, a couple of paws clenched against her body, and two trundle-bed legs with—thank God!—none of that tiresome peeny-weeny stuff in between.

"It's a girl!" the technician announces.

Like your average mall rat, she's just hanging out—not doing anything to indicate she's Harvard material. Then with one tiny fist she reaches up and—waves at us!

She's a genius. She's the gal I love. She's the most beautiful girl I've ever seen.

Writers are supposed to have fertile, perverted imaginations. Why, then, after seeing You (for after having been mugged on the sonogram, the Baby has become flesh and blood, a real entity capable of being addressed in the second person)—why can I only imagine You in a lifetime of the most middle-of-the-road situations, smiling your Kodak grin as I take endless shots of your life like a photographer searching for the perfect moment? All right, it's barf city—the most sentimental hogwash on the planet—but I picture you prancing in your first pink tutu, playing *Für Elise* on the piano, marching down the aisle at your high school graduation, your mortarboard sitting cockily on your head to indicate it's no sweat, baby, to be valedictorian. You are brilliant because you are homely. And because you're such a smarty-pants, you save me scads of money. You have a full scholarship to become the first female Whiffenpoof at Yale. You will be the best goddamn—well, *whatever,* as long as it's financially lucrative—on the East Coast, and support me in my old age as I try to write feeble essays such as this for a hundred dollars a pop (if I'm lucky). You have the same exact bra size as me. You say, "Mom, Tolstoy never made the best-seller list either." You say you hear the voice of God in every syllable of my penned words, and then you screech at me, "I'll never forget—never forgive you for—that time Grandma pointed at me and asked 'Is this child going to be Catholic or Jewish or—'and you answered, 'Just plain old fucked-up, I guess.'"

In the ninth month, the evil truth surfaces: My father-in-law has six toes.

"Six altogether?" I ask, horrified, and my husband says, "No, on one foot. I'm sure I've told you this before. He's got a toe extra."

The logistics of this are beyond me. How does my

father-in-law find shoes to fit? Does he have to admit to this deformity to those smarmy salesmen in the white shirts at Standard Shoes who ask "What size, sir?" Does he feel empowered by his extra toe? What if he had an extra finger? No wonder he doesn't like to go to the beach.

This news inspires me with such wonder, terror, and dread that I have to go to bed early just to forget about it. I wake at midnight, thinking, "Jeez, my stomach hurts." Then, glancing around the dark room and barely making out the faint outline of the empty crib in the corner, I remember I'm full term. Four days overdue. And I think, "Jeez, sure would be nice to get some sleep." But you, Baby Cakes, are determined not to give me a wink of it, as if to prepare me for all the sleepless nights to come.

We drive to the hospital. Three hours into labor I get a shot of Demerol to take away the pain, which causes me to vomit, and makes me drift off into half-sleep.

"Are you ready to push?" the nurse asks, and, taken by my pain back to some preverbal state, I grunt and snort, which she—experienced at this sort of thing— knows how to translate into a firm *yes-sirree, ma'am!* The bottom half of the bed is unlocked and rolled away. The nurse points to the mirror in the corner of the room, a convex affair that reminds me of the kind our local pharmacist used to glance into to make sure we deprived neighborhood kids weren't stealing Smartees and petal-pink Maybelline nail polish from his drugstore.

"Watch your baby being born!" the nurse urges me.

"Fuck you!" I holler. Then: "Take it out!"

"Push it out!" she commands me, and I squirt seven pounds of blood, sweat, and tears into the doctor's hands.

"You have a beautiful baby girl," the doctor announces and plops the shivering red bundle, still attached by a pulsing, bulbous umbilical cord, on my belly. The rude, squinched face of a succubus stares up at me, and then Baby Cakes lets out a tongue-vibrating cry. *Well,* I think, *I'd scream if I looked like that, too.* Consumed with love and repulsion—and my first maternal impulse, the urge to say "Go get yourself washed and clean, and don't let me see such a filthy little face again, young lady!"—I repeat, "Take it away!" and after a quick clip of the cord, the nurse makes a move on my progeny.

"How many toes does she have?" I ask my husband, after they take Baby over to the sink to clean her up and bundle her into her heated crib. My husband doesn't look at me. He doesn't even answer me. He's got a new love, now. Might as well get used to it.

"Ten," the nurse says. "I always count them."

Later she gives me a sponge bath and takes me back to my room in a wheelchair. "So what do you think of your baby?" she asks, and I have to admit I can hardly even remember those brief moments they let me hold her in my arms, except the uncanny replication of my mother-in-law's nose, my father-in-law's ears, and my husband's cute cowlick on her pookie little head.

"She looks exactly like my husband's side of the family," I say.

"They always look like their dads at first," the nurse says. "It's Darwinian. I guess it kept cavemen from accusing their women of being unfaithful and dashing their children to bits against the walls of the cave."

I pause. "You'd think men would have gotten over that by now."

"You would have thought so, yes," she says.

And now it's just Beautiful You and Fat Relative Me, kid. On the first clear, sunny day after we're home from the hospital, I bundle you in your bonnet and bunting and take you out for a stroll in your spanking new blue carriage, feeling oddly like an eight-year-old girl pushing her new Pee-and-Poop Dolly down the street. As I command the stroller toward the country club, wincing (will my stitches never heal?), I look into your wet brown eyes, which are about as Sicilian-looking as a chocolate *biscotto* dunked in *cafe latte*—and about as far from those blue eyes of my husband's family as you can get. Your smooth cheeks are so intensely pale, I vow to buy stock in Banana Boat, knowing the company is going to make a mint off the amount of sunscreen both of us will have to apply to ward off the burns and moles that could ruin our too-white skin.

I stop the stroller on the ninth green of the golf course, and lift you up so you can see, for the first time, this mindless addictive sport that I pray you will not engage in when you retire. "Mine," I murmur, as I hold your cheek against my face. "You're all mine."

Two older women stand on the green. One turns her gaze away from the tee and looks over at us. "What a pretty little girl!" she calls out to me, looking from the baby's cap of blond curls to my dark mop. "Is she adopted?"

MORTAL TERRORS AND MOTHERHOOD

AMY HERRICK

I will say first, I was not a girl carried away by a passion for babies. I didn't avoid them, but neither did they loom large in my ambitions.

When the King of My Mountain announced that he had set his heart on one, I was taken aback. We're too young, I said. We don't know what we're doing. What if we drop it? What if we ruin its character?

He brushed my fears aside with a wave of his hand. He said that we'd do as good a job as anybody else. More was not necessary.

I was nudged along on some current I could not name. I wanted to know who was the responsible party in such matters. Was it destiny? Were we just dupes of nature?

In the end I agreed to give it a try because I figured it might be one of those things I'd regret never having done, like eating sushi or riding the Cyclone at Coney Island. It wasn't that I exactly wanted to do it, but I was worried that if I didn't do it, I would always wonder what I'd missed.

If this was not an ideal motive for bringing a new and innocent person into the world, still, I think it was the only one that could have carried me over the pass.

Several months later I peered down at the little blue line which had appeared on the home pregnancy test kit. Beneath the great thrill of absurd pride that I experienced at this accomplishment, I felt a cold shadow of fear slide by, silent and sharklike.

I went into the other room, where my husband was blithely reading the sports section and leaving coffee rings all over everything, and told him the news that he'd better get his act together, as things were about to change. Then I went into the kitchen to make myself breakfast, but found myself, again, gripped by a queasy chill of fear.

What was it? Was it the thought of the method by which this thing had gained entrance to my insides, or the thought of how it was—even now—wildly doubling and tripling in size by sucking up my juices through a cord attached to its bellybutton? Or was it the rather unbelievable idea of how it would eventually make its exit?

I didn't know exactly, but who in their right minds would volunteer for such an experiment?

When the Other Party came in a little later and sat down nervously next to me and asked me what was the matter, I, naturally, could not really tell him. He patted me in that lame way guys pat you when they don't really want to know what's going on, and then, when that didn't seem to be sufficient, he put his arms around me. "What is it? Tell me."

"I'm afraid," I said at last, sobbing.

"Afraid? Afraid of what?"

"I don't know."

"But it's going to be great, really great. We can take it to the zoo and the museum. We'll have an excuse to buy Hawaiian Punch and you can put it in your lap and go down that twisty slide in the playground you always wanted to go down. We're gonna have a lot of fun. Really."

Of course, he was right. What was there to be afraid of? Zillions of people had babies. There was no reason I couldn't pull this thing off.

And for the next few days, although I was nagged by a sense of unease, there was nothing of any substance that I could put my finger on and I began to relax.

Then, one afternoon, I went into the kitchen to have some tea and I happened to pick up one of my Everything You Need to Know About Being Pregnant handbooks and my eye just happened to fall on the section about Toxoplasmosis.

Toxoplasmosis is a disease you can get from handling cat poop and it's very sinister because the mother often has no symptoms or she thinks she's just got a cold, but meanwhile it slips across the placenta and causes the baby to go blind and deaf. When you're pregnant, the book said, it is wise to wear gloves when gardening in case you inadvertently brush up against any leavings of any stray cats.

Just an hour before I had been gardening and I had not been wearing gloves.

I was instantly plunged into a state of the most frantic despair and gloom, certain that I had contracted this hideous germ. I refrained, however, from mentioning what was on my mind to anybody, because a part of me was pretty sure I was a lunatic.

After a couple of days, when my husband finally threatened to put his head in the oven if I didn't tell him what was wrong, I told him.

Being a wise man, he did not bother to get into an argument with me, but suggested I call our obstetrician (which was what I was dying to do, but hadn't been able to get up the nerve for) and talk to him about it.

When I called my obstetrician, he suggested I go to the lab and get a blood test done.

The blood test came back negative. I was almost prostrated with relief.

On the other hand, all I could think about was what a terrible person I was, what a horrible mother I was going to make. What good mother would mind that her child was deaf and blind?

I wept with sorrow and relief and vowed to take the experience as a warning that if I was going to survive the next few months I must learn how to sit back and relax.

On Thursday night our friends Kate and Steve invited us to dinner. Kate made a lovely meal of asparagus and pasta which I actually ate most of, in spite of my queasiness. After dinner she and I were in the kitchen commiserating with each other on our husbands' complete lack of familiarity with the basic principles of housekeeping and she told me how last night she was cooking dinner and the oven caught on fire because Steven had left a pan with two uneaten pork chops in the broiler. She'd had to clean the oven herself this very afternoon before we came.

I stared at her in horror. Oven cleaners were one of the toxic substances pregnant people were supposed to avoid. How could she have done this to me? How could she have been so stupid?

I spent the rest of the evening in preoccupied silence, imagining in detail all the possible cellular mistakes that even now could be repeating themselves over and over in my little one's tiny defenseless body because of the food I had just eaten that had come out of Kate's just-cleaned oven.

When it was time to get in the car and head for home, with a great sense of courage and self-sacrifice, I decided not to say anything to my spouse because I didn't want to have him spend the next few months worrying and tossing sleeplessly, as I was going to do. However, we were not halfway home before he pulled the car over to the curb and turned and looked at me resignedly.

"OK. Out with it," he said.

"Out with what?" I said nervously.

"Out with whatever it is that's making you look like you've just been taken hostage in a bank holdup."

I burst into tears and told him the whole unthinkable story.

"But, sweetheart," he said, laughing, "what we ate tonight was pasta. It wasn't cooked *inside* the oven. It was cooked on the range. It wasn't anywhere near that oven cleaner."

I stared at him. Of course, he was right. How could I not have realized this?"

"I'm not going to be able to handle this for nine months. You're going to have to stop. It's like you're looking for trouble. The baby's going to be fine, but if something goes wrong we'll handle it. So, chill out, OK?"

I nodded, grinning weakly, and rode home feeling the ecstasy of reprieve.

But, of course, what happened in the next few months was the same story over and over again. Some small incident would set off a chain reaction that would lead to an emotional crisis. My husband, after awhile, got tired of bailing me out. He would come home and find me in a funk and would go grab a bag of potato chips and turn on some ball throwing or kicking spectacle on TV.

Who could blame him? I worried about every conceivable mistake I might have made—from eating a hot dog, to having amniocentesis, to whether my worrying hadn't already blighted the spirit of my baby.

It was, all in all, a long and difficult period of time. It seemed to me I should have been able to put my finger on whatever the root anxiety was, but somehow I could not. All I knew was that I wanted this baby out of the darkness where I could get some control of the situation. Then, I was sure, I would feel better.

My water broke at around one in the morning. I had just fallen asleep when I felt this strange trickling sensation on my thighs. I stumbled bulkily out of bed and rushed to the bathroom. As I stood frozen with excitement on the tile floor, there was another small gush of water. The doctor had said check the color of the water to make sure the baby wasn't in distress. Clear water was good. Green water was bad. I caught a small splash in my hands and tried to examine it.

"Get me a cup!" I yelled.

"Whaddaya mean?" my husband yelled irritably. "I'm asleep! Get your own cup."

"For crying out loud, I think my water just broke!"

In the next instant, my beloved teammate, who up to this point had seemed to take the prospect of becoming a father as casually as he would a shopping trip to buy socks, suddenly appeared in the doorway in a crouch, with a strange look on his face, as if he were a quarterback, as if he thought I was about to throw the baby to him.

"Did you get the cup?" I asked him.

He looked at me intently, as if I were speaking Portuguese. Then he spun around and disappeared. He returned a moment later with a clean coffee mug. I opened my palms and emptied the water into it.

We both stared down into the water as if our lives depended on it, as if we expected to see down there a map, a sign, a face. Something to tell us what our next move ought to be.

But all we saw was baby pee, a little funky smelling, but perfectly clear.

Several hours later, I lay in my hospital bed waiting for my newly arrived son, who was sleeping next to my bed in his little plastic bassinet, to wake up and have a feed.

As I lay there I was filled with a delicious anticipation. It was almost as if, in some confusion of identity with the little one who lay next to me, I was waiting for some exquisite food that I could not name. He had been sleepy and calm when he'd first arrived, not interested in eating, and I couldn't wait to see what nursing would be like.

I had had a little anxiety when, an hour earlier, they had brought him in to me from the nursery where they had been giving him his post-delivery clean-up. I had been afraid that I wouldn't recognize him, that I was not a good enough mother to recognize her own child. But as soon as they lowered him into my arms I was completely reassured. All was right with the world. I was home free. He was slimy and squish-faced, but he was perfect, and I knew that I could have picked him out of a crowd of ten thousand.

Now I lay there, waiting peacefully for my little one to wake up and have his first dinner. After an hour or so, he stirred and flexed his little hands and did not cry, but began to make tiny, comic little animal sounds. I lifted him carefully out of his bassinet and fumbled with the buttons of my gown and stuck my breast in his face.

For a brief minute, he opened his eyes and looked up at me with a frown as if he were wondering who the hell I was. Still frowning, he made a sleepy, completely uncoordinated attempt to get the nipple in his mouth and then he fell back asleep.

I was filled with panic. Something was wrong. He hadn't nursed in the delivery room and he still didn't seem to be hungry. What could be going on?

Failure to thrive.

When the nurse came in I was weeping. "Something's wrong," I told her. "He won't suck."

She raised her eyebrows and, with a deft and casual hand, grabbed the baby and directed him to my nipple. With the other hand she gave my breast a quick squeeze. The baby opened his eyes very wide, bicycled his tiny legs in excitement, and with a ferocious lunge clamped down and began to drink like somebody who'd been lost in a desert for nine months.

He was fine. He was perfect.

I looked down at him in adoration and then I looked up and saw hanging over our heads, like a grand piano on a piece of dental floss, the mortal nature of all that we are. In a flash, I knew that not only were all my worries not over, they were just beginning.

All I had done was to get us to the starting line.

Now it was only a question of willingly hostaging the rest of my life to the job of protecting him and also myself (so I could be there to protect *him*) from every possible random catastrophe and misfortune.

When my husband returned later in the afternoon, I saw that there had been a great change in him in the last few hours. The whistling, carefree youth was gone. He came down the hallway silently, and stood in the doorway staring nervously around the room.

"Where's the baby?" he asked in a whisper.

"He's right there in his plastic baby-mobile. He just finished nursing," I said proudly.

He tiptoed over to the bassinet and peered in with dumbfounded awe. "God, he looks different already. Are you sure that's him?"

"What? What do you mean? Who else could he be?"

"Well, you know," he said shamefacedly. "You hear so many stories about hospitals getting babies mixed up."

"Nah, that's him," I laughed. "I'd recognize him anywhere."

My spouse was silent for a moment.

Then he said: "I was having the most terrible fantasy on the way over here. I was imagining that some terrorists had set off a bomb in the hospital and that the firemen wouldn't let me go in, but I fought them off and went into the building and was trying to find you and the baby."

I looked at him for a long moment. "You wanna try to burp him?" I asked. "I couldn't get him to burp."

"Jesus!" my husband said. He said it so loudly that the baby startled in his bassinet and threw up his arms to ward off whatever danger was coming our way. But he didn't open his eyes, and slowly his arms sank back against his chest. "You didn't burp him? You gotta burp him."

"Just make sure you support his head," I reminded him.

"I know that! You think I don't know that?"

He slid his hands in under the swaddling and lifted the baby up. I see him there still, in my mind's eye. He is terrified. He is sweating. He is in love. He is holding the baby stiffly out in front of him because he does not know how to bring it to his shoulder without dropping or breaking it, because he fears that what he is holding will shatter in his big, clumsy hands.

I felt a certain vengeful triumph to have, at last, my husband's company in this matter.

When I look back on the world as it was before I became pregnant, I can see that it was not, in reality, so very different from the way it is now. Yet today it appears infinitely more threatening.

My husband's fears still often seem pretty laughable to me. Before his son arrived, would he ever have feared riptides at Rockaway Beach, or the teenagers next door who test drive their motorscooters the wrong way down our one-way street? Would he have gotten up on a perfect summer morning and imagined thunder and lightning before the day's end, or a grocery store holdup when the little one and I strolled out to get some bread?

My own worries are far more reasonable, of course. They are much more about the mortal dangers that spring out from within.

When my son was tiny I worried that he would cease to breathe at night. I worried that he'd fling himself out of his little rocker seat and crash to the floor. When he was at the cruising stage, I'd lie in bed and picture him pulling the bookcases down on top of himself and getting crushed. I'd get up in the night and start moving the furniture around.

Now I often think back to being one and twenty, blithe and childless. Did I ever, for a second, foresee myself being concerned with such matters? And often I wonder, if it had been given to me to know beforehand what I now know about motherhood—the swift and merciless loss of innocence, how you are transformed overnight from being someone's child to being someone's parent, handed summarily a love so incandescent and irrevocable that you have to stay awake twenty-four hours a day to protect it from all the dark dangers out of left field—if I had known all this beforehand, would I have agreed to have a child?

My little one sits in his bath splashing around contentedly. I am not prepared, my breath is taken away, when suddenly he looks up and asks me point-blank if it's true that we all must die.

The answer I give him, of course, is not good news. I wait for him to say something, to rise up angrily and punch me in the nose at this, the greatest betrayal. But he just looks away and busies himself with his rubber frog.

I'm washing his face when he says, "And then after you die, you get to be a baby again?"

"Well, I don't know. Some people think after you die, you get to come back and be another person or animal."

"Do you think that?"

"No. I think after you die, you go back to nature. You become part of the trees and the grass and the sky."

"When are we going to die?"

"I don't know. I hope not for a long time. I hope I don't die until you're grown up and have your own family and children."

"What about me?"

"Oh, I don't think you're going to die till you're very old and have your own grandchildren."

"Maybe it won't happen."

"Maybe not."

I hold my breath and think about it. Who knows? Then I laugh and see how I've been duped, duped by the cunning and perfect beauty of nature's system, which uses babies as a way of securing our allegiance to life, of commanding us to go forward and grow better, even though we are burdened with the certainty that in the end we must all return to dust. It is no use to ask the question would we have had them if we had known? There is no going back. We are all driven headlong by a force that has only one thing on its mind, which is to make something out of nothing, pattern out of chaos, babies out of the dust motes dancing in the void.

It is the most darling of paradoxes that as fast as the universe makes itself, it is falling apart.

One picks oneself a baby out of the pot and in an instant the world is transformed into a gigantic booby trap. You are forced to see, not only how heartrendingly fragile a child is, but also that your own childhood is over, that there is an inevitable time limit to all things. Yet, faced with this, do you throw your hands up in despair and sink down into lassitude and indifference?

Certainly not, because here before you is that which you would jump into a burning building, or out of a speeding locomotive, for. Here before you, by a trick of light upon the bathwater, is the little stroke of genius— the face, the sign, the map—to show you your next move, to lead you through the doors of your own mortal confines to where you will outlast yourself.

A PAINLESS LABOR

CELINA SPIEGEL

I was twenty, on a ferry from Brindisi to the Greek island of Corfu. It was the summer before my junior year
of college, and I was traveling with a friend, both of us
in Europe for the first time. I have a poor memory for
details, but I remember so much so vividly from that
summer: a young girl with a parrot and tambourine who
sang for us in our hostel in Amsterdam; the blueness
of the Aegean, both transparent and dark, my ideal of
blueness; the night Adele and I slept in the arch of a
castle through a night of pouring rain—we lit a candle
and read to each other to stave off the cold. And the
stomach cramps that hit me out of nowhere on the ferry
boat. They were so severe that I believed I wanted to
die. It is hard to recall harsh physical discomfort, once it
is over; but the image of me sitting on a folding chair,
doubled over, in a blue and somewhat (I later realized)
transparent dress, Adele on the seat next to me—maybe
it's not even a true image, but it's the image that comes

to my mind as best embodying sharp and horrendous pain. What helped me get through it was the thought, which I repeated over and over to myself, that this was preparation for labor. Labor, I knew, was the most intense pain a woman would ever experience in her life. If women had survived it over centuries, I had to believe that I would survive it too—and I would most certainly survive this, its mere shadow.

Throughout my pregnancy I lived in a constant dread of delivery. Everything, in a first pregnancy, is unknown and unknowable, and I was convinced of two things: that whatever it was that was growing and wiggling in my belly could not be human; and that it would never come out—that I would burst before I would deliver. Actual labor was unimaginable. The thought of the pain terrified me. We have all heard stories of endless, agonizing hours, or even days, which culminate in Caesarian sections; we've all read Victorian descriptions of the grueling labors of idealized Dickensian females (the most womanly of women), which result in the welcome relief of death. I began to view women differently when I saw them on the street or on the subway: each a possible mother, they became heroic in my eyes.

In the end, I faked pain during my labor. I knew I was ready to deliver—my water had broken that morning (instinctively, the night before, I had moved the carpet away from the bed), my contractions had been five minutes apart for over two hours, and I was three days past my due date. My cervix was almost completely effaced, and had been for a number of weeks. And yet, the pain was bearable—a sure cramping, a tight balling of muscles that was uncomfortable, that hurt even, but that was nothing to scream over. It was easiest to deal with when I sat still and waited for it to pass.

Even though my doctor had told me to come to the hospital around noon, my husband was reluctant. He didn't say so, but he couldn't stop cleaning the apartment, straightening up this and that, dawdling. I knew he didn't believe I was ready. And when we arrived at the hospital, I was afraid no one else would believe me either.

So I moaned a little. I bent myself over and tightened my fists when I felt a contraction. Even though I was rigged up to a machine I didn't have faith in, which recorded contractions.

What I really felt was excitement. And the strange calm that often accompanies the inevitable.

I exaggerated the pain I felt because I was sure that if I weren't writhing and moaning (at the very least), the nurses would send me home. Even as I lay on the hospital's birthing table, with the doctor, nurse, and my husband standing around me monitoring my contractions, I felt like a fraud. When euphoria arrived, between pushes, and I felt as clear-headed and light as I've ever felt in my life, I told the doctor that I thought something was wrong with me. I had never heard of endorphins, the body's morphine-like natural painkillers—or perhaps I simply dismissed them (my husband claims he told me about them) as back-to-nature propaganda that had nothing to do with how real women feel; and yet I wondered why women everywhere weren't singing their praises. It's true that when the baby's head engaged in the cervix, the spectacular high faded and the cramping gave way to pain. But before I knew it, I had given birth. In just two hours and nine minutes, I had my first baby, a thoroughly human baby, whose thoroughly human fingers and toes were the most miraculous appendages I have ever seen.

When I first exultantly began to tell other women of my brief, natural (no-time-for-drugs) labor, I quickly realized that I should be more cautious with my exuberance. Either they responded with their own story of a long and difficult delivery, which embarrassed me, or they dismissed me as more lucky than they would ever be. I began to understand the silence that surrounds an easy labor. First of all, there's the natural inclination toward bravado—it's always the gory details of survival stories that interest us most. But even for women who have not yet given birth, as was the case for me, the mythos of pain in labor is so powerful that we cannot accept that our experience might be otherwise. When we hear of Chinese peasant women squatting in the fields to deliver their babies and then continuing with their usual labor, we dismiss these tales as charmingly exotic but of no consequence to our own lives. In Lamaze class we watched a film of four women giving birth: Two of them screamed and contorted themselves, one began to hit her husband, and the fourth smiled beatifically through her delivery. The first three responses seemed normal to us, but we all thought the fourth woman was crazy.

But slowly I began to hear of experiences even more astounding than my own. A colleague told me of driving herself to a doctor's appointment she had almost forgotten and then, upon examination, being rushed to the hospital, where she delivered five minutes later. (She hadn't even felt the contractions.) Or the sister of a friend: Her second delivery had been so significantly shorter than her first brief labor that for her third pregnancy her doctor trained her and her husband to deliver the baby themselves. (She did in fact make it to the hospital.)

I wish I had heard these stories before my delivery. Even if I hadn't believed that they would be in any way relevant to it, they might have provided some kind of hope, which is why I offer my own experience here. The hope that labor can be the most thrilling physical and emotional experience imaginable—even though it may in fact turn out to be the most painful; that—as the !Kung women believe—the fear of labor may indeed cause as much suffering as the process itself. Perhaps, pragmatically, it is in our best interest to prepare for the worst, or perhaps the myth of inevitable excruciating pain in labor is too strong for women to discount. But might it not also be that women have something at stake in believing in a difficult labor? Why are we, why was I, so eager to accept that labor must be painful?

"I will make most severe/Your pangs in childbearing;/In pain shall you bear children," God told Eve—a frightening promise that is difficult to discount, even in our secular age. After all, isn't the human condition in part defined by our painful origin, with each new birth reminding us of our inevitable death? And isn't pain, after all, in some way a signal that a physical experience is authentic, a way of feeling, of knowing, that we are alive?

I do believe that through our physical vulnerability in childbearing we are made not just to understand but to experience through our bodies just how valuable the life we have created really is. And one can argue that the pain involved grants an aura of exclusivity to what from the outside can appear to be a privileged fellowship. But what is even more convincing to me is that labor is one of the few experiences through which women truly become heroic. Men have war; women have childbirth. And, as with all heroic enterprises, the greater the challenge, the greater the feat.

Was my labor less than heroic, since I didn't suffer through it? What does it mean that my memories of ordinary stomach cramps on a boat ride in Greece can rival the most profound physical experience of my life?

One evening this past summer, when I was two-and-a-half months pregnant with my second child, my stomach began to ache badly. Throughout the night the cramps intensified, nausea set in, and by morning I could barely stand. It was ninety-degree weather and I was dehydrated. Yet I couldn't even hold down water. What I first thought to be food poisoning and then feared was a miscarriage turned out to be appendicitis. By the next evening my appendix had ruptured; but because I was pregnant I found myself undergoing surgery with only an epidural. That same calm I felt when I went into labor came over me. I feared that I would lose the baby; I felt acute discomfort as the surgeon and resident poked and pulled at my organs (as he operated, the surgeon instructed a class of residents, which is how I learned I had made it to the operating table in the nick of time— for the fetus, and possibly for myself as well). But I no longer held the pain up to some imaginary, impossible standard of the "real" pain of labor. And afterward, when all proved well, I had no reason to fear that my delivery would be even more traumatic.

If we acknowledge that the pain of labor is like any other pain, without any symbolic weight and with even a brief respite between contractions, then we no longer

have to fear labor as the trial of our womanhood. And
we do not have a reason to minimize other physical distress: severe cramping, exposed dental nerves, appendicitis. We may even have to consider (perhaps most
difficult of all!) that men's pain may at times rival our
own.

It's true that after my two-hour labor came the real
pain, just when I thought the greatest challenge ahead of
me was caring for my new baby: the episiotomy, which
was excruciating; contractions of the uterus—when I
was sure that I had survived all possible contractions; an
infection accompanied by high fever (what one friend
assures me Victorian women died from); and then the
six weeks of continuous bleeding that no one had prepared me for. And the pregnancy itself, with its six
months of nausea and vomiting, extreme exhaustion, and
sciatica, had not been easy. More than nine months, including recovery time and nursing, of enormous physical exertion—*What to Expect When You're Expecting*, the
pregnant woman's bible, tells us that during pregnancy
the body at rest is working harder than a nonpregnant
body climbing a mountain!—is that not heroic enough?

Now, nearing the end of my second pregnancy, I am
too busy with my family and work, with trying to make
some time for friends, to think much about what my
next delivery will be like. Unlike my first pregnancy,
this one has been so easy that at times I forget I'm pregnant. When I do think about the impending labor, I find
I'm even looking forward to it. I'm wondering whether
it will be even faster than the first, which is how, I'm
told, the second one usually is. But even though a part
of me wonders if my luck will simply be reversed this
time—easy pregnancy, difficult labor—or whether my
knowing that it may not be the most painful trial of my

life has made me too blasé for my own good, this time I'm not afraid. The entire process, from conception through birth, is—and I feel sure of this—the most amazing and rewarding physical experience a human being can undergo.

But perhaps we are so attached to the notion of a physically painful labor in order to prevent ourselves from thinking about the greater and more unimaginable emotional challenge beyond it—that of having and raising a child. For if labor itself is a heroic enterprise, how much more heroic is motherhood. Now, as my daughter begins nursery school, I have only an inkling of what lies ahead. I can only hope that I will be as wise, as patient, as firm, as loving, as my own mother. And in the face of the dangers and rewards we know of as life, these qualities are heroism enough for me.

MOTHER'S NATURE

JESSICA SABAT

It's not that I have blue hair, a ring through my nose, or spit in public. I don't. Physically, socially, education-ally, and financially, I am a typical middle-class New York woman. But I do have a tendency to stray from the beaten path, mostly just for the exercise, partly to get away from the crowd.

The majority of the women I know do motherhood by the modern book. They deliver their babies in the hospital, stay home for their few months of maternity leave, and then head back to work. Years before becom-ing pregnant I knew I'd be taking a different route. To me, hospitals are for the sick, injured, and dying, and pregnant women most often are none of these. As for work, well, financially, the choice to remain at home to raise our child is one that I'm fortunate to have, thanks to my husband Bob's income. Emotionally, it's one that I've never regretted.

Being an at-home mom struck me as rather bold.

Nowadays, not working is cast as either the best thing a woman can do for family and nation, or the worst thing she can do for herself as a vital part of the modern world. To Bob and me, it was just logical. We could not see ourselves bringing a child into the world and then allowing someone else to care for it most of the day. Besides which, I wasn't particularly tied to my career as a radio producer. My plan was to do freelance work from home so that I'd have some sort of income, but focus on parenting at least for the first few years. It was the way my mother had done it, and it had worked well for us.

A couple of years before becoming pregnant, I left my job to start my own business producing P.R. interviews for musicians. In theory I was gaining time to work more on my opera singing, a long-term project; in reality I was beginning to nest.

This moderately well-thought-out career shift revealed one of my dirty secrets. While I enjoy being busy, without outside pressure I can be downright lazy. In other words, I am not a born entrepreneur. It wasn't all bad, though. My little business was just that—little—but within the year I had landed an ongoing gig writing scripts for the host of a national television program. So I set up shop as a part-time busy person and a part-time tree sloth.

I envisioned my pregnancy and delivery as a defining event in my life that would be, possibly all at once, earthy, heavenly, and hell on earth. The only way to fully experience giving birth would be to pass on the drugs, bite the bullet, and see what happened. Just how much pain could I endure? I believed I had a high threshold—but then again, I had never given birth before. Convinced that I could only truly maintain control if I dared to risk losing it to the unknown, I decided to go natural, armed with only my wits and strength.

The morning I found out I was pregnant, after Bob and I came to and photographed each other holding the test stick, I set out to find a particular birthing center I'd heard about. Friends of friends and someone from work had delivered there with glowing results, but being sieve-brained, I never managed to retain the name of the place. I eventually checked the monumental Manhattan phone book under "Midwives." There it was: the Elizabeth Seton Childbearing Center, 222 West 14th Street.

I called the center, which garnered me my first congratulations and an appointment for an orientation tour the Monday after Christmas, a few days away. I felt triumphant, confident that I had found the perfect way to dodge the medical establishment's mainstream maternity machine and in the process, forge my own bold, new path.

Christmas passed. Although Bob was worried that a midwife would insist on moonlit field-childbirth and then make him eat the placenta, he accompanied me to our first session.

We watched two videos, one about the center and one on natural childbirth. I was totally engrossed. Bob got about as far as gross. He is very supportive, but he is also the most squeamish person I have ever met. As my birth coach, he knew his problem could be our Waterloo.

Bob hid his eyes. I winced and wiped my tears as the video baby, a small, slimy squirm of a thing, squeezed out and was swiftly deposited on its mother's chest. It surprised me that, aside from grunts of effort, gentle encouragement, and baby cries, there were no other sounds. No monitor beeps, no recitation of statistics, no chorus of congratulations from an attending medical team. Just deep emotion enlarged by silence.

After the videos we toured the two birthing rooms. Not exactly like home—no dirty socks on the floor or littered desk—but certainly far homier than the average hospital. The bed was a platform bed just like ours; there were nice print curtains on the windows and soft lights. I particularly loved that each room had a big whirlpool tub to labor in, which, the midwives assured me, helps cut the pain.

What we didn't find was evidence of technology. No machinery or wires. Just an oxygen tank and a decidedly dated-looking baby warmer/transport unit. Bob jabbed me and whispered, "This must be for the gerbils." I smiled, although I, too, was taken aback by the warmer's age and prayed we'd never see it again.

We went home with lots of paperwork and things to discuss. Despite my confidence, the cold medical realities that the center had laid out jarred me. "No high-risk pregnancies, no multiple births, no women over forty-three who are having their first babies, no deliveries before thirty-seven or after forty-two weeks of pregnancy." And, we'd been informed, of those who are accepted as low-risk clients, a full 20 percent will end up delivering in a hospital anyway, due to complications that arise during pregnancy or early labor. So, in addition, each client must select one of three attending obstetricians as a backup.

I started feeling disillusioned. Here I thought I had found my dream, and now I had a 20 percent chance of getting a nightmare. I wanted assurances and rewards for my courage, and all I was getting were out-clauses.

Eventually I started to see the bigger picture and realized that midwives need a spotless record built on expertise and caution to help their profession gain wider acceptance and support. But after our visit Bob was, if anything, more skeptical. The tour had convinced him that I wouldn't be dropping his firstborn in a field, but it wasn't going to be with the latest technology a heartbeat away, either.

We talked at length about what constitutes "the best." Sure, it can be machinery, medicines, and monitors, if one needs them or simply wants them around. Then by all means choose a hospital.

But isn't it also "best," I argued, to have consistent hands-on attention from one expert who, during labor, has only me to worry about? Someone who truly believes that, with preparation, women can deal with the pain without drugs? And since a hospital is available if needed, "then," I argued, "the balance is right. Let's give nature's course first dibs, and if it doesn't work out, then, in good conscience, we can allow medical science to take over."

Knowing my dog-with-a-bone tenacity, Bob cautiously assented.

But there was resistance from other interested parties. My own mother wasn't so much worried about me—she was quite proud, actually—but what if there was something wrong with the baby at birth? The best I could tell her was that out of 180 births at the center in the previous year, only one baby had needed to go to a hospital. The rest were just fine and went home with their parents as planned.

Bob's mother got jittery when an obstetrical nurse told her *she'd* never consider delivering outside a hospital. It wasn't until my mother-in-law discovered that her cousin's well-liked and respected daughter had delivered her kids with a midwife, as had the daughter-in-law of a dear friend, whose family is full of doctors, that she found her own peace with our decision.

Meanwhile I discovered that the center's style suited me perfectly. The midwives treated my pregnancy as a natural, personal, emotional, hardy-yet-precious development, an attitude that was manifested in some pleasantly surprising details. At each routine monthly visit, I pulled my own chart from the files. No asking, no waiting. The message was "You're a grown woman, we trust you." Next, I headed to the bathroom, peed in a cup, and dipped in the test strip. I noted any color changes and recorded the results on my chart. Then I weighed myself (oh joy), wrote it down, and plotted my weight gain on a graph. (We TRUST you!) Then I returned my file to the office manager and waited to see the midwife on duty.

No one whisked my urine off to perform seemingly delicate scientific tests too complex for me, a mere layperson, to understand. And, gratefully, no one peeked over my shoulder the happy day I confronted the frightening truth that I now significantly outweighed my husband (especially scary since neither of us was particularly thin to begin with). At the Elizabeth Seton Childbearing Center, one is left to confront this special kind of hell in private.

Then a midwife would examine me and answer questions. Any questions. Stupid questions, misinformed questions, even personal questions. And, since the midwives rotate shifts, I never knew who I would see, or even, in the end, who would deliver my baby.

The sum of all this trust, inclusion, and empowerment was faith. Faith and responsibility. However much I had had that got me to the birthing center in the first place, it was nourished along with my embryo. They both grew exponentially. I was asked and encouraged to be an adult. Pregnant and soon to be a parent, I was deeply grateful not to be treated like a child.

Halfway through the pregnancy, Bob and I were offered an extended series of childbirth classes at the center. Twelve sessions instead of the usual six, with our midwife visits to be conducted in class with assistance from our coaches. Bob was in the midst of a heinous work schedule, but in support of me and to help himself strengthen his weak stomach, he agreed.

Along with breathing and relaxation exercises and parent education, we learned to do our own prenatal exams. The same weigh-in and urine check as before, but the coaches took the measurements and used Doppler stethoscopes to listen to and count the baby's heartbeat. Coaches were also supposed to take the mother's blood pressure, but Doctor Bob never got the hang of it.

But Bob did get to the point where he could actually watch childbirth films—if they were in grainy black and white. It was the early-public-access-television aesthetic that won him over. He even laughed at one surreal moment when, after only the video baby's head had emerged, it suddenly popped its eyes open and started looking around. Ever on our side, our instructor offered to make a practice of turning down the color on the monitor, but Bob quickly grew bolder, which was a good thing, because I planned on delivering in Koda-chrome.

All in all my pregnancy was pleasingly uneventful— which, of course, secretly made me worry that I would be paying the price with a torturous labor and delivery.

A full two weeks before my due date I awoke with contractions at 3:00 A.M. I called the midwife and she said, "Could be labor. Try to relax, have a drink if you want, get some sleep, and call me back in a bit." So I did. The contractions, like slightly more intense menstrual cramps, continued. At about six o'clock I called her back and we decided this was probably the real thing.

I gently woke Bob and broke the news. The rest of the morning and early afternoon were spent climbing in and out of my warm bathtub, breathing through reasonably manageable contractions, timing them religiously, eating bits of food, and watching my apartment go from cluttered and dirty to orderly and spotless thanks to Bob, my mom, and my mother-in-law. I called the midwife periodically to check in and let her listen to me breathe over the phone, and by one o'clock I could tell things were moving along, since making any kind of conversation was beyond me and the contractions were getting longer and closer together. By two o'clock I knew it was time to go.

We got to the center just before three o'clock. I found out I was already seven centimeters dilated. They led me to the birthing room and I sank into their tub, seeking the pain-lessening powers of the warm water.

Did the tub help? Well, if I'd had to go through transition out of the tub and it was any more painful than it was already in the tub, I don't know what I would have done. It was like demonic possession, an out-of-control, wild ride, during which I could only yelp, squeak, and groan. Thirty killer minutes later, I began pushing. After a few efforts in the water I reluctantly climbed out onto the bed. For an hour on all fours, I pushed and pushed. Bob pressed hard on my lower back at each contraction. It hurt, really hurt—exponentially worse than the worst pain I'd ever experienced before—but, far more than that, the exertion was wiping me out.

Between contractions I put my head down on the pillow and whimpered like an overused sled dog. Pathetically, I begged, "I just want to rest."

"You're almost there," Laura, the midwife, answered.

After what seemed like endless contractions, Laura asked if I wanted to reach down and feel the top of the baby's head. She gently took my hand and guided my fingers.

As I stroked the warm, wet skin rippling over a hard skull, my distress receded. My kid was almost here and needed my help. After a few more pushes, Laura suggested I turn around and sit up against Bob and bend forward with each effort. This position made the backs of my legs knot into torturous spasms with each push, a pain more dreadful than the contractions. But the baby was moving out. Thirty minutes more and it was all worth it.

Nathaniel Benjamin Sabat came into the world with his left index finger hooked in his little mouth, and thanks to Laura's expertise at perineal massage, not only didn't I need an episiotomy, but I didn't suffer any tearing at all, not even an abrasion.

Nathaniel was immediately on my chest, umbilical cord still joining us, howling with tightly clamped eyes. Then, without warning, his lids flew open and he gazed with silent wonder into his mommy's and daddy's faces for the first time. Tears spilling over, we caressed him gently and with awed murmurs welcomed our new love to the world.

We stayed like that for many minutes. When the cord had stopped pulsing, Laura gently asked Bob if he'd like to cut it. I knew he'd decline, but to my complete amazement, the most squeamish man on earth said yes. He took the scissors and gave our boy his freedom.

Our first photo of Nathaniel shows me in profile with his face peeking out of my cradled arms. It was taken twenty minutes after he was born, at just about the same moment that I surprised myself by saying, "You know what? I could do this again." I had had the extraordinary privilege of giving birth just the way I wanted, and I was already game to see if lightning could strike twice.

The startling assuredness of that moment stands in sharp contrast against the often cloudy, uncertain path of motherhood which I've followed now for a year. Paradoxically, this mapless journey has somehow imparted a new clarity to my own path, and narrowly focusing my life on Nathaniel's has broadened my perspectives. As an at-home mom I've given up many freedoms, but in exchange, my life has grown a hundredfold more fun, a thousandfold more important, and a millionfold richer. Motherhood is undeniably slave labor, but I knowingly allowed myself to be dragged into captivity. I don't want emancipation. Twenty minutes into the game, I did indeed know the truth: I just want more.

THUMBELINA:
THE COMPLEXITIES OF
HAVING A PRETTY LITTLE GIRL

ERICKA LUTZ

Getting over my childhood was a matter of growing tall enough to be taken seriously and growing old enough to forget. But there is no real forgetting. Essential issues merely dive beneath our surfaces to feed, then rise again like the dark forms of sea mammals ready to blow. So motherhood has been for me.

A year ago I birthed a tiny, beautiful girl-child who looks like me, and who I fear the world will dismiss. From the beginning of my daughter's existence, the pregnancy, our lives have orbited around the same issues that tormented my own childhood—size, looks, gender. I am the daughter and granddaughter of feminists, and as a new mother I find myself asking the same questions they asked: Who will society force my daughter to be? How can I minimize the damage? How do I make her feel OK about her appearance if I still feel confused about my own? How do I mother her?

———

But I begin with expectations, I begin with bliss.

My pregnancy was wanted, planned for, unmarked by ambivalence, the first time in my life I've ever been so completely sure. It was, at first, a textbook pregnancy. I was thirty-one, in great shape, eating conscientiously, with a doting husband who'd been through it all before and calmed my mother-to-be nerves, gave me a back rub every night, and made sure I took my multivitamin. During my first prenatal checkup I watched on the video screen the sonogram of my fetus: arms and legs not yet complete, heart almost as large as its head. I laughed and it bobbed up and down inside me. The doctor smiled, froze the image, and handed me the first picture for our baby album.

I grew, I swelled. I imagined I carried a little boy inside me. I saw myself entering his world, driving a car full of his ten-year-old boisterous friends, and I was glad. For the rest of the pregnancy I held the image of a dark-haired little boy, freckled and serious, grinning up at me. And one day I felt my baby move inside me, a gentle, friendly squirming as I rolled onto my puffy stomach.

In my thirty-fourth week, my O.B. went on vacation and a doctor I hadn't seen before felt my belly, measured it with the tape, hastily rechecked the numbers on my chart, glared down, and demanded, "Are you smoking?"

"No, of course not."

"I need a sonogram!" he yelled out the door, and to Bill's and my frantic questions he growled only, "This baby is not growing!" and the pregnancy was suddenly high risk, and my body was no longer my own.

The first sonogram, done by a silent tech with a grim look on his face, confirmed the fetus was undersized. Diagnosis: Failure to thrive. Possible placental detachment. I was put on bedrest, prescribed two stress tests a week, and referred to a specialist for a fetal EKG to determine if the heart had holes in it.

Sonogram after sonogram. Sometimes a younger doctor joined the specialist to observe the procedure: "*This woman's baby is too small, let's take a look at why.*" Still the results came in: a tiny fetus, though the reasons were unclear. The fetus had no visible deformity, I had no bleeding, the placenta showed no sign of visible detachment.

"*Lie still,*" the doctors said. "*If the placenta is loose it may reattach. If it is loose exercise might detach it further and the fetus could die.*"

I took bedrest literally. I lay on the bed, on the couch, afraid to move. All day on my left side waiting for the death inside me to happen. Getting up only to go to the bathroom. "*Is it hungry?*" I asked the doctors. "*Is it suffering inside me, not getting enough food?*" "*No, no,*" they reassured, but I panicked when it didn't move for an hour. And then the familiar friendly flutter, thump, roll, and I relaxed again. What had I done wrong? Was my body defective, unable to grow a strong enough placenta? I obsessed about the days I hadn't eaten enough, hadn't drunk enough milk.

Bill made me fruit shakes. Breakfast, lunch, dinner, snacks, more protein shakes. That last month when everything inside was tight, I ate anyway, forcing it down. All my energy focused on the being inside me. I willed it to live, grow, flourish. Twice weekly, the trip for the non-stress test. Afraid to walk the hospital hall, imagining the placenta peeling away, my baby choking, dying.

Sonogram after sonogram. "*Well, the head's about the right size but the body is small. If it continues to stay this small we'll have to induce early, we can nourish it better outside your body.*"

Not yet a mother, I was already unable to care for my child. I imagined it taken from me, tubed and incubated. I pictured the little monster inside me. A little boy with a shrunken body too weak to lift its head. Would I love it? I felt pity. Poor little monster. *I'm sorry. I'm sorry.*

There were respites. Doctors, nurses, seeing the chart, then feeling with their hands, "*Well it doesn't feel that small.*" One kind doctor finally explained, "Oh, the length is OK, a little small, not too bad. That's how fetuses grow. It's just a skinny baby. A Gandhi baby instead of a Gerber Baby." I looked around the waiting room. Large people with tall Nordic backgrounds. I was born at six pounds; as an adult I stand 5'2", no giant. Were they expecting me to push out a nine-pound baby?

Twice weekly they hooked me to the monitors and measured the baby's movements. I lay there pushing a button each time I felt activity and fretted, *Is it passing the test? Am I?* And when the fetus slept and didn't move, a nurse with a mild electric shock zapped me and woke it up. Others were waiting for the bed.

"*We must induce at thirty-eight weeks,*" the doctors insisted. My parents, solemn, supportive, urged us to get a second opinion. Bill and I consulted other doctors. We forced our O.B. to sit down and answer lists of questions.

"I really don't have time today, I have other patients waiting," she said.

I hit the roof. "They can wait. We've waited for you many times."

Her feet tapped in their expensive flats. In transit from

her office to the lab for more tests I ducked into the bathroom and stole a look at my chart, the chart they'd forbidden me to review. Inside, the familiar numbers.
Notes about my "resistance" to the upcoming induction.

Four weeks of bedrest. In between office visits and
tests I lay on my left side and ate. Halfway through it
my therapist paid a house call, and I talked about my
concern about having a tiny baby, the tiny bright-eyed
boy I expected. *Poor little boy, going through life too small.*

My therapist looked puzzled when I mentioned my
own feelings of size inadequacy; we'd never discussed
those elements of my childhood: Slow developer, late
bloomer, not fitting in, mistaken for a second grader in
fifth grade. Missing out, undesirable, too weak; Easy
Out, Butterfingers; *"Do we have to have her on our team?"*
Mascot. Shrimp. First in line. Front row. Peanut. Short
Stuff. *"How's the weather down there?"* Later: Flatso.
"Let's pick her up." Carried around, physically mastered;
Steve Aviso, the class jock, laughing as he carried me
screaming and fighting to dump me in the garbage can.
My hardest punches landed soft and ineffectual on his
back.

*"They only tease you because you're a pretty little girl and
they like you,"* the teachers said.

"How did this make you feel about yourself?" my
therapist asked.

Powerless. Confused because I wasn't just small, my
size combined with my delicate features to present a
package that people seemed unable to take seriously.
Being pretty made it easy for people to dismiss me. *"Oh,
she's so beautiful, she's so cute."* My physical attractiveness, which should have been a gift, felt like more of
a burden. I hated being small and cute, for the world

patronizes small and cute. *"Be a big girl."* *"Oh, that's big of you."* *"Don't be small-minded."* *"Aren't you big."*

I remembered being thirteen, standing, shouting for silence so I could make my speech to the school assembly, head too low beneath a lectern. The microphone, lowered as low as it could go, still hung high above my head. My small voice was too high to be heard over the noisy crowd. The other kids laughed at my rage, and I swore to myself that I would lower my voice, grow tall, or at least powerful.

In time, I grew taller, tall enough. I rebelled hard. I pushed myself into adventures. Eventually I learned to project myself into the world, intense, concentrated. To enjoy my looks. I grew strong. I learned to be taken seriously, and to celebrate my individuality. Yet I'd never lost that sense of being too little. Now I felt inadequate carrying a tiny baby not as large as other women's, not as large as it was supposed to be.

"You are risking your baby's life, your baby could die at any minute."

Bill and I fought the doctors for more time to let the fetus mature. Then we knuckled under. We scheduled the induction.

We packed my bags. My mother bought a tiny preemie outfit so the baby, now estimated to be around four pounds, would have some clothing. Ten days before my due date they hooked me to monitors, IV'd me for pitosin, and induced a hard labor of double contractions every two minutes for twenty-two hours and an almost cesarean section before things suddenly worked: I opened. The universe relented. The nightmare changed to wonder and I easily pushed out my baby, unripe, covered with the glue of white vernix, with no eyebrows, a single eyelash poking through the upper lid of her perfect left eye, and a shock of long black hair.

"It's a girl!"

"It is?" I said, unprepared.

"Well, she's not that small," the nurse remarked. "Just keep her warm." And then, "Oh my, isn't she beautiful?" They placed her on my belly, put a cap on her head, wrapped us both in a blanket, and wheeled the empty portable incubator back to neonatal intensive care.

A girl. A tiny girl. A tiny beautiful girl.

I held my daughter, amazed at the real human being that had emerged from the pregnancy-turned-nightmare, from the arduous labor. Five pounds, twelve ounces. A healthy placenta. A medical mistake; the many sonograms had been wrong. Left to term, she would have weighed at least six pounds. I clutched her tight, ready to protect her forever, angry at how wrongly she'd been forced from my body. This was not how she should have been born.

Annie remained tiny. For a while she bounced along the third percentile, occasionally hopping up to the tenth. For the first few months I eagerly brought home from her pediatrician visits the little Health and Growth Record booklet in which the nurses entered her physical progress. I plotted her height and weight on the charts in the back of my child development book.

Then at eight months her growth plateaued, and she dropped off the charts completely. Once again the tyranny of the tape measure. Questions about my growth patterns, Bill's *"When did you stop growing?" "When did you have your first menstrual period?" "How tall are your parents?"* and, for Bill, questions about his older two children's growth patterns. In the drawer now set aside for Annie's important papers the Health and Growth Record booklet sat, a source of distress, and I kept the child development book with the charts on the shelf. The charts were an admonition.

I'd failed to grow her well enough.

I'm sorry, baby.

The pediatrician discussed the possibility of hormone treatments should a simple blood test determine any growth hormones were missing. Bill and I held down Annie's screaming body as three phlebotomists tried to insert their thinnest needles into her thinner veins.

The results came back—no hormones missing, nothing truly wrong with the baby, just genetically small, estimated to grow to five feet, maybe a little taller if, like me, like her nineteen-year-old half-sister, she has a late growth spurt.

Inside the doctor's offices Annie is considered not quite OK. Outside the doctor's offices, Annie's delicacy, bright eyes, and brown curls turn heads, draw crowds. *"What a perfect little child! "Does she do commercials?"*

The words rile me. Mothering Annie turns me face to face with my own past. The demons of my own childhood return. I fear for her childhood. Annie looks so much like I did as a baby, and looking at her is like finally seeing the reflection in that old mirror. I finally know what I looked like as a child.

"She looks like a porcelain doll!" No matter what she may look like, my daughter of the serious stare and already-strong will is not ornamental.

"Oh! Look at her! She's so petite!" I fear what awaits when Annie interacts with other, more "average" children. I worry about her in a world of large, loud kids who no longer just use garbage cans to express aggres-

sion, who might torment her for her size or strength, or make her feel small inside in a world where large matters.

Occasionally the comments are not so kind: *"That one is small but cute." "Well, at least she's pretty." "She's lovely, though."* And my favorite: *"That's OK, your mommy loves you anyway."* I meet these comments with dropped jaw, unable to retort, and lie awake wondering what I could have said to wither these people, educate them into shame, and send them on their nasty way.

"At least she's not a boy, it's easier to be a small girl than a small boy." I guess they say this believing it is OK for a girl to have no power while it would devastate a boy. If Annie had been the boy I'd imagined during my pregnancy, I wonder if the pressure for hormone treatments would have been more intense.

I want Annie to feel strong and wonderful inside her body. To be able to stand up against a bully. To celebrate her ability to whip through crowds and squeeze in places bigger people can't. I don't want her to feel she is too small or too delicate. I don't want her to believe she must rely on feminine wiles to get what she desires. Yet I fear that the quality of attention she gets will affect her psyche no matter how much we try to counteract it. She will be different from the others, and different in childhood can be disastrous.

At twelve months, Annie weighs fifteen and a half pounds and stands twenty-six and a half inches tall, far below the three percent marking on the size charts. After pediatrician appointments, a day of pointed comments, or seeing a child her age loom over her in the park, I fear my Annie isn't thriving. I wake in the middle of the night and watch her sleeping on her back, hands behind her head, knees bent up and open. Her froggy position. She looks so tiny.

But she is perfect, damn it. I want to tear up the size charts that rule us. There is nothing wrong with this child. Inside our relationship Annie is not too small, she is not a little doll. Oh Annie, I feel her warmth against me, thrill at the love in her voice as she murmurs my name. A bright, healthy child, already verbal. One ear is pointed like an elf's. Wild brown curls. Adamant mind. Amazing to have a daughter.

Around Annie's first birthday I relived the month of bedrest, labor, delivery. I was unaware of how strong my reaction would be. I still wonder if I failed her. I could have, should have said, "Screw you, there's nothing wrong, I'm keeping this baby to term," and had the baby at home naturally, surrounded by my family and friends.

Questions continue to haunt me. I know a parent does not risk their baby's life to show they are strong and defiant. But if I was not strong and defiant then, how can I expect to be strong and defiant when it matters in my daughter's life? A child needs love, care, values, and an ally. In the lurch, can I be that ally? How can I make her feel smart? How can I make her feel strong?

I don't raise these questions rhetorically. I need to know. When adoring acquaintances, the neighborhood members of her "fan club," pick her up, when she flinches and I don't register it until retrospect, I am not parenting her well.

I could dress her always in pants, hand-me-downs, or boy's clothes to deemphasize her femininity. But I don't want to create more separation from the other little girls. She should be able to enjoy her beauty, not be stifled by it, and I know what pain my family's lack of clothes-consciousness caused me.

Part of it is that I don't believe, despite the women's movement, that things have significantly changed for little girls. If anything, for a child in the nineties there is even more emphasis put on size, on looks. The size charts did not exist when I was a child, the modeling industry was not as pervasive. My baby daughter has already been defined and typecast. A *girl*. A *tiny* girl. A tiny *beautiful* girl.

This is my first job of parenthood, to draw the delicate lines I will walk as Annie's mother: to acknowledge her small size and outstanding looks yet teach her that they are not the only things that matter; to help her learn to have a big personality, lower her voice and have her presence and intelligence command attention, and help her feel comfortable with who she is, others be damned.

And perhaps being Annie's mother will move me beyond the shadows of my own childhood. We are all born into a set of circumstances, some advantageous and some to struggle against. Perhaps the set of struggles I discuss are only my own. She is so young and I can only speculate, I do not know what her world will be like, or whether these issues will flow innocuous past her. *I can only promise not to denigrate your concerns, Daughter.* I will observe, I will listen. Annie will teach me.

II. INITIATION

MOTHERHOOD AS SUBVERSIVE ACTIVITY

VALERIE SAYERS

Pregnant with my first child, I was twenty-five years old and innocent as a babe myself. I thought having a child meant rocking the handhewn cradle to the tune of "Bread and Roses." I thought that I would bring this new baby to cafés and bars and political meetings, where everyone would admire my new maternal glow.

I was so innocent, in fact, that I tried to proceed with motherhood as if this gentle delusion might become reality. My son Christian, born in a cold December, came home to Christmas lights that would festoon the apartment his entire first year. His father had made him, by hand, a cradle. I bundled him under my coat to listen to fiddles and penny whistles in smoky bars, where he slept content.

At the baptism, the old priest railed on about communism and my son howled in outrage at this misreading of the sacrament. *Don't you have a bottle?* the priest asked, and my giggle threatened to escape. No bottle for this

baby. Later, when he was safely nursed and the cham-
pagne was opened, I held my child close and threw my
head back, giddy from the strange ceremony and egged
on in my giddiness by the friends and family who
crowded into our little apartment. My husband snapped
our picture in front of the Christmas tree and to this day
I can feel, when I see the picture, the joy that possessed
me. I was pretty sure I would have a dozen babies at
least.

All that year, when I held my son at the movies or at
a party or safe with friends and family, my head would
tilt back with that same dizzy happiness. And much of
the rest of the time I battled a domestic desolation so still
and so thick and so hopeless that I could only push
through its cloying curtains by reminding myself that it
was not right to leave a newborn baby in the care of a
mother so sad as this.

I had always thought that I would raise a baby in the
middle of raucous life. I have six siblings, the best of
company. In college I embraced all philosophies with
the words *social* and *communal* as their roots. I have never
liked to stay home nights.

And I certainly had never felt, before I had a child,
burdened with domestic duties. My husband and I had
entered into an egalitarian marriage without so much as
a discussion about whether we would take turns to clean
and cook and shop. How else could you do it? *Rise up,
sister,* we would laugh when a suburban relative com-
plained about her husband's distaste for her cooking.

But from the beginning, my husband took the whole
business of making a living more seriously than I did.
After college, I worked as a waitress, a tutor, an information clerk for the Parks Department, an editorial assis-

tant at an anarchist-libertarian publishing company (the descriptive adjective depending on which way the wind blew). By the time I was twenty-five, I had finished an M.F.A. at Columbia and was teaching part-time, the most precarious of jobs: They called you the night before the semester started. All I really wanted to do was write. I had a stubborn faith that if I only held out—if I didn't buy a suit or start making pension contributions—I could eventually call myself a writer.

My unwillingness to calculate whether we might ever have a real kitchen or a trip out of town (both of which I craved as much as the next consumer) left my husband carrying the financial burden. When we discovered that I was pregnant, though, he took his own leap of faith and left his staff job as a video engineer to do freelance production. We had no health insurance, but we had a sense of elation: *I never want my child to feel,* my husband said, *blamed for what I didn't have the courage to do.* I worked my desultory hours, my husband worked maniacally—a freelance life meant taking the jobs when they came, to save up for lean times.

Meanwhile there were childbirth classes (shared), hospital tours (shared), decisions (shared) about where a crib might fit in a two-room apartment. Even in childbirth, in a long, hard labor, I did not feel alone. My husband played cards with me, joked with my jokes and grimaced with my grimaces. At the very end, when I wanted to leave my own body, the look of pain on his face connected me to reality. A minute after our child was born, my eyes were fixed on father holding son, the father with that same look of anarchic joy he would later capture on film, on my own face.

I remember profound shock that there was a real living baby at the end of this ordeal. Father and child looked designed for each other, but when they put the baby in my arms, I couldn't make anything fit. I was all elbows and tensed shoulders, and my son wasn't the least interested in nursing. Everyone around me swished in brisk efficiency while I lay bloody and pale and clueless, my great belly deflated, mysteries issuing from my body.

The sharing ended here. We didn't have long together that night: It was after one in the morning by the time the baby was suctioned and wiped clean, and the crew was eager to whisk him off. I remember the moment of cold panic when they took him away and my husband bent to kiss me goodbye. I had been in labor a day and a night, and I was hungry and exhausted and possessed of a loneliness I had never experienced before or since.

There was no room for me in the hospital that night: I was wheeled onto a sunporch, roomless and hopeless, in a predictive metaphor for that first year of motherhood. I did not sleep until dawn. It wasn't pain that kept me awake, though I was conscious of pain, and it wasn't any anxiety I could name as such. It was that loneliness that kept me from sleeping, an inchoate longing.

The next morning they moved me to a room the size of a closet: solitary confinement for the only new mother on the ward who'd chosen rooming-in for the baby. Weak, hungry, tired, I struggled to rise whenever he cried, and time telescoped—in my imagination, my little son cried for hours. The wearier I became, the more loneliness yielded to terror. I had no idea how to feed him, even bathe him. I had no idea how to convert this crazy love I felt for him into practical maternity. My mother was in South Carolina, my brother and my sisters scattered around the globe. I did not have a single friend who so much as dreamed of a baby, though they all seemed to think it a swell adventure that I was having one. The fathers' visiting hours were over before they began. I was alone in this.

When I came home, there *was* company again, for a little while: My husband took a week off, my mother flew up, friends streamed in to see the baby. He slept and slept and slept. The more noise, the more music, the more perfect a baby he was. I went back to teach the last classes of the semester: My husband rushed home to relieve me. Our child smiled earlier than any child has ever smiled.

But soon enough everyone went away again, and at their departure I climbed on the seesaw between joy and desolation. What made me such a failure at this mothering business? If I looked at the evidence from the hospital rationally, I could see the cold institutional causes for my early dislocation. But as time went on, I was not inclined to look at evidence rationally or to blame social structures; I was inclined to blame my own personality. When I stepped out with my new son snuggled close to his father's chest, I felt again the reassurance of a marriage that defined its roles loosely. Then my husband went back to work, and I was trapped in Betty Friedan's feminine mystique without even the consolation of an earlier generation's community of mothers around me.

The semester ended, and I came down with a bad cold that worked its way into bronchitis. My husband worked around the clock. No more egalitarian marriage as I had known it—who else now had the time to shop and clean and cook? Often I sat on the staircase connecting the two rooms of our apartment, holding a sobbing child, sobbing myself. In my despair over my hacking cough, I called my department to tell them I couldn't teach the next semester. A bad mistake. Now there was no money for sitters, even if a sitter could be had in a neighborhood with a two-month waiting list for a Saturday night. Now I did not have even semi-adult conversation to anticipate twice a week. It was a bitter winter, and when I took the baby for a walk, he trembled. I made myself sick with longing for the pine woods I had wandered as a child, and hauled my son back to our two city rooms. I read to my baby, wildly inappropriate passages from trashy magazines I picked up in the checkout line, and George Eliot, who saved our souls.

My friends, childless, were all at work, their hours and their commutes long. No one dropped by in the afternoon. The loneliness stretched out. January and February were too cold for the park, and when I did meet another mother, I invariably made a crack about antifeminists to a sweet traditionalist. I thought I'd moved to a neighborhood full of writers and artists, but I was invited into the double parlors of the wives of Wall Street lawyers. I wasn't sure what I was doing there, but I was pretty sure we weren't going to be talking George Eliot in those Victorian rooms. Solitude began to look seductive after a long discussion of designer wallpaper.

I despaired that I would find a way to be a writer and a mother. This son of mine cried without talk or music, and I would have looked a pretty fair lunatic to anyone who peeked in at five o'clock, when I spent an hour dancing him around the tiny living room. The minute the baby's eyes closed, I dashed for the typewriter and wrote without so much as a blink to collect my thoughts. Sometimes I was so tired when my baby slept that I longed to sleep myself, instead of slogging off to work. Sometimes, eating my lonely lunch, I pictured

myself wearing a suit I didn't own, accumulating a pension after all, flirting by the coffee machine.

One day the fantasy of returning to the real world
filtered into the real world's consciousness. It had been
a long and lonely morning filled with the baby's cater-
wauling, and near the end of it, a friend called to ask if
I would like a job. Her job, in fact. The money was not
great—most of it would go to child care—but the work
was decent and would take me away from home. I
would emerge from my lonely rooms, find company for
my son more suitable than my own.

I entertained the notion for all of three seconds. I cannot tell you in what order the images that stopped me
from accepting the job entered my mind's eye, but I can
tell you what they were: my son's sweet smile, offered
with his uncanny possessive stare; his tense body in the
middle of a crying jag, fists jabbing; my typewriter, in
a corner of the living room, to which I flew whenever
this demanding child closed his eyes.

There it was: I was a writer and I was a mother. For
the first time, I understood the symbiosis of this relationship. Up until the moment I was offered a full-time job,
a chance to be a real person in the real world, I had
seen motherhood as the obstacle to my writing. Before
motherhood, I had worked whenever the mood—or the
light, or my energy—was right. Motherhood had sen-
tenced me to hours of domestic stasis and, I thought, no
chance to dive down into a writer's semi-consciousness
while my child was awake. After motherhood, I worked
whenever I could: while he slept.

And did not have the sense to realize, until someone
asked me to follow a more normal course of earning a
living, that I was producing more prose in those first
months of motherhood—those dizzying, terrifying

months—than I produced in years of posing as a writer. It came to me as I stood at the phone that the will to finish my first novel was delivered along with this child, that the discipline to write whenever it was possible had made its appearance with my son.

I will not lie and claim that this epiphany changed motherhood for me. The rest of that first year was a daily struggle, even if my son's first word was *i-i-uh,* a sound we interpreted as *typewriter,* as in my constant refrain *If I could only have an hour at the typewriter.* (His second word was *shit,* which was, I'm afraid, the sound I made when interrupted at my work.) But the dual revelations that I really did want to spend most of my time with my son and that motherhood might provide a cover for this secret life of novel-writing were a comfort. I came to see, gradually, that a morning spent with a little boy on my back while I scrubbed or walked or cooked or even paced was a morning when my work was stewing on a low flame; and the moment embracing his round body before I put him down for his sleep was often the moment of my emotional unwinding. I wrote fast and hard, and came back to him kinder.

I do not want to romanticize this first-year experience with my baby. What my husband and I kept trying to learn all through that first year (and again when we had our second child and still, as we take turns earning money and watching our boys growing into men) was that if we did indeed reject the notion that one of us should give up a chunk of herself for a long while, if we decided that we should both follow—if you'll excuse the corny expression—our dreams, then we would have to reinvent our marriage and come at egalitarianism from all sorts of unequal angles. We would both have to give up time, lots of it, and money, and we would have to put up, often, with the loss of each other's company, because we were on the peculiar shifts that occur when child-care money is tight. We would have to rearrange our lives week by week, sometimes hour by hour. Our obligations to our child could not be divided evenly down the middle—and whose can?

I know now that babies grow and time increases, but I didn't know it that first year. I think, given my own stubbornness, that my fierce blindered insistence on keeping the work going probably did allow me to claim the life of a writer. Other women are not so single-visioned, artistically speaking, and have the good sense to know that they can take a year, or two, or ten, and come back to their art the richer for what they have learned in their mothering. Nothing saddens me more than hearing one mother criticize another for the way she has tried to work out the balance of child and self and work in those early mothering years. Some of us are actually good at domestic jobs, and some of us need to be sprung from the kitchen before we go berserk. Some of us need time out, and some of us need to push on. Some of our children need us to be self-fulfilled, and some of our children need us to put ourselves aside for a few years and attend to them. It seems to me that we should celebrate all mothers who figure out the time to go to the bathroom in the first year of motherhood, much less the perfect balance of work and child.

As it happened, at the end of my son's first year—and before I had properly figured out the time to go to the bathroom—the three of us moved to a large apartment building in a cheaper neighborhood. I discovered there an edgy, happy collection of women, all wobbling as they tried to balance children and work and art. Around mothers who scrambled financially and intellectually, as hungry to talk books and politics and movies as I was, I began to come out of my first-year isolation. I could look back and see its causes with a clearer eye.

And I was able, too, to look back at those moments of self-imposed domesticity that had added to my sense of myself as a writer. I saw my son's dark eyes, almost black, bearing down on me with equal insistence in delight and in demand. He was a beautiful child who looked nothing like me, but we shared tempestuous personalities: He was easily engaged, easily frustrated. And he loved language—he chatted away from the earliest weeks, before he had any words, and as soon as he had them he flung them around with relish. *I-i-uh. Shit.* Sometimes, when he asked that I give over all my time and energy to him, I saw him as a subversive agent, a rebel child insisting that I leave this workaday world and engage in some irrational exploration of body and soul, some dancing around the living room, some tramping through city streets, some chanting of syllables. What writer could ask for a better child?—he disrupted everything and brought everything into sharp focus. In my dark moments I thought that motherhood was keeping me from myself, but again and again that first year my child reminded me that motherhood was only deepening my sense of mystery at this world, only deepening my sense that if I was a writer, I had better run to that typewriter and write.

A CREATION STORY

JANET MALONEY FRANZE

There was a big open shower next to the toilet. Light tan ceramic tiles—"hospital beige"—covered the floor and walls. I sat there naked on the john with my legs shaking. There wasn't a shower curtain, it was just an open space. My body was shaking as I sat staring at the chrome of the drain cover. I don't remember there being a shower curtain. See me? I see me. I'm down there, sitting, and shaking, on the john, wondering why there's no shower curtain. "I will never do this again. I will NEVER do this again."

I had just given birth to my son.

I noticed myself in the mirror as I moved to the door at the nurse-midwife's soft knock. It was as if I were seeing myself seeing myself, a reflection within a reflection. There always seem to be two of me hovering in proximity. One is the reactor, who feels and acts on impulses. That's the one noticing that every blood vessel in my face—including those in my eyes—had broken from pushing, and the one wondering about shower curtains. The other me is detached, disembodied, transparent . . . watching, thinking, and hoping. That's the one wondering why in the hell, after enduring hours of excruciating, graphic childbirth movies and practicing natural childbirth techniques, after reading nearly a hundred books on pregnancy, childbirth, and the newborn, it had never occurred to me that after birthing I would feel like I'd been hit by a Mack truck. And I was pissed.

See me? I'm the exhausted, over-exhilarated one nursing my gorgeous scrunched-up son, Nathan, and talking all night with my sister. He was born at 6:11 P.M. and weighed seven pounds, ten ounces. It hadn't been a particularly difficult labor, as labors go, my son was born healthy and whole, but at the end of it I was one terrified mother.

One mother, terrified.

I'd tried for years to deny that one day I would ultimately be a mother, and I hadn't looked forward to being pregnant. I didn't want to look like that. When I am not pregnant I find "with child" bellies distasteful and discomfiting. Ours is not a culture that glorifies big bellies, Demi Moore's cover shot aside—or as a case in point. Most representations of pregnant bodies aren't pretty. Every single time I visualized my belly pregnant, scenes from a movie I'd seen years before popped into my head. Scenes from *Alien*.

No, I definitely had not looked forward to pregnancy. But even now, years later, when I hear a baby, my breasts tense and tingle, mimicking the familiar lactation "let-down response" that happens just before your milk begins to flow, even though I've no milk to let down. When I see a baby, my knees dissolve and my heart pulls me toward it, arms reaching, "May I?" and once again I feel my son's tiny foot pushing against my lower right rib. Like the phantom feeling an amputee is said to experience. Real yet unreal. I used to give Nate foot massages in utero, and all my maternity clothes became pilled and worn in that one spot. Whenever I think about it, my hand instinctively finds that spot. Nate's place; the Nate who was yet to be Nate.

I loved that first pregnancy. Never had I felt more real, more there. Twitches metamorphosed into discernible body parts under my hands, my heart burned, my stomach heaved. The more bizarre it became, the more melded I felt. I had a purpose. I had status. Once, miserable and uncomfortable and huge, I said "screw it," and parked in the handicapped space nearest the drugstore. One glance at me heading toward him and the cop tore up the ticket he'd been writing. Pregnancy was power.

But the act of separation, the giving of birth, the awkward re-entrance of my pre-baby house . . . I wasn't there for any of those things, not really. The symbiotic woman carrying life within her body and soul became another creature altogether: a mother carrying life in her hands. See me? I can—unfortunately—see me on the videotape, over and over, year after year. There I am big and blotchy, on the outskirts of all the new baby commotion. Displaced in my own home.

The lines of my definition are fluid to me, ill-fitting to everyone else.

There's a grating suppression in the pit of my stomach. It's a resisting, guttural reaction to the fact that my life is inescapably constructed around motherhood. Biologically and psychologically, as a social construction and as a familial one, I am defined as a mother and always will be. I'm the product of a stay-at-home mother, a product of a culture that hollowly exalts women who are mothers. At the moment of my son's birth, all that motherhood implies became *me*. All the images that have surrounded me, that have seeped into my consciousness—and more importantly into my subconsciousness. The Virgin Mary, Mother of God. The TV moms. That crazy, artsy mom who lived next door when I was a kid. She painted her living room black and had a spider monkey that lived in the hedge between our houses. Her daughter always looked slightly unwashed. My mother always looked slightly disapproving. The daughters in romantic novels, who never seemed to have mothers, but who always had adventures and lived happily ever after. My good friend Carole, who bakes and gardens and volunteers with handicapped kids and is calm. Mothering requires a strange combination of depth and shallowness, an ability to shift gears on the fly, shoot from the hip, and juggle widely disparate activities simultaneously. It's a skill I cultivate with difficulty. American motherhood—as I saw it—was selfless, kind, available, understanding, restive, organized, and well fed.

I'm messy, often selfish, sometimes mean, easily self-obsessed and distant, and frequently stubbornly obtuse. I'm emotional and moody, cluttered. I sneak chocolate cookies for breakfast. But I'm a mother now, and for me that means I need to shape up. I try to fight it, but I do believe I must come to a placid acceptance of it—a sense of integration with it—if I am to become at all. Motherhood inescapably defines me. If I write what I know, I write motherhood. If I read what I know, I read motherhood. If I walk, talk, and eat what I know, I walk with a child on my hip, I talk in a high, engage-the-baby voice, and I eat gone-cold food while I pour cups of apple juice.

In short, sudden moments of suspended animation— between the second I notice all is calm and the next second when all isn't—I wonder what happened to what I used to know. I wonder if it matters. If it ever mattered.

> *By the time I gave birth to my son I didn't believe in God anymore.*

One day my friend's five-year-old boy turned to her in the car and declared, "You know, Mom, God is a girl." Today, if I believe in a God, that's the one I believe in—God the Mother. Motherhood is too powerful, too weird, too awful to be anything less than the province of godhood. It dissolves bones and explodes brain cells and utterly disintegrates hearts. Sleep deprivation, comic relief, towering rages and bittersweet tears, wave after wave of unexpected emotion, are all part and parcel of the motherhood routine. Its never-ending responsibilities are stifling; its salvations are so thick with love that sometimes you can't breathe. See me? I'm rocking. Crying. Rocking. Crying. Hating this infant in my arms. Loving this infant in my arms, this infant Nate who won't stop crying. The room brims with midnight lightness. A disembodied baby cry floats eerily from the monitor at my left elbow. The monitor's picked up some renegade radio waves; someone else's baby somewhere else in space is crying in my home. Nate latches on, but struggles; I don't dare move to try to turn the monitor off. So as I struggle to calm my baby, ghostly baby cries invade my night. I can't get away from them. And it frightens me, sickens me, that I rock and cry and think about people who throw their babies against walls. That I visualize a woman like me, a nightmother, sleep deprived, half dressed, unwashed, scared, feeling inadequate and out of control, hurling the perceived source of her insanity against the wall. The room stills, the air melts, my son stares up at me, not sucking now, one tiny, perfect hand poised mid-air like a dancer's, all dark bright eye-pools and shadowed softness. Still and knowing. Still and loving. My heart shatters from completion, happiness, grief . . . and shame. Patience, sadness, forgiveness, authority, love, "infiniteness" . . . godhood.

And I guess that makes me a goddess, as are all the women who gather together in the name of The Playgroup. I used to think that Thursday morning playgroup was the only thing that stopped my life—our lives—from imploding in those early years.

When you're a stay-at-home mother your life keeps compressing tighter and tighter, your focus narrows to a point that materializes as your child. You don't go out much, because by the time you feed the baby, clothe the baby, change the baby, change your baby-stained shirt, and slick back your still unwashed hair, it's time for the baby's nap. I don't know a single stay-at-home mother who will willingly screw up naptime.

But almost all of us agonize over what to do while the baby sleeps. We'd talk about it at Playgroup, between whispered nightmother confessions, relieved to find others who understood completely. We all knew that June Clever had never passed an unproductive naptime when "the Beav" was but a babe. She would have checked her curls, tied on her apron, and started dinner. Mrs. Brady would have had "the girls" over for coffee and crafts. Our husbands seemed to believe that the housecleaning, laundry, coupon-clipping, bill-paying, and "just-because-you're-special" baking could fill that empty time slot, no problem. Mostly, I just wanted to sleep.

Except on the weeks when Playgroup was at my house. Knowing that my four neighbors would be coming for coffee—and that their four babies would be crawling on my dirty floors—sent me into a baking/cleaning frenzy. Knowing that for four solid hours I would have four other adults to talk to made it all worth it, even though the main topic of discussion was invariably our infants and our home lives and motherhood.

It's not nice to fool around with Mother Nature.

"Once there was a tree . . ." I was full of anticipation as I settled Nate down into the crook of my arm and read the first page. The book was special to me, I'd purchased it not long after Nate's birth, relishing the thought of reading it to him in the then-distant future: *The Giving Tree* by Shel Silverstein. I wanted to share the wonder with my baby boy, to read to him a book I'd read as a child. I turned the page.

". . . and she loved a little boy." Oh no. My brain was freezing, alarm bells ringing. Consciousness clicking in, albeit tinged with regret. I'd studied traditional literary representations of women, of mothers, though I'd pretty much glossed over the seemingly tired discussion of the virgin/whore dichotomy. The recognition that usually both nature and culture are represented as female—with nature as the seductive virgin to be deflowered, society and culture as the corrupt mother or whore to be escaped—had irritated me, but I had filed it away as something to be aware of as I studied the canonical books. I didn't want to find it in my childhood books. In my children's books.

The Giving Tree is about the evolving relationship between an altruistic tree—always "she" in the lower
case, and never named—and a male character. When the
male character is very young he comes to play in and
around the tree; "he would gather her leaves and make
them into crowns and play king of the forest;" he'd
climb on her, swing on her, eat her apples, carve his
name and the names of other women into her skin.
"And the boy loved the tree very much. And the tree
was happy."

But then the male character starts to grow up and begins to find the tree inadequate for his needs. He neglects
her, abandons her, returns only to make demands of her.
Still and always calling him "Boy" with a capital B, the
tree gives herself away to the boy for his gain. She urges
the boy-man to cut off her limbs, saw off her trunk, de-
capitate her, so that he may build a house, sail away in
a boat, be happy. Years pass between these gracious,
selfless offerings, years when the tree remains rooted,
alone, stripped of her virtues, as "Boy," perpetually dis-
satisfied, explores the freedoms of his life. Becomes a
man. Becomes an old man. The "boy" never once, never
ever, thanks the tree for her sacrifices or reciprocates in
any way. When he finally returns, the glorious tree has
been reduced to a depressed "old stump," who knows
herself to be worthless. " 'I am sorry, Boy,' said the tree,
'but I have nothing left to give you . . . I am sorry,'
sighed the tree. 'I wish that I could give you something
. . . but I have nothing left. I am just an old stump. I am
sorry. . . .' "

My stomach was in knots, icy cold knots. Nate's eyes
had widened in reaction to my reaction. My mind was
rebelling. I wanted to either scream or throw up. I
couldn't decide which. This was too close to home. I

didn't want to be a mother who noticed these things and was upset by them. I wanted my saccharine sweet memories intact. I didn't want to acknowledge that early readings such as these could have had any effect whatsoever on my development. I wanted denial. But these days denial is hard to come by. In all aspects of my life now, different voices speak and intertwine truths I once thought unrelated. The girl who had first heard the story had become the new mother who bought the book who had become the becoming-conscious mother who cannot close her eyes, for the love of her babies, who will always be babies and who are no longer babies. I finished reading the book.

"I don't need very much now," said the boy, "just a quiet place to sit and rest. I am very tired."

"Well," said the tree, straightening herself up as much as she could, "well, an old stump is good for sitting and resting. Come, Boy, sit down. Sit down and rest."

And the boy did.

And the tree was happy.

The End.

I gave my innocent, sleepy son a long, heated lecture about how ungrateful, how badly behaved that boy had been, about how no *person* should treat any other *person* with such disrespect. But he'd already slipped off into dreamland. I buried the book in the back of a kitchen cabinet.

Four years later, a flyer came home with Nate from kindergarten. His elementary school was soliciting donations for a fund-raiser. The theme was *The Giving Tree;* all the children were encouraged to buy a leaf.

See me? I'm *very* carefully wording a note to my son's twenty-three-year-old teacher, trying to "commiserate" with her about how difficult it is to address, on a kindergarten level, the sexism in *The Giving Tree.* I'm trying to remember to print in roly-poly upper- and lower-case letters, to show that I'm setting a good example. I know this note won't fit her picture of me—the mom who is happy to help with class parties and read funny poems to the kids—and I'm trying to make sure my other voice doesn't create a negative distortion.

Ms. Sebastian called and left a message on my machine that I ought to call her as soon as possible. She didn't sound as if she appreciated my insights. Though she didn't say so, I could tell poor Nate had just been branded: "Franze, Nate: child of radical feminist." In giving birth to my son, in wanting the best of worlds for him, I'd given seed to a new woman. And now my growth had branched out to encircle him, to mark him. Bits of me glint in his sturdy little body, noticeable to outsiders.

A mother is a mosaic . . . shattered, fragmented and
awesome to behold.

See me? I am a fragmented woman, as are all the mothers I know. Indistinctly lovely, frightening, disoriented, and sometimes dangerous up close. Awesome when viewed from without and away. Sharp fans of milkglass, shattered by the ball-peen hammer of disillusion, held intact by deep knowing and love. Skeins of Maryblue veins on a sweet-smelling neckfold, tucked up close under a pocked patch of ruby. Lackluster pieces of tired eyes . . . hazel-brown, cerulean, slate, and amber. Pinpoints of neon consciousness. Grounding lines of jet that lead up and back and around and away in random patterns. Broad expanses of beige boredom. Shots of light insight and dark doubt framed in leafy green revelations. Crystal infant teardrops throwing off rainbows of life so intense you must stand back.

To see me.

To see us all.

To see.

A Dangerous Thing to Hope For

Gail Greiner

When my son Nikolai was born after eighteen hours of excruciating back labor, the crown of his head banging against my tailbone with every contraction, the delivery nurse said, "I don't like his tone." The doctor, hanging him upside down and slapping him on the back, couldn't get him to cry. "You didn't have Demerol, did you?" she asked, having arrived just in time for the pushing. "He looks like a baby on Demerol." And when we saw the enormous black and blue bump on the side of Nikolai's head, my husband and I feared that our child was brain damaged.

Our fears about Nikolai were, thankfully, unfounded. After my failed attempt at getting him to latch on—"You can try," the nurse had said, "but I don't think it's going to work"—Michael followed our drowsy baby down to the nursery where he let out a forceful wail in protest against the bath, assuring us that he was OK. Our pediatrician, to quell our fears, ordered a cranial sonogram. "This is just in case he can't get his shirt over his head when he's three," he told us. Up in radiology we were able to see, through the soft spot on our baby's head, his beautiful, perfectly formed brain. "He's going to Harvard," the technician said. Michael and I both breathed a sigh of relief, but secretly I felt terrible guilt at what I saw as my rejection of him during those milli-seconds that seemed like hours after his birth. I pulled away from my newborn, in an effort to ready myself in case he were going to be taken from me, as if I could protect myself from this terrible love.

Now, as Nikolai's first birthday approaches, I see that both my fear that he was brain damaged and the way I withdrew in reaction to that fear were part of what has become a familiar cycle. This pattern of fear and with-drawal manifests itself in my feeling that I won't be able to connect with my child and that, one way or another, I'll lose him.

Of course the pattern didn't start with Nikolai's birth or his conception. Not long after my parents separated, when I was eight, my mother gave me a book about divorce. I remember turning immediately to a chapter called "The One-Eyed Monster," thinking that whoever wrote this book understood that ever since my parents' divorce I'd been afraid, and maybe they'd be able to tell me something comforting, something I could use at midnight when I couldn't sleep and thought the squir-rels on the roof were really a murderer coming to take what was left of my family. What the authors had meant was that a child of divorce is like a monster with only one eye—read *parent at home*—afraid of losing that as well and being left blind, read *alone*. In a more general way, the authors were exactly right: Out of my parents' divorce a monster was born in the form of loss. Not only did I lose my family as I knew it, but I lost my sense of competence and entitlement, my sense that I was both lovable and capable of love.

As commonplace and banal as it was in the late sixties, my parents' divorce was a sudden death to me. A death of home, a death of happiness, a death of love. "Mommy and Daddy both love you very much," my mother told my brother and me, "but Daddy doesn't love Mommy anymore." With those words we dissolved into tears. Because we knew about love, we knew that our house was built on it, that our lives depended on it, and without it we couldn't survive.

Another chapter in the one-eyed monster book explained that my parents' divorce wasn't my fault. I never thought it was my fault. Whatever had killed my parents' love had done it quickly and silently, with no warning. From this I learned an important lesson: If it could get them, it could get me too. No one is safe. Twenty-six years later, that message is still embedded in me. That and the feeling that because it happened to me, because my family imploded when I was eight, I am somehow undeserving of a happy family, that now, as a mother, I am unworthy of this bounty. I don't think my parents' divorce was my fault, but I guess on some level I feel it was my fate.

When I was older the monster manifested itself in anxiety that I wouldn't get married, which turned into the worry that I wouldn't be able to get pregnant, to the fear that I'd miscarry within the first trimester, to the fear that my baby would be born with some horrible malady. Somewhere I felt that such perfect happiness— from finding my soul mate to cradling a baby so that her warm head fit in the curve of my neck—would never be granted me, a daughter of divorce, a child of family unhappiness.

When I was pregnant I refused to let myself imagine holding my baby, as if I could protect myself from the devastation I'd feel if something did go wrong. My only indulgence was imagining dressing him or her in different hats: a little baseball cap, a Moroccan skullcap, the little three-pointed knit hat, a gift from my office.

I bought nothing for the baby. My due date was in early September, but when August rolled around Michael and I still hadn't gotten a single onesie. Gifts sent to us, tiny white beaded moccasins, a Peter Rabbit rattle, a stuffed Noah's ark with miniature pairs of cows, zebras, lions, and alligators, I secreted away on a shelf in the linen closet, scarcely daring to look at them.

Maybe because I hadn't let myself imagine holding my baby, I was completely unprepared for the ferocious love I felt for Nikolai as he lay on my chest in the hospital, his head no bigger than a doughnut. Hand in hand with that terrible love came a sickening fear. "Your children will take you for ransom," a friend once warned me, and I didn't know what she meant until I felt him against me, his breath so determined, his brow intent on sleep.

Home from the hospital, I barely left the house for a month. I blamed it on lack of sleep and an exhausting labor, but mostly, I think, it was because I was exhilarated by my love for Nikolai. I didn't want the magical bubble surrounding us to burst. At the same time I was devastated by my love and by the knowledge that I would never be safe again.

In those first tender days after bringing Nikolai home, I was pained when my in-laws held him. I wanted to be holding him. I couldn't breathe easily again until he was back in my arms, where he belonged. When I looked at our dog, our sweet, docile Rosie, I saw only a carnivore. I feared that some not-so-atavistic twinge would kick in and she'd steal Nikolai from his bassinet, snap his neck, and eat him for lunch.

When friends dropped by unannounced with their toddler, it was all I could do to be civil. Their child, earlier a sweet baby, was a huge unwieldy creature teeming with germs from day care. What were they doing bringing him into the same room with my pure, untainted, vulnerable newborn? The first time Michael and I took our tentative steps outside with our baby, I was shocked at my reaction when acquaintances tried to peer into the Baby Bjorn. "Keep away," I wanted to say.

Suddenly I saw and heard everything through the eyes of a mother. I couldn't bear any bad news, much less the news on television. One reported death meant the infinite pain of one mother, a plane crash meant that pain multiplied by infinity. I had entered into the secret club of motherhood with its combined joys and terrors, but no one was talking about the terror.

"I wasn't prepared for how much I'd love him," I said, looking for communion at a meeting of new mothers at the local Y, my first real outing, when Nikolai was little more than a month old. In the circle we were sharing what had taken us most by surprise. "I didn't think I could love anything more than I loved my dog," I added, trying to lighten it up a little, feeling self-conscious as my statement was met with an awkward silence. But what I'd really wanted to say was "Aren't you terrified? Aren't you afraid that something's going to happen to your baby? Or to your eight-year-old or to your teenager or to your grown son? And then where would you be? What would happen to you? How can I leave him with a babysitter who might let him fall out a window, how can I take him to day care when the building could explode? How can I let him take the school bus when it could slip off an icy embankment or be hit by a speeding train?" But these new mothers expressed only concern about their lack of sleep, or the difficulty of getting around the city with a stroller, or whether or not to return to work.

Afterward, though, one of the moderators said she'd been moved by what I'd said, and that in Anne Tyler's *Dinner at the Homesick Restaurant,* one character tries to lessen that feeling of terror and vulnerability by having another child but finds, instead, that the feeling has doubled. Here, at last, was acknowledgment that what I was going through might be normal, that once a mother, I had no escape.

It was during a walk with Nikolai and Michael that I began to realize my fear was intrusive, that it obstructed my time with my family and interfered with my joy. A little boy, perhaps eight or nine, rode by on a red bicycle and Michael said to Nikolai, "That'll be you, little guy," and instead of picturing Nikolai at eight speeding around the flower beds on his bright red birthday bicycle, I pictured my husband's grief should his son not get to grow up.

I don't know if I worry more than the average mother, but I know the toll it takes on me. I can only imagine how it will affect Nikolai. When I am afraid, whether it's a fear of not being able to control his crying or manage his crawling, a fear of illness, a fear of random violence and natural disasters, I withdraw emotionally. My myriad fears compromise my sense of connection with my baby. Taking me out of my little world with him, they leave me hovering above, a fearful observer.

Not only am I robbed of the present with my son, but something is taken away from him, as well—his right to an untainted, unadulterated vision of his future.

Now, the day before Nikolai's first birthday, I not only feel guilt about those moments in the delivery room when I hung back, suspended in limbo, as if I were deciding whether or not to keep him. I feel guilt about all the times I am withdrawn from him. Being with my baby, really being present with him, is something I have to actively give myself over to. It still doesn't come naturally. Nikolai seems particularly demanding now, crawling into things he shouldn't, forever asking to be entertained. Exhausted, I get into this "my turn, your turn" thing with Michael, in an effort to get away from Nikolai. Part of my need to escape comes, I know, from my own expectation that I should be totally present, that I should stimulate Nikolai constantly, and that I should always enjoy it. Trying to make up for what I fear I lack, my presence alone isn't enough: I have to be an *uber* mother.

"When you roll a ball to him, does he roll it back?" my pediatrician asked me at a recent checkup, and I had to say I don't roll a ball to him. My cousin has taught her baby how to clap and how to throw away an acorn she's plucked up from the lawn rather than putting it in her mouth. Another cousin knows just where Nikolai is ticklish and makes him laugh a laugh I've never heard, never elicited. My friend says "Give mummy a kiss" to her nine-month-old and her baby happily obliges, leaning forward and putting my friend's nose in her mouth. The same friend hands my own son a toy, stopping his crying instantly while I futilely bounced his seat, pleading, "Baby, baby . . ." At times like these I feel like I'm a bad mother, like I'm missing something other women were born with, some secret knowledge of how to *be* with a baby. Instead of simply rolling the ball, or asking for a kiss, or teaching my baby to clap, I worry that there is some magic mothering formula that I am not privy to. I forget that Nikolai and I have our own routines and rituals, that we polka around the house, play peek-a-boo and the kissing monster, that I made up new words to "Twinkle, Twinkle, Little Star" just for him. I forget that when I'm nursing him to sleep, my hand holding his foot as he softly strokes my chest, I am with him entirely.

So now when I find myself pulling back, afraid that my happy family will somehow be snatched from me, I remember these things, and I remember Nikolai, so capable, so full of life, so generous in his love. He embodies life and connection, and I'm learning through him. For if there's any formula for being a good mother, it's to let my child unfold, and to be there with him when he does.

Nikolai is standing on his own for the first time today. As I watch him and clap wildly, I am filled with that mixture of happiness and sadness peculiar to mothers. Almost a year into motherhood, I have come to revel in this strange concoction. Because as I clap, tears streaming down my face, I see that it is this clapping, these tears, that are the weight and measure of my love.

INITIATION

AMY LEVINE

My old robe pulled around my still-flaccid middle and my hair matted to my head from the shower, I stood in our tiny hospital room shivering and blinking at the sight of my husband cradling our new daughter. I was pleased by how calm and gentle he was with her, relieved that his usual equanimity had made the leap to fatherhood with him. But, where was my own confidence? All I felt was panic. Despite my determination to maintain the elation that overcame me upon her birth, I was dizzy with bewilderment.

Before I had a chance to comb my hair, Sonya stirred with a whimper and my obstetrician came by for rounds. She looked rested and professional in her work clothes, especially in contrast to the way I felt: a bedraggled and harried mess. After pressing down hard on my belly to check that my uterus was contracting, the doctor glanced quickly at my reddened nipples. Standing in the shower, I had been amazed by how raw they had become overnight. Bill had stayed with us and neither of us slept much because Sonya didn't. Most of the night I had lain on my side, my left arm cocked painfully over my head, trying to breast-feed. During her visit my doctor assured me that the soreness from Sonya's nursing would subside, but that I "really shouldn't let her suck longer than ten minutes" on each side. Ten minutes! I knew Sonya could go for an hour if I let her. Such advice worsened my sense of unease.

I might have gained some perspective on my harried feelings that morning had I been inclined to trust in Bill's teasing words about how I rarely take change well. In recent weeks he'd made much joking mention of it. With the exception of my wedding day, which for some reason I met with serenity, I have faced each milestone in my life with a mourning period for the old me. I will never forget lying in bed the night before I entered junior high school, crying in my mother's lap, scared to go. "Nothing could ever be as great as North Main Street Elementary School," I sobbed. Needless to say, I did the same thing the night before high school and college, with my nostalgia focused on the place I most recently left. Now I was graduating from independent, professional, childless wife to "Mom," and crying in my mother's lap seemed an entirely inappropriate option, although—truth be told—I did just that the day we brought Sonya home.

When the doctor walked out it was time to nurse again. I settled into a cold vinyl chair, opened my robe, and unhooked the trap door in my maternity bra for the fourth time that morning. It was only seven-thirty. When Sonya latched on to my cracked nipples, the pain made me swoon. Bill stood in front of me and instructed me to breathe until it subsided, as he had during my labor contractions. Meanwhile, gifts and greetings from the outside world—symbols of the reality of what had just transpired in our lives—began pouring in. Suffice it to say that my gratefulness didn't come till later. With a crooked smile, I accepted the vases of flowers, mylar balloons, mammoth teddy bears, and heaps of frilly and oversized baby clothes, worrying about where I'd put them in our tiny apartment.

While I was breast-feeding, several nurses popped in to check on us. Their presence relieved me, but I also resented them for their youthful vigor and weekend plans. I was struck by how vastly different our worlds had become overnight. Just a day ago I was carefree enough to do for and worry about others, or myself. Now I didn't give a damn about anyone else; I was astonished by my baby's needs and my own discomfort. Fifteen hours after Sonya's birth, I felt unable to slow this Ferris wheel of change. When I seemed to be getting on top of things a new problem or hunger pang would strike and my confidence would be pitched down again, just to swoop back up with the calming feel of Sonya's gentle grip or her sweet slumber.

My parents got to the hospital at eleven-thirty, having stalled for a few hours. The night before they'd rushed into the labor and delivery room minutes after Sonya's birth, encroaching on a time I wished I'd made the point of reserving for my new family. Just the sight of them that morning exasperated me; my life had evolved, and the emotion evident on their faces augmented my anxiety. I tried to chat with them, but the tension in the room was monstrous, and it all emanated from me. I had been nursing intermittently since that dawn shower and the exhaustion and hunger that I came to associate with nursing were overwhelming.

I felt horribly guilty for my brooding because I was already so in love with Sonya; her tiny starlike hands, searching mouth, and soft cheeks thrilled me. But I was distracted by the frightening loss of control I felt. I told myself to push these feelings away, but I couldn't. Finally, reading my mood, Bill asked my parents if they would mind going out for lunch to give me a little rest. They happily obliged, probably relieved to get away from their Jekyll and Hyde daughter. When they left I sank down on the bed and watched Bill rock Sonya in his arms.

It didn't get much better when we first got home, although I was happy to be back on familiar ground. My new responsibilities were a thousand times more confounding than my old desk job, although when asked I still told people that I wouldn't be "working" during the coming year. (I soon stopped phrasing it that way.) I was amazed at the ease with which Bill laughed at the hallmarks of infancy, but I rarely found humor in them. I realize now that early motherhood is a very different sensibility than fatherhood, with its own occasions for laughter, but during those days my seriousness clashed with Bill's joviality. A loneliness borne from our dichotomy set in somewhere deep inside me.

The plan among the grandparents was to spread out their arrivals, but there was some overlap. Bill's parents, who arrived with the intention of helping us through the second week, had much the same effect on me as my parents did, with the added sting of strangeness. They'd never seen me in an emotional state; I showed myself involuntarily, but self-consciously. My method of exerting some control over my life was to shrink from everything they tried to do for me. For example, they would suggest that I take a nap when the baby did. Take a nap?! I couldn't relax. I was so relieved to finally have a moment to myself that I didn't want to waste it asleep—despite the fact that I'd be happier if I was rested. Little inconveniences, like my dad and father-in-law sitting on the couch across from me as I clumsily attached Sonya to my sore nipples or knowing that people in the next rooms were within earshot of the gurgling water of my perineum bath, grated on my nerves. When they urged me to eat, saying that nursing was zapping my energy, I ate less. I didn't understand then why I wasn't hungry, but now I realize that I used eating as a means of control. I knew my nutrition was something I could navigate and their telling me when—and even what—to eat robbed me of the very thing I most yearned for. When they'd tell me to lie down, I would announce that I wanted to go for a walk. And on and on. It would have been so much better if I'd simply expressed my needs at the time, but I was shackled with a fear of disappointing them and of confrontation.

What I realize now is I was so hard on myself about my ability to properly care for Sonya and, paradoxically, so convinced that only I could appease her that I didn't want to let anyone else fulfill her needs. For me, "help" meant keeping me company, not the hands-on approach. I was even territorial about passing her to my husband. In the nursery I was sure I'd figured out the most expert way of cleaning Sonya's umbilicus stub or closing her diaper or getting her T-shirts over her head without startling her, and I stiffened when he attempted to get into the act. It would have been nice if I could have learned from the loving and experienced example of our parents, or laughed with Bill at his clumsiness (and mine), but who was I kidding? "Nice" is not what brand-new motherhood is about. It's about exhaustion, uncertainty, and soaring, thrilling, startling emotion. For better or worse, no way but my own made me comfortable.

After the first two weeks passed and everyone left, there were other challenges. The simplest routines became big—even nervewracking—events. Taking a shower was a race against the clock. I'd prop Sonya in her bouncy seat, place it on the bathroom floor, and yank a pull toy that played "Twinkle, Twinkle, Little Star." Then I'd jump in the shower and as soon as the last bars of the song played out I'd peek from behind the curtain and begin singing, "Hi, Sweetie. Sonya Be-elle. I love you." If I allowed more than a few moments of silence, I'd hear little whimpers that soon gave way to grumbles and tears. I didn't feel better until I was out of the shower, dripping and holding Sonya, watching her smile at her reflection in the mirror. I had such a hard time letting her cry. I needed to know that she felt secure. Or was it me?

Mealtime was not an issue because I simply had no meals, per se, during Sonya's first few weeks—unless Bill was home to feed me while I breast-fed Sonya. (During dinnertime, I covered her comically with a napkin to shield my crumbs.) When Bill was not home, I did eat, but in jagged hunks and huge unseemly bites and loud slurpy gulps. My days of a fresh salad and the newspaper were gone. If I toasted something I usually ended up eating it cold and if I chilled a drink I drank it warm. I ate finger food such as a dry bagel or a handful of raisins when I took Sonya out for a walk and I kept a bag of M&M's in the diaper bag for a quick zap of energy—anything I could put in one hand and have the other free to carry her or push her stroller.

I was most at ease when Sonya fell asleep during our

walks. It was like a time out, a moment to take a deep breath. Watching her pale face and nearly transparent eyelids as she dozed reassured me that all was well. After a feeding I would dash for the stroller, put a bottle of milk and freezer pack in the diaper bag, and pray for a good hundred yards of strolling peace. I'd go to great lengths to keep her asleep. Because the cracked and bumpy sidewalks in our Boston suburb often jolted her awake, I took to walking her on the road. One day I was scolded for my "carelessness" by an older man with a tan who clearly regarded me as a negligent mother. If he only knew how harshly I judged myself!

If Sonya as much as whimpered I was there in a flash. I monopolized her and relished my work, but my power was also my vice. My insistence on being Wonder Mom—to flit into her room at her first sounds, and to assume the majority of caretaking tasks—kept most of the responsibility in my camp. Although it was my initial means to control, it excluded Bill and ultimately left me feeling suffocated and resentful.

My bitterness showed itself in passive-aggressive ways. I became insistent that we "be quiet." No matter how low the television was, I asked Bill to turn the volume lower. When he was on the telephone I'd scold him. I insisted that he turn down the volume on his (5:30 A.M.) radio alarm so as not to wake Sonya, so much so that he overslept on more than one occasion. I spoke so softly that everyone began telling me to speak up. My defense? If I was going to be there for Sonya any time she awoke, we had to treat the times she was asleep as sacred.

Bill was immensely patient with my intense response to motherhood, but there were times that my will drove a wedge between us. Whether or not I was being fair to

Bill was low on my list of concerns, as awful as that sounds. And it took its toll. There were more than a few nights when I would fall hard asleep while we tried to make some sense of our latest tiff. I would get angry and frustrated by the littlest things he'd done, or worse, didn't do. Yet I felt a striking need to dictate how everything for Sonya should be and became annoyed by his protests. I picked and criticized, stewed and sulked. Never mind that I'd had full days to master the art of folding a dirty diaper, I couldn't bear to watch Bill do it. I remember one night hovering in the nursery doorway, watching him change Sonya's diaper, my knuckles turning white as I gripped the molding. He closed the tabs in a downward position instead of stretching them across her middle, as I did when I found that slanting the labels led to leakage, and it made me cringe. I just couldn't allow this way of diapering her, or that way of burping her, or this way of bathing her, or that way of holding her, if it wasn't MY way.

In spite of my overpowering instinct to monopolize Sonya, I romanticized Bill's opportunity for escape. He was able to get in the car and drive off. So what if it was to go to the hospital, where he was in the grueling last weeks of his residency? He had open road and—I thought, naively—peace of mind. He interacted with other adults, joking about movies and current events. His body did not hurt. His shower was never interrupted by Sonya's impatient cries because I was home when he showered. He could eat lunch without being interrupted; he was able to wear nice clothes. He could run out to the store without worrying that Sonya might need him for breast-feeding. Me? I rocked day and night in the glider rocker, inhaling her sweet scent and savoring her infancy, but also resenting Bill's freedom, with the gnawing, irritated buzz of sleep deprivation.

But what I didn't realize was that Bill envied *me*. One day I heard him talking on the phone, unaware that I could hear him from the next room. "I wish I could stay at home and watch her grow," he said. "It's very hard to leave every day. I feel like I'm missing so much."

As the days and weeks and months have passed, Bill has missed things, but I report them to him with a joy and pride that sustains me. The simple favor of experience has given me my much-groped-for sense of control. Time has rescued me from my chaos. Time, and the wonderful sense that Sonya is happy and developing normally. Her naps fall into a firm schedule; she is resilient and easily appeased. When her daddy comes home from work she flaps her arms and legs and smiles, just as she does when I reappear over her crib as she wakes up from a nap. Bill and I spend entire evenings together after her 7:30 P.M. bedtime. We talk, watch *Seinfeld*, and order Chinese food, like before. Bill still points Sonya's diaper tabs down and I still notice, but we look back, and ahead, with a sense of humor gained from experience.

As I write this I realize that I've more than become a mother. I AM one—a condition that defines me as much as I define it. The awesomeness of parenthood rarely escapes me, and I feel its blessing. Despite my tendency to be hard on myself, I have learned that Sonya needs a happy and relaxed mother too, not a neurotic one. With time I have learned to nurture myself as well as her— and even to entertain the notion of letting go.

BABY BLUES: A JOURNAL

SARAH BIRD

AUGUST 22. Day Three with Wee One: Mom is with Gabriel, so, here I am, for the first time, sitting down to jot a note about the most psychedelic experience of my life: childbirth. After a fairly shitty pregnancy—nine months of ambivalence about a surprise conception at age thirty-nine—I was stunned by how glorious the birth was. I fully expected to be yelling for drugs like Elvis and am glad I didn't. They really need to have different words for pain. Childbirth is more like doing a marathon without moving an inch.

Oops, sounds as if my mom isn't having any luck calming Squidgepot down. I expected crying, but, my God, it sounds as if the little guy is hooked up to electrodes. Better go make sure Grandma's not cranking the generator.

AUGUST 25. Day Six with Wee One: Obviously, we have a complete night shift guy. I'm trying to reset his bat-baby clock by putting on bright lights and loud

music during the day, but they're not having much effect. It doesn't matter. I love to watch him sleep. I love
the way his eyes roam, wide open, when he's asleep.
His little sighs and slurps and gasps and hicks. His
twitch of a smile. The mouth pursing in a rosebud of
theatrical surprise. I love his spine of pop beads and his
breath of milky caramels.

AUGUST 27. Wee One saw his first movie today: *sex,
lies, and videotape.* What would Penelope Leach say about
such a choice? The lobby was mobbed with *cinéastes,*
serious devotees of "film" all dressed in black. So we
waited, then sneaked into the back row, hoping we
wouldn't bother anyone, and I plugged Gabriel in. He
nursed away happily through most of the movie. Yes!, I
congratulated myself, I *am* going to be one of those mothers who just slings her baby over her shoulder, then
charges in just in time to deliver those searing closing
arguments to the jury! This cozy illusion continued
right up until the film's climactic moment. A notably
quiet moment: No background music, no one onscreen is
talking. It's all just telling glances and SILENCE. At
this precise moment, Gabriel explodes with the loudest,
longest, gassiest poop ever unloaded into a diaper. The
looks of disgust and horror from the *cinéastes* sent me
fleeing to the lobby.

SEPTEMBER 2. Two weeks of motherhood and I am
officially Very Tired. Gabriel seems to be sleeping *less*
every day. And night. George has taken to bunking on
the couch since he's having to put in such long hours at
work. There's no reason for him to be awake too since
what happens mostly at night is nursing and, supportive
as he's been, George has completely failed to lactate.

SEPTEMBER 3. Gabriel nursed or fretted from ten
until four in the morning last night. Usually, he conks

out for an hour or so around one or two, but when I tried to put him down at three-thirty, his eyes were wide open, glowing like coals. He seems hungry all the time, then, as soon as he starts to nurse, he pulls his legs up to his tummy as if he's in pain.

This is the fourth time I've called Dr. Finberg. Her nurse assures me that it takes time for "these little ones to get organized."

SEPTEMBER 6. My God, it's been eighteen days! I'm so glad Mom is here, especially since George's enlightened employer granted him exactly one day of paternity leave, then sent him off to El Paso. One day! Just about long enough to boil some water and cut the cord. So, thank God for my mother. I mean, who could ask for more? Mother of six children? A pediatric nurse? If she weren't here I'd be a lot more upset about Gabriel's crying, which gets worse every day. He never sleeps for more than two hours at a stretch, then, when he does, he remains tense and fisted against the world. The worst of it is that I feel it's all my fault. That he spent nine months marinating in the toxic waters of my doubt. This thought tortures me. I am perversely comforted by the fact that even my mom can't seem to calm him down. She spoke to the nurse for me today, whipped a little nurse lingo on her. The word "colic" was mentioned.

SEPTEMBER 7. My mother leaves tomorrow. The other night, just before dawn, when Gabriel finally dozed off, Mom and I sat on the back porch listening to the deer feed and trying to catch a breeze. I steadied myself for a long time before I confessed to her that I was tortured by the fear that I should never have become a mother. She insists that I am a wonderful mother, but I know what is in my heart and feel even more of a fraud that I could fool the person I'm closest to in the world.

She reminds me of how happy I was when we first got home and how little any of us have slept since.

SEPTEMBER 8. George took Mom to the airport today. I couldn't go with him because the slightest noise now causes Gabriel to start shrieking. Literally. The sound of the air conditioner clicking on causes him to absolutely lose it. I felt like clinging to my mom, begging her to stay. But she's already postponed her departure two times. Before she left, she told me I had to speak to my pediatrician and ask about colic. As my mother drives away, the last of my early euphoria goes with her. I feel as desolate and lonely in my suburban fortress as a pioneer woman on the windswept frontier plains.

SEPTEMBER 9. Finberg's nurse has taken to calling me "Mom." "The first few weeks can be awful tough, 'Mom.'" I reread the sections on colic in my baby books. They describe colic as a couple of hours of crying in the evening that can be pacified by putting a baby on top of a rocking washing machine or driving around in the car with the baby strapped in a car seat. Both of these "cures" send Gabriel into shrieking fits. His crying— high-pitched and desperate as a cat being tortured— grows daily in ferocity. The only thing that does console him is the Daddy Dance. The Daddy Dance requires George to sproing around violently. Only maniacal pogoing will make Gabriel stop crying. I try it when I have the energy. One thing I haven't had to worry about is losing the preggo pounds. Between the Daddy Dance and prisoner-of-war sleep deprivation, I weigh less than I did in high school.

SEPTEMBER 10. My nipples are ringed in bruises. When Gabriel nurses I think of Bill Pickett, the famous black cowboy who invented steer wrestling. Pickett could pull down a bull by clamping down on the animal's lip. I swear, watching Gabriel as he writhes and jerks on my nipple that that is what he's trying to do. Yee-HAW! Ride 'em, cowbaby!

I finally got Finberg on the phone today and let her listen to Gabriel shriek his wild banshee shriek. She was infuriatingly dismissive. I swear if I told her Gabriel was breathing fire and eating pig iron, she'd tell me that that too is "pretty much in that broad range we call normal." She admitted that he "might" have "what we call colic," but all that really is are just immature nervous and digestive systems. That I'd just have to give him time to "get himself organized." What is this "organized"? She acts like everything will be all right as soon as Gabriel gets that little miniature Filofax. She says there's nothing to be done except wait. That most colic disappears by the third month. Three months! I can't survive three months. Then she adds with crushing condescension, "Babies generally sleep more than moms think they do."

SEPTEMBER 14. Kept a precise log of *exactly* how much Gabriel slept yesterday. Five hours and thirty-seven minutes. Total. In a twenty-four-hour period. Some of that in twenty-minute snatches. The rest of the time he was either writhe-nursing or shrieking unless I was pogoing with him. I called this information in to Finberg, but there has been no response. Surely this can't be within "that broad range we call normal?"

SEPTEMBER 16. I cannot last another two months. Alternative solutions: I've eliminated all dairy products from my diet. I've given Gabriel a tea with some homeopathic remedies. We tried acupressure. Still he shrieks. I'm almost too tired to feel sorry for him and his immature nervous system anymore. George is under a lot of pressure about the El Paso project. I know his job is shit; still, when he walks out of the house in the morning, he could be going to Tahiti, I am that jealous. I count every second until he returns. I turn Gabriel over to him at the door, go to the bathroom, lock myself in, turn on the shower, and cry.

SEPTEMBER 19. A new variation in sleep deprivation has appeared. When Gabriel *does* finally conk out, I can't sleep. Probably because I get so tense transferring him to his cradle. It's like deactivating a bomb. I sit up, then move in minute increments, not breathing, inching forward with reptilian movements of the butt muscles to the side of the bed. I stand and walk the few steps to the cradle as if I had a glass bowl of water on my head I am trying not to upset, then lower him in. About half the time, he blows up anyway and wakes up shrieking in pain or terror or I don't know what. If not, I lie in bed, rigid, waiting for him to explode. It would be heavenly to sleep with him, but Finberg has warned me against doing that.

SEPTEMBER 25. Awake since three, I dragged myself out of bed when I heard the paper hit the porch. On the front page was a story about a boy who was abducted at the age of seven, then held for eight years until he was found. The boy grew up, married, and had two children that he wouldn't let out of his sight. "I'm okay if I can see or hear them," he would say. The man was killed in a motorcycle accident. When George found me still sobbing a few hours later, he said something had to change. He would take over at night. We'll switch to formula. This prospect panics me. I've done the research. I know Gabriel needs the antibodies from my breast milk. More than that, though, nursing is my strongest link to Gabriel, the only way I have now of showing him that I love and want him, that if I can't completely give my baby my heart then I have to give him my body. Though he wants to, George is able to help less and less. His high-impact Daddy Dancing has aggravated an old back injury, and it's painful now for him even to lift Gabriel out of his cradle.

SEPTEMBER 28. I haven't been answering the phone much since Mom left, but I got several insistent messages from Clare. I guess only your best friend can order you to come to dinner. We tried. Got Gabriel strapped into his car seat. Got halfway to her house, then just couldn't stand listening to him shriek another second and, knowing that he'd continue shrieking at Clare's house, we turned around and headed back. When we got home and I released Gabriel from the torture-rack car seat, the night air seemed to calm him, so I decided to try a walk. Two blocks away, he started screaming again. A man inside his house pulled back his curtain to look out and see who was being tortured. I hurried home as fast as I could.

SEPTEMBER 30. George had planned on coming home this afternoon at three. When he called to say that yet another crisis had flared up and he wouldn't be able to leave, all he heard for a minute or two was me sobbing and Gabriel wailing, then he said, "Go to the car. Drive to Finberg's office." I started to protest. I hadn't had a shower in two days. Hadn't washed my hair in a week. "Go to the car," George repeated. "I will meet you at Finberg's in fifteen minutes. I'm leaving now."

At the office, the receptionist thought there had been an accident from the way Gabriel was crying. Finberg wasn't in, so we saw the famous Dr. Ben White, of Ben White Boulevard. He listened to Gabriel cry for about thirty seconds, then said, "I've been a pediatrician for sixty years and that's about the most ear-shattering crying I've ever heard. I almost never do this, but . . ." He wrote out a prescription for something called Levsin's Drops. We gave Gabriel the prescribed two drops and he slept for two hours. It terrified me. I hauled out the PDR and discovered that Levsin's Drops are in the same family as belladonna. Can I give an opiate to a six-week-old baby?

OCTOBER 17. Had a couple of utterly dreamy days. Gabriel and I both had colds. We had a great night. He slept from twelve-thirty to four-thirty. Nursed, then we both went back to sleep again until eight-thirty. Amazing how sleep brightens your attitude. Still, I must give voice to the forbidden words: If I had it all to do over again, I would not. These are the words a mother must never utter. The words that negate the existence of the being she brought into the world. The words I will bury.

OCTOBER 25. I plugged the phone back in last week and have heard from my agents on both coasts, my book editor, two magazine editors, and the movie producers about missed deadlines and manuscripts I should be working on. I have to find some help.

OCTOBER 31. Happy Halloween! My God, what a freak show we have endured interviewing babysitter candidates. We came so close to hiring a woman George and I both perceived as warm, caring, and competent right up until the moment she said, "If you call that last name on my references, I never did hit that child." And she was the best! At least I will be working at home. My heart goes out to any mother who has to leave an infant. We finally did settle on a young woman from Iran. She's here studying early childhood development at the university and is the oldest of six children, so I'm hopeful.

NOVEMBER 3. Eeek! The Iranian is a disaster. I'm holed up back here in my office, listening to Gabriel wail, counting the seconds until I can ask her to leave. She showed up with her mother, who was in a rage because I had asked her daughter if she could do some of Gabriel's laundry while he slept. Gabriel and the Iranian mom break into full shriek at the same time. So, while I jump around doing the Daddy Dance trying to calm Gabriel, the mother goes through the family's illustrious pedigree and close connections to the Shah, citing the many servants they had employed back in Iran, and what an insult it was to the dynasty to have asked her daughter to do baby laundry!

NOVEMBER 15. I am exhausted. Black whirlies dance constantly in front of my eyes. I've had a hacking cough for the past week. I can't allow myself to remember my old life. I was in paradise and voluntarily walked out. Why? There is something that feels so incurably hormonal about my mood that I've looked up depression in all my pregnancy and baby books. They talk about the "baby blues," about feeling weepy the third or fourth day after the delivery as hormones settle out. They suggested going out for a special dinner. "Weepy" and "special dinners" sound so pastel in contrast to the violent colors of my own emotional palette that I can only assume my problems are something else entirely. Something caused by a diabolical combination of health misfortunes and bad character. That I do not have the "baby blues." What I have is a decision that was wrong for me and that I must learn to live with.

NOVEMBER 19. Three months. The magic three months. Gabriel cried for ten hours today. I wouldn't say the colic is gone quite yet.

NOVEMBER 22. I've had a strangely lingering case of

stomach flu. We hired a woman to help out. She has eight grandchildren. When I tried to warn her about Gabriel, she assured me that "Babies love me. *All* babies love me." After a couple hours with our little panther cub who can only be soothed by some major slam-dancing, she handed Gabriel back to me. Then, while I nurse him, she plunks down next to me and starts in on this endless recitation of surgeries and medical anomalies. So I am now haunted by stories of relatives whose bones "were just a-snappin' like twigs, she was that et up by the bone marrow cancer." Even worse are the tales of births gone bad. Of uteri that "set up like concrete" and "third-degree tears right up to the rectum."

DECEMBER 26. Day after Christmas. George just got out of the hospital today with an eight-inch incision zippering his spine. Whatever toll his years of football and Frisbee took on his back were fatally exacerbated by the stress of the colic months. The experience was terrifying. First his pain, then the creeping numbness in his left foot. The night before he went into the hospital, he lay in my arms and cried. He's had to be so strong and so stoic for so long.

Oh, I just remembered: I turned forty today.

DECEMBER 30. A wonderful surprise. Diane came over last night with a Greek salad and a couple of bottles of good red for a late birthday celebration. We polished off both bottles. In spite of a hangover, I felt incredibly good the next morning and realized that Gabriel had slept through the night for the first time.

JANUARY 6. It was the wine. Gabriel didn't sleep through the night. *I* did.

JANUARY 25. Odd as it sounds, this past month, with George recuperating at home, has been lovely. We've all spent a lot of time together snuggling in bed.

Life would be fairly cozy if I could switch off that constant thrum of anxiety about the deadlines I've missed, the books I fear I will never write.

I was talking on the phone yesterday to a friend, male, who was complaining about having to put in forty-eight hours straight to finish manuscript revisions on time. As I listened to him complain about spending the kind of uninterrupted time I won't have for years, I had this very clear image of being on the starting line of a race track with men and childless women lined up on either side of me. The gun fires, they all burst out of the starting blocks, and there I am clutching Gabriel, trailing after them, trying to keep up while I burp, diaper, and breast-feed.

FEBRUARY 10. Gabriel is finally, officially "organized." Now that he is no longer in pain, he is an utterly charming fellow. He's starting to fill out and, best of all, he sleeps. Six hours a night and two naps a day. Unfortunately, I'm still not sleeping. A wonderful new addition to our lives is the Snugli. I pop him in that and we're off. He also tolerates the car seat now, so our world is opening back up. I took him to the library yesterday and checked out all the books they have on insomnia. I know my world would brighten if I could only sleep.

FEBRUARY 25. Gabriel is delicious. His new nickname is Mr. Creamcake. He is all pink and creamy. I've been battling cabin fever. George won't be allowed to lift anything heavier than ten pounds for a year, so I can only dart out in brief snatches. I've been getting a fair amount of work done during my insomnia hours: I wake up at three or four every morning. The first moments are the worst. I am vaulted into consciousness drenched in dread and foreboding. It takes hours to build up the energy to haul myself out of bed.

I'm making a conscious effort to memorize Gabriel. The way he bugs his eyes and opens his mouth in a tight "O" like a Kabuki actor displaying comically theatrical surprise when I read to him. The smell of the steam vaporizer mixed with the cozy, cheesy odor of the diapers in the pail as we nurse by nightlight at midnight. Someday I hope I will look back on these mental snapshots and feel the joy that is out of my reach right now.

MARCH 1. Had another bout with that odd stomach flu. George goes to physical therapy three times a week. Since this is my journal for telling all the truths I can speak nowhere else, I might as well confess my irrational resentment when he goes off to exercise and be massaged by a (good-looking, young, semi-worshipful, female) therapist.

MARCH 15. Jeez, I hate it that this sounds like the Book of Job, but I pulled my back out. Ligaments. The doctor said it would be fine in a week or two if I don't do any lifting. I asked if he could explain that to my six-month-old. The doctor looked at me as if I were delusional and I probably am. I've been calling around trying to find some sort of hydraulic device for getting Gabriel in and out of his crib. Surely there must be something for handicapped parents, but I can't find it. Looked at a couple of infant care centers and they drove cold wedges into my heart. The worst was The Children's World Learning Center. Ammonia smell of pee when I walked in. No one was at the front desk, the checkpoint. Wandered back. Peeked into nursery. Rows of cribs stacked on top of each other like chicken coops lined two walls. Only two workers for a couple dozen children and they were both gossiping away to each other. Even worse, when they caught sight of me, they broke into this animated charade of caregiving. Then the receptionist spotted me and told me state regulations forbid visitors from coming in without first "registering." She gave me a brochure that talked about curriculum and caring. The picture on the front showed this very made-up young woman bottle-feeding an infant. She had awful red talons, nails as long as a Mandarin princess. I hate to imagine parents more desperate than myself who would leave a child there.

APRIL 1. Beth, queen of all twelve-step programs, dropped by today without warning. I was mildly embarrassed. It was three in the afternoon and I was slopping around in the same sweatsuit I've worn for the past week. Hair not combed. My house a total wreck. Beth, never one to beat around the bush, informed me that I was "clinically depressed" and needed to call her therapist. Immediately. I tried to let her know how far from possible that was. That if I had the time to see a therapist I would use it to sleep, or clean up my house, or, who knows?, take a shower. She just left this therapist's number and said, "When the pain gets bad enough, you'll call."

APRIL 15. Finished my manuscript. I like it. Got the news yesterday that my last novel was chosen by the New York Public Library as a Book To Remember for the year. Intellectually, I recognize that these events should be causes for happiness. Just as I recognize that Gabriel should be a source of joy. I feel close and connected to him when he nurses, but the rest of the time I look at him and simply wonder what a good mother would be experiencing. I'm certain my outlook would improve if I could sleep, if my back would heal.

MAY 15. Have to chronicle this amazing small person, this little man with the big mission. He wakes up and I take him back to bed to nurse, then he gets down to the important business of ripping my face off with his razor-sharp nails. When we finish, he studies his hand like he's on his first acid trip, "Oh, wow, what *is* this many-pronged thing?" Cracks me up. I hold him up on my stomach and he immediately starts doing his hoedown dance, tapping his left foot into me. I blow into his face. He shuts his eyes and, completely enraptured, grins his big toothless grin. I wish I had the typical reactions to all this baby bliss. Doing motherhood without the right hormones or whatever the hell it is I'm missing is like having a tooth pulled without Novocaine.

JULY 15. Eleven months on. I came across an article today about post-partum depression. I was utterly galvanized reading this account of PPD that exactly mirrors my experience—insomnia, exhaustion, loss of joy, feelings of hopelessness and doom, loss of appetite, disappearance of libido, overwhelming guilt. Hope glimmers as I recall the article's closing imperative. "Remember: Depression is an illness, not a weakness."

JULY 25. Visited my gynecologist with this PPD information. He listened sympathetically, then suggested that I do what he and his wife did after the birth of their third child: take a trip to Hawaii. I must find another doctor. He gave me a prescription for Xanax. I tried it once and sank from depressed and hopeless to depressed, hopeless, and zombie-ized.

AUGUST 25. I write this from a hospital bed. That odd, recurring "stomach flu" turned out to be appendicitis. It struck exactly on Gabriel's first birthday. The night of his party, I was in the emergency room having surgery. I've been here on a morphine drip now for the past four days, sleeping around the clock, and am reborn. God, I wish I had had emergency surgery ten months ago.

SEPTEMBER 12. Had to return to that trip-to-Hawaii gynecologist to have my diaphragm refitted. He informed me that prolactin, a hormone produced by breast-feeding, depresses L-dopamine levels or some such thing. Whatever, it usually makes women sleepy but, for some sensitive few, it can have just the opposite effect. Why, I asked him, had he not shared this information with me before? Oh, hadn't I? he answered in an offhanded way.

SEPTEMBER 25. I've gotten myself back again. I took Gabriel to the park today and watched him stagger around like a wee drunk and just laughed out loud. I was flooded by happiness. For the past year, happiness ran off into ravines of regret and melancholy. Now it soaks in and saturates me. Even fairly upsetting events like how badly the movie adaptation of my second novel turned out don't rock me that much. Slept right through some fairly scathing reviews. It's going to be all right.

SEPTEMBER 25, 1992. Three years later. Spent the evening with Clare and Joe and three-month-old Baby Bryan. Bryan slept almost the entire time. Clare had to wake him up so he could do a host of adorable baby things. I still feel pangs whenever I'm around "normal" babies, a mourning for that perfect pastel babyhood we never had.

DECEMBER 12, 1995. Six years later. Went to an open house last night hosted by George's new division chief. I was just putting in an appearance, being the spouse, when I ran into Kevin. It was great remembering how we saved each other's sanity when we worked together. Hard to believe it was twelve years ago. He said that his wife was expecting and their worst fear was a repeat of their older son's colic. I almost never talk about colic with other parents. What would I say after they confess that they both almost lost their minds when their baby cried for A WHOLE HOUR every evening? But I heard something in Kevin's voice that made me ask, "Colic? *Real* colic?" Kevin's face came to life. He sensed he was talking to a veteran. " 'Real' colic," he assured me.

We were like the survivors of some horrible disaster no one else could ever understand. "How many hours?" he asked. "At the worst," I answered, "Gabriel was either crying, nursing, or we were pogoing with him eighteen hours a day." Kevin glanced around, then whispered conspiratorially, "There were several twenty-four-hour periods when, I swear to God, Drew did not shut his eyes for one second. All the doctors said it was impossible. Drew's eight now. We'd planned on having three, maybe four kids. But it's taken Janey this long to even consider the possibility again. She finally decided to do it because she says it's like she never really got to have a baby. You know what I mean?" Tears pooled in his eyes. I hugged him, one survivor to another.

"Yeah," I said, "I know exactly what you mean."

NEGOTIATING VIOLENCE

MERI NANA-AMA DANQUAH

The entire first year of motherhood for me was tainted by violence: physical violence, emotional violence, social violence. Giving birth itself seemed to be an act of violence. The landscape of my body became a battlefield during labor. There was excruciating pain, screaming, blood from the tearing of flesh, and well-earned scars, which, like tattoos, will be forever etched on my thighs and abdomen. I was plagued by an undiagnosed depression that debilitated me throughout the greater parts of both the pregnancy and my daughter's infancy. By the time my daughter, Korama, was born, the partnership between her father and me was crumbling. We had drained the pleasure from our romance and were left with only harsh words and hardened hostility. On top of everything else, in April of 1992, the month of Korama's first birthday, Los Angeles was brought to its knees by racial injustice and riots. Indeed, Korama and I took a journey that year that led us through fury and fear, through alarming confrontations with my past and necessary negotiations for a peaceful future.

In hindsight, I see now that I have always had a proclivity for turmoil and individuals who created or sustained it, as well as a predisposition to depression. This is a toxic combination for a new mother, but it was brewing in me long before I discovered I was going to have a baby. My own childhood was full of emotional disorder. I grew up in a household that mistook control and intimidation for love, the rush and intensity of anger for passion. There were never broken bones, just broken spirits, but we danced dangerously close to the threshold of domestic violence. And in the wake of our emotional wreckage, we concealed our pain with silence, retreated, like phantoms, behind facades.

A native of Ghana, I have lived in the United States since I was six years old and alternately embraced three disparate cultures: Ghanaian, mainstream American (read: white), and black American. My family strongly believed in traditional African values and principles such as the prerequisite respect of elders, the unspoken second-class citizenship of children, and the collective endorsement of corporal punishment. To not physically discipline one's children is akin to not feeding them three square meals or not providing them with an education. It is virtually unheard of. As a result, I spent my youth in blood-curdling fear of my parents' power. Their words—whatever words—were law. There was no freedom in my child-world to challenge or reject, no license to question. I held no rights that could be exercised without the threat of violence.

As it turned out, all that fear only translated into politeness, not sincere respect. No child of mine, I promised myself, would grow up the way I did. I wanted to have a relationship with my children based on love and genuine respect, not fear or obligatory deference. At the same time, though, I wanted to pass on to them the honor of heritage. I wanted them to eat the food and speak the languages of my primary culture. It is a classic desire: wanting to mold a child into something other than a reflection of yourself, while refusing (or simply not knowing how) to abandon the tools and models your parents used to shape you. My better judgment told me that it would be a difficult, if not altogether impossible, task, so at a very young age, I vowed to never become a mother.

Ironically, I was the first among my peers to get pregnant. At sixteen I had an abortion. At nineteen I had another. At twenty, I had a miscarriage two weeks after I found out I was, for the third time, pregnant. Had I not miscarried, I would have most likely had another abortion. The fourth and last pregnancy I carried to term. Like all the others, it was unplanned and, initially, unwanted. I was twenty-two years old, a college dropout who feared that having a child would mean forgoing an artistic career. I ultimately decided to go forward with the pregnancy more because of cryptic dreams and vague longings than any strict logic or rational sense.

There may be such a thing as a "perfect" or "right" time to have a child, but by anyone's standards the timing of my pregnancy seemed all wrong. My boyfriend and I were still living together but we had reached an undeniable impasse in our relationship; we fought constantly, throwing insults, objects, and punches to injure one another. This was not the spirit in which Korama was conceived but until we split up, when she was eight weeks old, it was the tepid climate of our home. Given my history of low self-esteem and harmful liaisons, it was a climate in which I existed rather comfortably. I had never learned to expect anything more substantive than sex in a relationship, not even civility or consideration. Having a baby expanded my focus; it made me want to work things out in my life, especially with my boyfriend. I naively imagined that somehow our baby could bring us closer, if not erase the tension which was thick between us. I was wrong. The feuding persisted and eventually he threw me and the baby out of his home.

Korama and I moved into an apartment in a rundown building that I agreed to manage in exchange for free rent. I taught creative writing part-time, and more nights than I care to remember were spent working a phone sex line out of my home. A dense cloud of melancholy hung over my head. On my own, with a newborn, I began to reevaluate my decision to become a parent. *Did I make a mistake?* I wondered each night as I stared at the ceiling, swallowing worries. There was never enough money, and the only child-care assistance I received was from a small, makeshift support network of young, childless friends. Life began to seem too large and laborious to deal with.

Most of my time was devoted to obsessing about how much of a failure I thought I was. I felt as if I hadn't succeeded at anything in life—not in my education, not in my relationships, not in my literary ambitions. It was hard for me to move past all the guilt and self-loathing. Caring for an infant was burdensome. It required more energy than the depression allowed me to give. I became afraid of failing at motherhood as well, and that was a thought I couldn't bear to consider.

Luckily, Korama was a low-maintenance infant. She rarely cried except when she needed to be nursed or diapered, and she slept soundly for long stretches of time. Mostly, she would just lie there next to me in bed and stare. Her look haunted me. I felt as if she sensed my ineptitude, knew in her tiny heart that she had been shortchanged by the heavens and granted a mother who was no more capable of dealing with the world than she. The life I had planned for Korama and me was all too quickly moving out of my reach.

When I think back to those days, what I recall most vividly is the enormous amount of rage and frustration I fought to suppress. While trying to maneuver around the guilt and resentment to access the love I knew I had for my daughter, my own potential for abuse was exposed and, to my surprise, I had been engaging in a constant and precarious flirtation with it. In August of that year, when Korama was four months old, I had to file a domestic violence restraining order against her father. He had come to my house for a visit with his daughter that ended with him beating me.

It has been said that parents often raise their children to be all that they themselves could not or would not be. That is not the kind of parent I wanted to be. I had always hoped my child would inherit a few traits that genes alone could not translate. Traits like integrity, pride, perseverance, the spirit of compassion, and a strong sense of self. I wanted her to be familiar with the sound of her own laughter, but one is not able to give what one does not possess.

My turning point came on a frigid evening in January of 1992. Korama was nine months old. The depression had lifted ever so slightly, but I was still riding a flimsy seesaw of self-deprecating emotions. We were in the living room, Korama in one corner with her Christmas toys, I in another listening to my favorite cassette. I was flipping the tape over in the recorder when I caught the scent of burning food. Apparently I had forgotten to turn off one of the burners on the stove. I rushed into the kitchen. When I returned minutes later, Korama was crouched where I had been sitting, encircled by a spool of loose tape, the empty cassette still in her hand.

I could feel all the stifled rage traveling through every vessel in my body. I marched blindly toward her, ready to unleash it. My footsteps were heavy, thundering. Even the flesh on my palms was quivering in anticipation. I was no less than two yards away when I stared into her pupils. She looked as innocently petrified as a doe. She turned her gaze to the floor and curled softly into her body. I froze and studied the scene as if it were a photograph. I hadn't touched her with a cruel hand or uttered an irate word and there she was, helpless, at my mercy. *My God,* I thought, *what power!*

Korama was numb to my presence when, at last, I sat down cross-legged next to her. Instead of hitting her as I had planned, I hugged her, picked the tape up off the floor, and placed it in her lap. My hands continued to shake, but not in anticipation. They were shaking because I had almost held an infant physically accountable for things she had no control over—my lethal choices in relationships, my poverty, my feelings of inadequacy; clearly, those were the circumstances at the root of my rage—and for what? Destroying a cassette tape that was worth no more than ten dollars? She was simply exploring and dissecting the world around her. She was trying to learn and, as her mother, it was my duty to teach and guide her, not punish her.

That incident prompted me to take a look at myself. Every relationship I had ever had was, in some way, abusive. In each one, I played the role of the victim. It was always the fault of someone else that I was not the person I wanted to be. From one involvement to the next, I carried blame, like a bouquet of flowers, and placed it in the open arms of my partner. It became clear to me that I opted to be with those people because they fulfilled my subconscious wishes to be mistreated; they re-created home for me. The fact that I was living out a dangerous cycle came without question. What I was unsure of was whether I would be able to break that cycle.

The highest vision I had of myself was far removed from the reality of my actions. I wanted desperately to be the mother I always dreamed of having when I was a child; I wanted to become the person I knew I was capable of being. For days afterward, I combed my brain, trying to figure out a way to change who I was. Then it dawned on me that I had already changed. The woman who approached her daughter in a crazed frenzy was not the same one who sat next to her and offered maternal tenderness. Somewhere in the moment that separated those two women, I took responsibility for myself and for my emotions. I made a definitive choice to reject the patterns of my history.

Progress was slow. My financial troubles grew worse before they got better. And the anger, that righteous indignation which eased me into adulthood, did not automatically disappear. It lingered as depression for years but once I sought proper medical treatment, it too went away. However, during those first trying months, the bond I share with Korama found form and strengthened.

Crucial compromises were made. For example, my books, cassettes, and other possessions that might be destroyed by a child's curiosity were placed on high shelves.

I shamefully admitted to myself that my inattentiveness to Korama in her earlier months was a passive type of abuse, but abuse nonetheless. Rather than continue to let her lie idly in her crib simply because she was not hungry or in need of a diaper change, I played with her and held conversations with her, as I had when she was in my womb. When Korama's first birthday came, it was as much a celebration for me as it was for her. In the twelve months it had taken her to learn how to walk, talk, trust, cultivate a solid personality, and use it to relate to others, I had relearned many of those very same things for myself.

Exactly three weeks and three days after Korama's birthday, the verdicts in the trial of the officers accused of using excessive force against Rodney King were announced. The largest civil insurrection in American history followed. From the safety of our Los Angeles home, Korama and I observed the violence through the windows and on television. It was harrowing. Everyone was using their anger as a justification to hurt someone else. As we watched, Korama stood beside me clutching my leg. I wondered how much of what was happening made any sense to her. Surely she was registering something. We think so little of what impact our actions have on children, especially those who are still nonverbal. What do we know or understand about how they process hurt, disillusionment? Korama had seen so much in her first year.

Violence breeds violence. That night I made a resolution in my heart to never strike Korama and to never invite abuse—of any sort—into our household. Keeping that resolution has been no simple feat. Korama, now five, is an intelligent child with a will as strong as stone. She is everything little girls are not supposed to be: rough, aggressive, determined. She talks back—in several languages, using a patois of phrases pulled from English, Japanese, and Spanish, as well as Ga, my native tongue.

Needless to say, finding appropriate and effective methods of discipline that complement her development but do not involve physical force can be challenging. It requires patience, respect, and unwavering faith in the power of words. Admittedly, when I have been at my wits' end, the thought of spanking her has come to mind. It would be a quick fix, for the short run. But in spite of, or perhaps because of, my past, I recognize the importance of teaching Korama to understand that love and violence do not go together and should not be accepted when given hand-in-hand by the same person—be that person a lover, a friend, or a parent.

Several months ago, Korama and I were taking a trip together. A man seated next to us on the plane remarked, "What a cute little girl," then suddenly reached over to pat Korama on the head with one hand while pinching a chunk of her cheek with the other. Annoyed by the invasion of her space, Korama pulled back, looked him square in the eyes, and said firmly, "It's not nice for people to touch each other without asking. Please ask me next time." When I was her age, I didn't feel entitled to claim, let alone exhibit, such personal agency; I would have silently accepted the intrusion. That Korama did not made me proud. It was a sign that she—and I—were making great strides in our personal growth and that if we continued to travel the path we were on, both of us were going to turn out just fine.

BREAST-FEEDING: THE AGONY AND THE ECSTASY

CATHI HANAUER

Before I got pregnant, and then once I did, I imagined motherhood something like this: I'm sitting in a rocker in an earth-colored robe smiling down at my baby, who is lying in my arms, mouth fastened to my breast, dreamily nursing away. My husband is preparing us tea with milk and honey, and a feeling of peace pervades the room—one that will go on for months, as I fully intend to nurse my baby for no less than a year. Virtually everything I've read and heard makes it clear it's the best gift you can give yourself and your child. And for me, breast-feeding seems the essence of motherhood.

Here's the reality: I'm sitting on the spit-up-stained sofabed trying to balance my wailing three-week-old daughter, Phoebe, atop two pillows on my C-sectioned lap. I'm preparing her, but really I'm more preparing myself, for her ninth or tenth meal of the day. However I hold her, I'm in for some serious pain. First she'll clamp on with a grip astonishing for a person who could fit inside a shoe box. Then she'll suck off the scabs that have formed on my nipples since the last feeding, oh, two hours ago. For a good thirty seconds my milk will "let down"—something the books describe as a mildly tingling sensation but for me feels like having my entire upper body mashed in a vise. Sweat runs down my body, and I clamp the couch, or my husband, and yell, "Shit Shit Shit!" So much for the baby's virginal ears.

But the pain of let-down passes, and then come the reasons I endure the rest. My baby drinks plentifully, her gorgeous eyes affixed to my face; hormones cruise through me like some unearthly drug; and everything feels right, and even rather wonderful—for a little while, anyway. I sit back and remind myself I'm providing the ultimate substance in the ultimate act: feeding my baby something from my own body that will grow and heal and nourish her. I am Steinbeck's Rose of Sharon, El Greco's Madonna, earning my place among nursing mothers of history and literature and art—not to mention my peers, since every smart, hip mom I know breast-feeds. Many do this while working full-time office jobs; they get up at 5:00 A.M. to nurse the baby on one breast while pumping the other for the nanny's feeding, they rush home at lunchtime to get in a round, they pump in office bathroom stalls when their breasts fill up at work. And still, the "F" word—formula—is barely spoken in their homes, let alone the actual substance allowed to grace their baby's lips. Well, it won't touch my baby's, either, I tell myself as I gear up to switch breasts. I am the perfect mom. Here I sit, breast-feeding.

What I try not to think about, as my daughter suckles, is the bowl of now-tepid water sitting next to me that I've been using to apply hot compresses to my breasts, which are huge and rock-hard, absurdly uneven, and

crammed with gumball-sized lumps. To complement my
bleeding nipples I'm also experiencing my first case of
mastitis, a painful infection that results from some combination of clogged milk ducts, fatigue, and stress. If un-
treated it can lead to a breast abscess, which requires
surgical removal and other such pleasantries. Treatment
consists of antibiotics, compresses applied round the
clock, and bed rest. As if.

Let me interrupt to say that not every woman has the
breast-feeding experience I did. Some have no problems
at all becoming human pumps. Some find it blissful from
beginning to end, though I confess I've yet to meet one
of them. More women, I think, have a few problems at
first and then things click into place. My sister-in-law
breast-fed four kids for two years each, despite clogged
milk ducts at the start with each one. The leader of a
breast-feeding support group I went to proudly announced that she'd been "lactating" for eleven years
(three kids). If she'd experienced breast-feeding as I
did, I guarantee you she wouldn't have spent fifteen percent of her life doing it.

But back to me. Before I stopped breast-feeding—after
the nine weeks—I would get mastitis three times. I
would swallow a small landfill of antibiotics that
couldn't possibly be good for my kid, and spend endless
hours massaging, soaking, pumping, and applying ice
packs and heating pads to my throbbing breasts. I would
bare my chest to the midwife and the gynecologist, the
pediatrician and the breast surgeon who finally convinced me that, being literally not built for this, I should
quit. I would pay a lactation consultant to suggest, via
phone, that I had thrush, and attempt positioning techniques that required suspending the baby or my body in
Twister-like poses the entire time I nursed. I'd spend

hours talking to La Leche League volunteers and reading books and pamphlets for answers that don't exist, receiving contradictory advice at every turn: wear a tight bra, wear no bra; nurse more frequently, nurse less often; pump, don't pump, pump sometimes. I would spend Valentine's Day in the shower with my husband—him suctioning my breasts with a handheld plastic pump, me massaging the lumps from the top, and our baby, forever wanting more milk, wailing from her car seat on the floor next to us. It was hardly romantic, though if ever my husband performed an act of love for me, this was it.

Here is a sampling of what the baby bibles of the nineties and the breast-feeding zealots, or "Nipple Nazis" (as the slightly less determined call them), are quick to tell you about breast-feeding—the things I knew before I plunged in: It's easier, cheaper, more convenient than formula; it offers protection from allergies and constipation, and provides immunities and less chance of diaper rash. It may give your kid a higher IQ, and it makes him or her less likely to be obese. It also helps heal *your* body from the trauma of giving birth. In short, it forms an irreplaceable, lifelong bond between mom and baby. Read: If you don't do it, you're stupid, selfish, clueless. A freak.

Here is what those same bibles either fail to mention about breast-feeding or breeze over too casually—the things friends eagerly confess upon hearing my horror stories, the things I came to learn: Breast-feeding hurts. For me, in more ways than I ever imagined two otherwise healthy breasts could, and far more than my C-section incision (though, granted, I had morphine for that). I've already mentioned pain with let-down, clogged ducts, and mastitis. There's also engorgement: Your breasts blow up to a few times their normal size over a few hours and feel like they're packed with wet sand. (Mine went from a 34-B to a 36-D in half a day, leaving the stretch marks I otherwise avoided during pregnancy.) As for nipple problems, I'll just add that mine felt, for weeks, the way it feels just after you burn yourself on a hot pan, and nothing I put on them— lanolin, vitamin E oil, olive oil, breast milk—did a thing.

More breast-feeding reality: The baby sometimes latches on to one breast and not the other—which means you have to pump the other breast all the time or end up like those horrible haircuts of the Eighties, where one side was full and the other side shaved. Or—even worse—the baby won't latch on to either breast, which means you have to pump and feed it with a dropper, a cup, or your finger, since introducing a bottle at this stage, experts claim, could lead to "nipple confusion," which might make the baby reject the breast altogether.

When you're nursing, your breasts leak—meaning, they leak even when you're not. Mine did, anyway. They leaked in the shower, milk running down my body in streams, and they leaked as I stuffed them into breast-feeding bras with special leak-proof pads. Then they leaked through the pads, forming circles of milk on every one of my button-down shirts ("Ah, I see you've got on the uniform," one friend said of my stretched-out leggings and milk-stained Oxford blouse). They leaked when someone else's baby whimpered, even if mine had just been fed. They leaked through my pajamas and into my mattress, so my whole bedroom smelled like milk. So I woke up sopped and sticky night after night. This, by the way, is infinitely preferable to not having *enough* milk, which can also be the case.

Eventually, of course, one's breast faucets learn to regulate themselves. So I hear, anyway.

The truth is, in the first few months of motherhood, breast-feeding takes over your life. I suppose this is the point; newborn babies need their moms full-time, need to learn that someone will always be there for them. I knew and respected this need, and yet—whether out of stupidity, naivete, or simple lack of preparation—I still was staggered by the absolute power of breast-feeding to replace, or, rather, *dis*place, everything else in my life. And this at a time when life seemed to multiply into a mind-boggling mass: writing thank-you notes, fielding the barrage of post-birth phone calls, reading about why your baby projectile vomits after every other feeding, making up missed work deadlines. One woman I know recorded her feeding schedule in one early twenty-four-hour period: 11:30, 2:00, 4:30, 6:30, 9:00, 11:00, 2:00, 5:30, 8:00, 11:30. Keep in mind these are starting times, and a feeding takes twenty to forty minutes at least—not including burp time, bath time, time to re-place the many calories Baby nurses out of *you* so that you can keep making milk. I've yet to meet a mother who can do all this without feeling frazzled, not to men-tion a teensy bit resentful when Daddy heads off for a day of uninterrupted work—or you both do, but his briefcase is filled with documents and the newspaper and yours with breast-pump parts and Medela milk bags.

The truth is, breast-feeding does not allow for shared parenting—not by a long shot. And if you're the sort of couple my husband and I are, in which the woman earns as much as the man and both salaries are necessary, it shifts the balance so far over to the woman's side it's a wonder we don't collapse. My husband loves taking care of our daughter, and he did almost everything at first. While I lay recovering from my cesarean or navigated the arduous trip from the hospital bed to the bathroom and back, he learned to diaper the baby, clean her cord, wrap her like a sausage, rock her to sleep. Back home, we placed her bassinet on his side of our bed, and for a while he rose and changed her and delivered her to me for night feedings. But soon we stopped changing her between feedings (she was barely wet, we were barely functioning), and then Dan's job of transferring her from bassinet to breast didn't keep him awake while I nursed, so at the end of the feeding I had to either wake him, which seemed vicious, or get up and walk around the bed to put her back, which seemed absurd. So we switched the bassinet to my side, and from then on I got up and fed her every few hours while he snored. Did I resent him? *Hell* yes. But really, why should we both be exhausted when I had the goods, when there was nothing he could do but sit and watch me nurse? This is how it goes with breast-feeding.

The upshot of this, of course, is that it's the mom— the food source—whom the baby learns to adore, at least at first. And let me tell you, I relished this adoration. When I walked around the block and came back to find the baby wailing and my husband helpless, it was all I could do not to gloat. A breast-fed baby smells its mother. Even when you introduce a bottle of pumped breast milk, Daddy can't give it if Mommy's in the room. The baby wants the real thing, thank you. Never have I felt so desirable.

Perhaps because I failed at it, more or less, it seems to me the pressure to breast-feed creates a subtle competition among women these days—another thing (perhaps like having natural childbirth in the Seventies or the perfect body in the Eighties) to make us size up each other and feel we have to measure up or exceed. The best mother in the Nineties is the mother who breast-feeds the longest, who never supplements formula, who leaves work the most times to rush home and nurse. Once, just after I stopped nursing, I told a friend who'd also quit because of mastitis that I'd had to stop for the same reasons. She asked my symptoms, and I told her: painful lumps that sometimes made it impossible for my daughter to get my milk out; hot, red blotches on my skin; pain when I lifted the baby, reached for a glass, walked up or down stairs. She listened carefully. And then she said, "But did you have a fever?" "I don't think so," I said. "Then you didn't have mastitis," she announced. As if I were lying, or all the doctors had been wrong. As if I didn't have a *real* excuse to quit. Like she did.

Another time, on a weekend out of town, my husband and I met a couple with a baby just our daughter's age. "Are you still breast-feeding?" the woman asked. I said no, and then—of course—recounted the reasons I'd had to stop. "Oh, I had all those problems, too," she said. "But my doctor told me to stick with it, and my husband said, 'Honey, it's best for the baby,' and eventually it got better, and now I'm *still* doing it!" She grinned. I noted with satisfaction that her baby had cradle cap. And then my husband jumped in. "Well, it didn't get better for Cathi," he said. "She *had* to stop." I could have kissed him. But later, I pleaded with him, "Do you think I didn't try hard enough?" I couldn't stop thinking I was weak and selfish to have quit. No matter that our baby was moon-faced and lovely, the picture of health. I was a failure as a mom. As least compared to other women.

And yet, once I entered The Great Breast-Feeding Contest—even though I was losing—I couldn't seem to back out. I asked friends, relatives, mothers I met on the street how long they'd breast-fed, when they'd stopped, how long they'd go on. If they'd done it less time than I had or supplemented with formula, I felt deep relief. If they hadn't I felt not so much envy but admiration. But one thing I found both troubling and oddly reassuring was this: Almost every woman offered an excuse for why she stopped. "She got teeth at five months and started biting me," apologized one. "He got a cold at four months and wouldn't take the breast," said another. In turn, I recounted my own "Why I Quit" saga, always careful to mention that not one but *two* doctors— including the pediatrician—had advised it. And I wondered, even as I bored myself with the same graphic details, why I couldn't just say "I stopped at nine weeks." Or say nothing. But I couldn't. I still can't.

There's a quote I love: *Every man's life is a diary in which he means to write one story, and writes another.* For most of us—most of the women I know, anyway— there's a gulf between what we are and what we want to be. And for me, the experience of breast-feeding brought that gulf to light. On the Want To Be side I am earthy and breasty and maternal, never impatient, never glancing at the clock in my child's presence. Things will get done, or they won't. It doesn't matter. What's important is this: Motherhood. Breast-feeding.

On the other side of the gulf, alas, I am diminutive

and hyper, strung tightly as a fiddle. I flit around like a wind-up toy on Duracell overdose. I can't stand chaos, can't stand disorder, love a good steak now and then, can't stomach tofu. I wear black, not gauze, and I don't look good in baggy blouses. I give birth by C-section, without which my baby and I would both have bitten the dust. So much for au natural.

I had thought I'd be able to close this gulf when I had a baby—after all, what better motivator than the health of my child?—and I *did* close it slightly for the nine weeks I breast-fed. I sat still for hours, nursing and cuddling my daughter while dust bunnies floated by and dishes towered in the sink. And the truth is, I found those weeks to be among the most intense in my life, a time of exquisite passion, pleasure, and pain—like falling in love with a man you're not yet sure loves you back, or losing your virginity to the boy of your dreams.

But for every second of sweetness came a second of pain, for every moment of pride, a moment of stress. This is what I'd have liked to learn—perhaps during one of the classes at which we spent so many hours studying childbirth, something that takes a day or two before breast-feeding kicks in, 24/7, week after week, without a break. I'd like to have learned that some of us might not meet the nursing goals we'd set, and that, if we didn't, we could still show our faces. I'd like to have learned that breast-feeding might be a contradiction, as it turned out to be for me. And while I wouldn't trade a second of it, I'm glad to be done, at least this time around. Because the week I quit breast-feeding is the week the balance in our family began to shift back, the week I stopped hurting. The week that motherhood became fun for me.

And yet. Sometimes now, when I see a mother breast-feeding, I ache with all my heart to do it again. Like the pain of labor, the sensation of nursing is slipping away, and I want to hold on to it—to remember what it was like to look down and see my daughter's lovely eyes, feel her suckling, smell her sweetness, cradle her soft downy head. To proudly nurse in buses and parks and coffee shops, reveling in the stares I'd sometimes get. I tell myself that next time, if there is one, I'll concentrate on the pleasure instead of the pain. That next time I'll learn to meditate, I'll try harder to work out the lumps. I'll let my nipples heal in the sun. Which, *next* time, will always be shining.

And then I come back to reality. Next time, if there is one, I'll be happy to get through nine weeks. My daughter, formula-fed for almost seven months now, could not be more perfect. She took to the bottle in an instant, wolfed her Isomil and never looked back. Maybe she sensed the stress draining out of me when I stopped breast-feeding, the happiness and energy seeping back. It was a happiness I'm sure I transferred to her, in lieu of breast milk. And really, when it comes right down to it, isn't that what motherhood is about?

THE LAST NURSING MOMMY TELLS ALL

TERI ROBINSON

What do Venus di Milo, Marilyn Monroe, and I have in common? The answer is actually quite simple: The sight of our bare chests can incite my son Jake to babble on incessantly about his favorite pastime—nursing. In an Italian restaurant, he looks lovingly at a cheap knock-off of Venus di Milo, touches her breasts with slim fingers, and says "wanna nurse" over and over again. Posters of the buxom Marilyn draw a similar response. And, of course, my breasts—plain, ordinary Mommy breasts— evoke the same sweet mantra.

That he lumps my thirtysomething body together with these two goddesses is both flattering and discon-certing. Can't he tell the difference between breasts (quite literally) constructed to pleasure the masses and the ones that have nurtured him since birth? Could Mar-ilyn or Venus fill in for me? I'd like to think not, that, despite Jake's wandering eye, his heart belongs to me.

At just over a year, Jake is still an avid breast man—

his beautiful eyes literally light up at the prospect of nursing. He tugs at my shirt, demanding his due, and then, breast in mouth, nestles in the crook of my arm, content and peaceful. He's addicted, pure and simple. And, I must confess, so am I. Like codependents, we feed off each other. Breast milk is the magic elixir that always calms Jake, and those minutes spent each day with a baby at my breast soothe me more completely than do Mexican food and rainy days. That kind of peace is hard to come by, and harder to let go of, even now that he's becoming a toddler with a mouthful of teeth.

I never expected that the nursing experience would stretch out this long and that I would become one of the grand old dames of breast-feeding among my friends, doling out sage advice like some kind of lactating Yoda. And I can't really trace how I came to be such a nursing enthusiast. Brought up by a mother who bought into the formula craze of the Fifties and Sixties and surrounded by other bottle pushers, it's amazing I slipped so easily into the breast-feeding lifestyle.

In my conservative hometown down South, as in other places, nursing often carries with it the stigma of the lower class. Some of the women I know would rather spend a bundle on formula than suffer the impropriety of baring the breast. "Yuck!" says one friend, "I would *never* do that." Another, who could barely make ends meet, once dragged me into Wal-Mart to spend an ungodly fortune on formula.

But once the decision to nurse evolved, in my heart I knew I would go the distance. From the minute Jake's hungry little mouth first found my breast, my heart was filled with an indescribable mix of emotions—an achy happiness, strong passion, fierce protectiveness, deep contentment, satisfaction, joy, and an overwhelming bond to the flesh of my flesh.

We did it! I want to shout at that first coupling, but there's no one to hear except my tiny hours-old baby and an unidentified roommate sleeping behind the curtain to my left. My husband, Larry, exhausted by nearly twenty-two hours of labor, is at home asleep. My first real taste of motherhood is sweet, untainted by contortionist maneuvers to find the right position, discouraging pain, or tearful failures.

While I eventually have my bouts with sore nipples, engorgement, and sheer exhaustion, by some stroke of luck or good genes, I avoid most of the problems that some nursing mothers face. As the initial discomforts pass, I promise my son that he'll never know the taste of even one sip of formula. Over the next year I'll feed on praise for sticking to that conviction, but I'll curse myself as well, because long-term nursing, even when it's easy, is never, well, easy.

The early days seem like a perpetual cycle of nursing, burping, and changing diapers rather than the slow succession of coffee commercial moments I envisioned when I was pregnant. And I'm convinced that someone has shaved a few hours off my day—there's just no time to get everything done. Even if I get up at 6:00 A.M., I rarely leave my house before noon. By the time I bathe Jake he has to nurse, by the time I change him he needs to nurse again. And, inevitably, thanks to leaky breasts and even leakier diapers, I have to change my own clothes at least once.

Soon enough, though, the act of nursing becomes as natural as breathing, an involuntary response to a natural demand. A friend of mine says she knew she had mastered nursing when she argued with her boyfriend, following him from room to room, oblivious to the fact that she was topless with her son stuck firmly to her breast. For me that moment came when I ran to the front door to sign for a package delivery. It wasn't until I saw the look on the UPS guy's face that I realized my son was still nursing and our little dog was hanging, by his teeth, to my shirttail.

Indeed, Jake and I have nursing down to an art form. He can, and does, nurse in almost any position imaginable—standing up, sitting down, lying prone, feet flung to one side, under the computer table as I pound out an assignment on deadline. In trains, planes, and automobiles, he has latched on. The recollection of my pre-nursing days, like the memory of labor pains, has faded away. I vaguely recall being childless, freewheeling my way through the day on my own terms. Now, I find myself marching to the beat of a smaller, much hungrier drummer.

I would feel like the ultimate (albeit sticky and smelly) Earth Mother except that my not-one-drop-of-formula policy has driven me straight into the mechanical embrace of the breast pump. The handheld, battery-powered pump is my ticket to the movies, spontaneous shopping sprees, the gym, a much-needed haircut, and the world beyond. Its steady grind serves as the soundtrack for my new life. Wa-wuh, wa-wuh, it sputters while I interview executives over the phone or sit locked in a grimy stall in a public rest room. Soon, an impressive supply of milk bags lines our freezer. I can go anywhere, do anything—sans baby.

For Larry and me, even with all the changes it's wrought, nursing has given us a sense of freedom that often eludes other new parents. Instead of feeling trapped by the baby, we've found we can take Jake anywhere the breast goes—to the movies, church, a Bob Dylan concert, even to meet Jimmy Carter—with little concern that he'll disrupt anything. Except possibly the time alone that Larry and I used to spend.

Still, I never feel that we're growing apart. Larry has become an intimate part of the nursing experience. From the beginning, I often chose to feed Jake while leaning against my husband, wrapped in his arms, or sitting close enough to him that Jake's little hand can stroke his arm rather than mine. Gradually, we grow into a comfortable fit, a warm family unit melded together by our sweet baby.

I suppose that during the many months of nursing, a first-time mother could lose her sense of self, her self-esteem, confidence in her attractiveness. After all, you hit an all-time nadir of vulnerability—hormones rage, the responsibility of being the sole source of nutrition weighs you down, and you're on call twenty-four hours a day. Though I lost every pound of pregnancy weight within a week of giving birth (a grand benefit of breast-feeding), three months out my body's still better suited for Raphael than Calvin Klein. Lumpy, hard, leaky breasts look like implants gone wrong. My feel-good clothes—skinny dresses and slinky catsuits—lie tucked away in some drawer. (Although I do venture out to dinner in a unitard one evening, only to end up—in a feat that would put Gumby to shame—pulling my breast through my sleeve to nurse.)

Indeed, with a baby at the breast for more hours than I care to admit, feeling more like a dairy than a woman, self-doubt seems inevitable. Yet, I've never felt more attractive. Maybe it's the inner peace that nursing has brought. Or possibly the sense of accomplishment. My husband has never seemed so attractive to me, I think, since I've seen him as a daddy.

Though nursing seriously cuts into the amount of time we have to make love—hell, we don't have a lot of time to even think about it—the bond between us has grown strong. An unexpected bonus. Changing diapers and washing breast pumps become a sort of foreplay, the aroma of sour milk a powerful aphrodisiac.

So with my love life and self-image intact, I feel bold enough to gamble on a full-time job that has career advancement written all over it. (OK, so the money's great, too.) But the commute alone will add three hours (the equivalent of one bottle of expressed milk) to my workday, meaning I'll have to pump at least twice a day to keep up with Jake's demand.

Eventually my average day goes something like this: Get up at 5:00 or 6:00 A.M., fit disposable bags onto the pumps cleaned the night before—I can't help imagining big, ugly streptococcus germs invading them while I sleep—and pack them up for the trip to work. I pump a fresh bottle, get half-dressed, maybe grab breakfast (although I usually take breakfast on the run at Penn Station waiting for the train), wake the baby, dress him, nurse him, finish dressing, grab a couple of ice packs from the freezer (to keep the day's milk cool), greet the sitter, and dash out by seven-thirty to make a train that won't get me to the office until a few minutes after nine. Miss a step and I land in the train station half-dressed without ice packs, although ice-cold cans of Coke do nicely in a pinch. One harrowing week, after an over-zealous babysitter depletes my milk supply by offering Jake a bottle every hour, I find myself pumping three times during the day.

After several months, the grueling work schedule takes its toll. When a late cab keeps me from boarding the 6:33 train home one frosty evening, I am in a desperate state of panic. With a dwindling milk supply in the freezer at home, three bags of expressed milk in my bag, and no clean pump in sight, a thirty- to forty-minute wait for another train means my son will probably down another bottle before I get home, the fresh milk in my bag may go sour, and I have no way to eke out another bottleful of milk while I wait for the next train.

Like the assets of some blow-up doll, without a pump or baby, my breasts have ballooned, taking on exotic-dancer proportions. In pain, with a nearly two-hour commute ahead of me, the sound of an infant crying brings some relief as my milk lets down and spews out, soaking the front of my now very tight black dress. I silently thank the East Village for keeping black clothing en vogue and clutch my bag to my chest as I dash for the train.

My body and mind finally scream *enough*! I don't even have to consider what to ditch: the job. And I never regret it. I'd rather be dirt poor than do the Superwoman thing even one more minute. So it's back to the freelance life for me. Now I can relax, enjoy, nurse this baby for as long as I want. Of course, it's at this precise moment that I come down with the dreaded chicken pox, a farewell gift from one of the children at the company's daycare center. I celebrate my second wedding anniversary flat on my back in bed with a smattering of sores circling one nipple like a fierce wagon train. As for my son, he Hoovers on, oblivious to the pain that each touch of his lips brings.

Through all of this, though, the shadow of the bottle looms large. Despite a pendulum swing back toward mother's milk, we're not exactly a breast-feeding–friendly society—although we are certainly a breast-obsessed society. Perversely, the same people who drool over "Baywatch" babes or pore over the tabloids for the intimate details of celebrity sex lives often are horrified by the nursing mom. I can clear a room or reduce a crowd to uneasy silence simply by sticking Jake under my oversized shirt.

In a restaurant one night, a dear old friend and an ardent supporter of my breast-feeding efforts shifts uncomfortably in her seat when it becomes clear that Jake and I might do the dirty deed right there at the table. Go to a more secluded area, she tells me. "Try to find one!" I want to scream. Few establishments even have bathrooms equipped with couches or chairs. I've spent many an hour squatting on the floor of a small bathroom, resting my baby partially on one knee and holding him to the breast—all the while maneuvering clothes to offer him a clear path—until he's finished his meal.

Society has done such a good job of embracing the bottle that we, the newest crop of nursing mothers, haven't had much opportunity to view breast-feeding occurring naturally in our culture. Only a little over half of all new mothers breast-feed and less than half of those make it through a few months. Most of us didn't have the good fortune to see our mothers, aunts, and sisters nursing.

So in the Nineties, we have to learn how to do it all over again. Nursing classes and seminars coach us on how to feed, the best position to hold the baby in, and the proper way for the baby to latch on. I can't imagine that my grandmother had to ask anyone, other than her own mother or sister, for advice on how to nurse. But today we have to pay lactation specialists and call the La Leche League for advice and support.

As the year progresses and I extend my nursing tenure, I continue to stare down the naysayers. But as my child moves from tiny infant to toddler, their ranks are growing. Support wanes for my breast-feeding efforts even among other nursing mothers. Apparently some who champion a suckling infant are put off by an older child at the breast, vaguely uncomfortable that they might be witnessing an Oedipal complex in the making.

I've never bent to peer pressure before and I'm not about to start now, but I do secretly worry sometimes if I'm nurturing my son too much, creating a Mama's boy who will never, figuratively, leave the breast behind. In my worst nightmares, I see Jake as a forty-five-year-old man, still living at home, pants pulled up under his armpits, calling me Mother and usurping his father's place in my life. Just when does mothering turn into smothering?

The end of Jake's first year marks a turning point as I resolve to wean him from his morning nursing session. When first denied the breast he flings himself backward across the bed, letting loose the most pitiful, keening sobs. As my husband carries him, kicking and screaming, into the other room, I bury my head in the pillow and shed a few tears. Just when I think I can't bear those mournful sounds another second they diminish, and in the ultimate act of escapism, I doze off. But my dreams are a fitful tangle of horrors befalling my child at every turn. And I'm the only one who can save him.

A year after this exhilarating journey began, Jake is only a few steps closer to leaving the breast behind. I'm not sure I'm any closer yet myself. Yes, I relish the thought of my freedom—freedom from dietary restrictions, a limited wardrobe, time constraints, burgeoning, leaky breasts, and pawing little hands. But at the same time weaning frightens me, because I've come to depend on breast-feeding as much as Jake does. So weaning him means weaning myself. I fear breaking the bond with my child, forgoing the blessed assurance that I can calm him as long as a breast is ready and available.

I'm plagued with doubts and questions. Will my son feel rejected? Will he ever sleep through a movie again? Nursing has woven itself into the fabric of my very existence; will I unravel once it has ended? Can I bear the sadness of Jake not having conscious memory of the experience that bound us so closely together? Or, will I take comfort in the knowledge that he'll retain the security spawned by this nurturing, if not the actual memory of it?

In my heart, though, I know that the strength of my relationship with Jake doesn't depend on my ability to nurse. If the first year of my child's life has been about forming bonds and establishing a sense of security, then the second year will focus on helping him grow into his own person. In this framework, weaning is no different from any other area of child-rearing. This is the year when I'll deepen the cut in the umbilical cord a little more and try to accept the hard truth that this child of mine and I are no longer joined as one.

METAMORPHOSIS

CONSTANCE SCHRAFT

In a photograph of my son at three weeks old, he is lopsided in his car seat, a receiving blanket bunched around his head for support. I remember taking the picture. It was a bright autumn day, and my husband and I were packing our car, having spent the past few weeks at my parents' house in the suburbs while a crew of construction workers erected walls for a second bedroom in our loft in New York City. Now the job was complete, the Sheetrock dust had settled, and we were on our way home.

The shimmer of the Hudson River caught my eye for a moment that day, but mostly, I looked at my baby. I was sitting beside him in the back seat while my husband drove. Preoccupied with our own thoughts, we did not speak.

I had always wanted a child, only I did not know when. Not yet, I had said, if asked. When I became pregnant by accident, I was apprehensive. Observing my sister, a medical doctor, negotiate the first year of her daughter's life had made me aware of the demands of motherhood, and in the example of my own mother, who clearly sacrificed much of herself in the raising of my sisters and me, I saw how motherhood could come to define a woman. I didn't want that to happen to me.

Despite my concerns, I loved being pregnant. Every pound I gained seemed to give me ballast. The months passed swiftly, and my delivery was smooth. My son had a sweet and accommodating disposition; he slept most of the time. Now that we were returning home, I was ready to get back to my life.

In front of our building that morning, I struggled with the stiff buckle of the baby's car seat while my husband began to unpack the trunk. A friend of mine, who has no children, happened to be walking by, and she stopped to welcome us home.

I lifted my son carefully from the car seat and held him toward her. Then I waited, much as a knight might have awaited his accolade.

"Is he OK?" she asked in a concerned voice.

Looking at the photograph, I can see what she was seeing—a scrawny three-week-old with mottled skin and a heavy head. But I can remember just as distinctly what I was seeing at that moment—eyes with the variation and translucency of marbles, long fingers that would one day play the piano, a perfectly shaped head with hair the color of new straw.

"Oh, well," my friend went on, "I guess all newborns are a little funny-looking."

I was only momentarily hurt. My mother had prepared me well to absorb such offenses. In third grade a girl made fun of my boots, black, waterproof, practical. Tearfully, I reported this to my mother.

"She probably doesn't have such nice boots," my mother had said, to console me.

With the birth of my son, a disparity had arisen between my friend and me. I had something that she didn't have. But as I snuggled the baby that day, I did not believe for a moment that this was insurmountable. After all, she and I were the same people we had been before the baby was born, and we had been friends for years. We would carry on as before, I had no doubt.

While my husband and I acknowledged that with the birth of our son we were setting out in new territory, we were both determined to carry on as before. Like all new parents we found our child astonishing, but my husband would never be caught praising him in public, and I distanced myself from the image of the stereotypical new mother, endlessly recounting her child's accomplishments.

"We're not going to change just because we had a kid," my husband and I were both known to say.

So it had been during my pregnancy. Neither of us told anyone until I was four months along. Rather than buy maternity clothes, I wore big shirts or loose-fitting dresses. In the privacy of my home, I did all the things that pregnant women do, but I didn't want anyone to know. At night I read avidly books about pregnancy and lay awake feeling my baby wiggle and kick inside me. Periodically I ate enormous quantities of certain foods, and occasionally I cried, from a combination of fatigue, joy, hormonal changes, and anxiety.

Once we move back home, our life will become normal again, my husband and I had told each other lying in bed nights in the back room of my parents' house, and in many ways it did. The baby sat happily in his infant seat, cooing, tugging at his socks, or gazing into space while I worked at the computer or chopped vegetables. At hardly a month old, he attended a baseball game. He slept in the Snugli at a Robert Mapplethorpe opening and on a pile of coats at a friend's party. Out to dinner, I dribbled salsa over his sleeping head.

On the subject of my son, I was mostly brief. "He's wonderful," I would say, when asked. The first of my friends to have a baby, I intended to incorporate him into my life without ado.

My neighborhood friend stopped by often, as she always had, and over tea, we chatted about our usual topics—her painting, my writing. One of our pastimes together had been shopping, and when the baby awoke from his nap, one or the other of us would put on the Snugli, and we would stroll downtown to our favorite discount department store. If the baby fussed, we hurried to the nearest coffee shop so that I could nurse him. We giggled and confided in each other, the same as always. I wanted to say, You see? Nothing has changed.

Often on weekends my husband, the baby, and I would visit my parents. There it was impossible to maintain the status quo. When my father held my son, his expression became so vulnerable that I could hardly bear to look. My mother, under whose scrutiny I often felt flawed, softened at the mere sight of her grandson. With his birth, I had pleased my parents beyond their expectation, and happy as I was to have won their approval, still, it irked me. They seemed to feel that having a baby was the greatest achievement of my life.

"You're doing a wonderful job with him," my mother often said. But that was not how I thought of my son. He wasn't my job; he wasn't my achievement. He was simply a new member of the family.

When my mother rocked my son, she would sing, "Little man you're crying, I know why you're blue, Someone took your kiddie car away." I had never known her to be so tender. I was annoyed when she said that I was doing a good job, but watching the baby fall asleep in her arms, I felt a tremor of such intense emotion that I could not speak.

My life was split: With friends I made light of my new responsibility; alone, I was as foolish and ardent in my love as a mother could be. Looking at the thick photograph album of the first year of my son's life, it seems that no moment was too insignificant to warrant my rushing for the camera, always loaded and within easy reach.

I found my baby more absorbing than my husband, my work, my friends, and the world. I could and did spend hours that first year watching my son, and as I watched, my mind did not seem to me dulled. Rather, it roamed, much the way it had when I traveled by train in Europe after college, with a paperback copy of *The Magic Mountain* folded across my lap.

Watching a baby is not unlike watching scenery; afterward, I felt restored. My son fell asleep on my lap; I laid him gently in his crib, then sat down at my desk, where I worked undistractedly for a few hours until I heard him stir. He napped so regularly that I had no need of a babysitter. I paid for my quiet morning and afternoon sessions at night, when he woke often, but this was all right with me. Day for night, I was accomplishing as much as I had before he was born.

When my son was six months old, I took him to a baby gym class. Until then I had avoided organized mother groups, not because I had anything against them, as I was quick to say, just that I didn't need them. I already had plenty of friends.

What made me decide to go that morning was the sudden realization that my son had no friends. He did not have a babysitter to take him to the park, sit with the nannies, and acquaint him with kids his own age. He had been an infant during the fall and winter, napping or teething on a rattle while I worked. We had been alone in our own dreaminess. Now it was spring and he could sit up and play and make interesting sounds and I thought that it was time that he had other kids around.

That morning I found myself part of a circle of mothers, our babies secure on our laps. We clapped our hands, in hopes that our children would clap back. Song after silly song, we imitated the clownish gestures of the group's leader.

During free play, we hung around on colorful vinyl mats as the babies crawled and rolled, and some of the women compared notes.

"My son's been sleeping through the night since I brought him home from the hospital," boasted one.

"She already says Mama and Dada. I guess it's true that girls are quicker than boys."

"He's off the chart in weight and height. The doctor says he's never seen such a mature baby."

Then a woman who had been quiet spoke up. "Most of the time I am so exhausted I can hardly speak."

"Oh, me, too. I get home from work and I just want to hold my baby, and then I have to get dinner, do a load of laundry, and leave a list for the babysitter for the next day. If I get to bed before eleven, it's a miracle."

That was how it seemed to go. Essentially, comparing notes was comparing each other. I was silent. My son did not sleep through the night; he did not yet say Mama or Dada; he was of average size. I, too, was sometimes tired and did inordinate amounts of laundry, but complaining about it seemed a betrayal of my son, who, after all, was only a baby.

For the first time since he was born, I felt myself lacking. These women, with their practical hairdos and comfortable shoes and their satchels overflowing with baby supplies, seemed to know something that I didn't know. I didn't even own a changing table; I had considered it unnecessary. I changed my son's diapers anywhere—on the floor, on the bed, on the couch. In my purse was a spare diaper and a wooden rattle from Vermont—no Desitin, no change of clothes or extra sweater, no *Parents* magazine, pacifiers, or bottles.

Not only was I lacking equipment-wise, but I could not expound on my policies and beliefs about motherhood and child care. Until now, I had liked the way that I was raising my son, but I could not have described my approach. All I knew was that I wanted my life to remain the same, and that I didn't want to buy or carry around too much extra stuff.

I remembered traveling uptown on the bus with my son to visit my sister several weeks earlier. I prefer to take the bus when I am not in a hurry, rather than the rackety subway, but that day, the trip took over an hour, during which I hung from a strap. I could have had a seat; many people offered theirs. But every time I sat down, my son, who rarely cried, would start to cry. I had him bundled too warmly; there were too many strangers clustered around, and too many strange sounds.

I didn't know the words yet to "The Wheels on the Bus Go Round and Round." To calm my son, I muttered, "One Hundred Bottles of Beer on the Wall." The

more he fussed, the more embarrassed and overheated I
became, which only increased his unhappiness. I imagined people thinking, "She can't even quiet her own
child."

Once I got off the bus, though, the baby stopped crying, and by the time I reached my sister's apartment, I
was able to describe the incident so that she laughed.

"Why didn't you just get off the bus and hop into a
cab?" she asked.

We laughed more at how foolish I had been, but
thinking back, I knew the answer to her question. If I
had gotten off the bus, I would have been acknowledg-
ing that, at least occasionally, my son required special
handling. He couldn't always fit into the already-
established patterns of my life. Sometimes I was going to
have to get off the bus and take a cab.

Soon after the gym class, I went to a baby supply
store on the Lower East Side and bought a lightweight,
easily-collapsible stroller. "He's getting a little heavy to
carry around all the time," I told my husband.

"It's about time," said my friend the first time she
saw me pushing my son down the block in the stroller.
"I thought you were going to carry him around in that
thing until he was ten."

Sadly, it occurred to me that my friend made too
many barbed comments for my liking, and that my
method of tolerating this behavior, ignoring the remarks,
was probably not to her liking either. I wondered what
would have happened if I had confronted her at the very
beginning instead of presuming that she was feeling the
envy of a child. If I had said, "Funny looking? Are you
blind? He's the most beautiful child in the world." I
might have sounded ridiculous, but I would have stated

my case from the start. Instead, I had doggedly gone on acting as if I hadn't heard, pretending that the relationship between me and her, between me and the world, wasn't changing.

When veteran mothers hear that another woman is having her first child, they talk about their own pregnancies and deliveries. They talk about their happiness, their exhaustion, their babysitters. What no one ever told me and what I have never told anyone is that something drastic occurs with childbirth, and even though a woman may look the same soon afterward, sound the same, laugh at the same jokes, she is not the same. The change is ineffable. It has to do with the power of magnetic attraction. It has to do with the demonstrations of inhuman strength that you read about in the *National Enquirer,* a woman lifting a car that has rolled on top of her child.

I think back tenderly to my early days of motherhood, seeing myself as a lone weathercaster huddled beneath an umbrella near the eye of a hurricane, trying to look professional in a sodden raincoat as I shout, "Yes, Frank, it's definitely raining." Babies are mercurial creatures; mothers are, too. My inability to articulate what I thought and felt back then now seems perfectly understandable. One moment I was profoundly content; the next, I did not think I would survive the terror of watching my son grow. My life was changing, I could not control it. How would I end up? Who would I become?

This tumult is life, and life as a mother is one of its most extreme forms. Ultimately, the conflict that I felt early on, whether or not to accept the culture of motherhood, was beside the point. I had already accepted the position. Changing table or not, there was my son, after all, who will forever persist in calling me Mom.

THE ETERNAL NOW

ALISA KWITNEY

Finally, after a decade or so of teething, my son cut his
first tooth. It has been a long and eventful process. When
his gums first started hurting, Matthew could barely roll
over, let alone crawl; by the time the small white pro-
trusion knifed its way into the world, governments had
fallen, genetic puzzles been deciphered, and the wheel
of fashion had spun yet another revolution. Yet I can
barely remember the time before teeth, any more than I
can recall the titles of the courses I took in college.

Having a baby is living in the eternal now. Having a
baby means caring intensely about the stage you're
going through, while forgetting everything that happened more than a week ago. I can dimly remember how
terrified I was that Matthew's penis wouldn't heal properly right after he was circumcised, but that was eons,
months ago. Already the details have begun to blur, just
as other mothers told me they would. "I hate to say it,"
says one friend, whose child is four, "but you forget all

that stuff that means so much in the beginning." There is a reason for this memory loss: Time passes more slowly in the eternal now. My mother was the first person to warn me. "When you have a baby," she said, "days last for weeks."

And yet, as long as my days become, I still find it almost impossible to get anything done. There is some chaos theory involved, some entropy. I prepare some food for Matthew: He gets covered in winter squash and banana: I wash Matthew: He takes an enormous dump in his diaper: I change Matthew: Someone calls, wanting to go out to the store with us: Matthew takes a nap. Despite having so much ostensibly free time, I see my friends rarely, although we make plans to meet four or five times a week.

Reading, which has been my emergency escape since I was seven, is now nearly impossible. I used to read the way secret alcoholics drink, during lots of little stolen moments during the day, not really hitting my stride until sundown. Now the stolen moments are fewer, and all the little things I used to do so easily—balancing my checkbook, returning phone calls, washing my hair— must compete with the desire to find out what happens in chapter three.

Also, I find I can no longer concentrate on difficult plots because motherhood has made me obsessive and forgetful at the same time. I thumb through novels, trying to remember who Wolkowicz is, and why he is following Ilse. But for a new mother there are benefits to being obsessively forgetful. Today's strange vomiting through nostrils is an all-consuming crisis; yesterday's napless marathon is but a dimly remembered hell.

It is important to focus on whatever is going on in the eternal now.

On Duty

OK, so now my mother has left the house with the baby for a couple of hours so that I can get some work done, but for the past forty-five minutes I haven't even looked at the papers in front of me, I've been savoring the exotic slice of solitude, reading a few pages of one book and then turning to another, thinking about how good a hot bath would feel, contemplating hot chocolate.

Then my apartment gives a small floorboard and pipe groan and I look up from my book, suddenly aware that the baby hasn't made a sound recently. One of my heart's ventricles gives a little wheeze of terror and I think, very fast, *Oh my god he's not in his crib where's the baby did the cat* . . . and then the panic subsides as I realize that Matthew is out with my mother, safe and sound, and I am not on duty.

It's strange, not being on duty. I go to sleep on duty, knowing that I am allowed to sink into unconsciousness but not too far, in case the baby wakes (which he does, several times a night, even though he is now six months old and should be making it through twelve uninterrupted hours). I wake up on duty, which isn't too bad unless I have to go to the bathroom right away. If Matthew's in his crib, I can rush up, smile, and then go in the bathroom right off the nursery, but usually morning finds him in the bed with me, although I seldom remember exactly when the switch occurred. ("Three A.M.," my husband says.) I can't leave Matthew on the bed unattended, and if my husband is already halfway out the door I carry the baby into the bathroom with me and pee with him sitting on my knees.

I realize I probably shouldn't admit to this.

Being on duty, however, is not that difficult. Except for reading, which requires focused attention, and cooking, which requires some of the same, I find there is nothing I can't do with Matthew. I can flip through a glossy magazine while he plays on his back next to me; I can watch television while holding Matthew under the arms so he can stand on my stomach; I can exercise on the ski machine while Matthew swings in his electric swing.

I do not actually take advantage of this last possibility, although this morning I did put an old disco song on the CD player and danced around Matthew while he laughed. Then I picked him up and whirled him, which made him spit up, but he didn't really seem to mind.

But even though being on duty is not difficult, I find it's exhausting, like being a hostess. You can't really relax at your own party, even when everything is going well, because in the back of your mind you know that when it's all over you're going to have to get the sangria out of the couch. Being a hostess is probably good planning for being a mother. You need to sound happy and calm even while the shit is hitting the fan.

Being on duty is a constant pressure, like being queen of England. It never really stops, which is why mothers live for the moments when their babies are asleep. It's so exquisite, that brief respite when they do not need your constant care, when you do not need to feel the faint sting of jealousy that mars the interludes when someone else is watching over them. This is the difference between being in love with your baby and being in love with a man: When you're in love with a man, you don't pray for him *not* to call you.

Breasts

Matthew is entertaining himself in his crib, kicking his busy box, smiling these new huge smiles that are almost silent laughs, rolling around, drooling copiously. I am feeling testy with my mother, who fed him his first teething biscuit while I was out at the dentist. I am feeling testier with Holly, the last of my close, childless friends, who has just moved to Singapore—the kind of adventure that won't be happening to me anytime soon. Speaking of adventure, I am feeling jealous of my husband, who will be going to Australia on a business trip this summer.

My husband complains about business trips, but I am convinced that the ones that sound fun, are fun. Of course, my job doesn't involve a lot of travel, so I can think what I like.

This is my secret identity: I am a comic book editor. For three days a week, I sit in an office and edit comic books. Like tending to an infant, this is stranger and more difficult than it sounds. I read scripts, critique artwork, fix up pencilers with appropriate inkers. In meetings I discuss promotionals, production values, resurrected superheroes and decapitated heads. There is a feeling of camaraderie in the halls. Pre-baby, I used to work late against some rapidly approaching deadline, then go out for a drink in the Irish pub around the corner. Sometimes, when an out-of-town freelancer was around, I would call home to say I had just been invited to a dinner on someone else's expense card, and wouldn't be back till late, was it all right? And it always was all right with my husband, even though I came home smelling like the Irish pub. You'll be home late? Have a ball. But nowadays my breasts swell up like Cinderella's pumpkin coach, warning me not to stay out too long.

Breasts. Around three o'clock I have to lock the door to my office and pump, pump them. They are as demanding as infants. Ignore them at your peril. But there is something that all those books leave out when they describe the fast, convenient new mini electric pumps: that distinctive, carrying, buzzing noise. Does it sound like a vibrator? Does it ever. I worry what my co-workers think. I borrow a radio, to no avail. In the end, I put up a sign on my door: DO NOT DISTURB. MATERNAL BOVINE THING IN PROGRESS. (WHAT DID YOU THINK THAT NOISE WAS, ANYWAY?) Even so, I am embarrassed, and slink down the hall on the way to the little refrigerator trying to hide the bottle of expressed milk in the folds of my sweater.

More Breasts

I think I may want to wean Matthew now. I meant to do it when I first went back to work, just keeping the morning and bedtime feedings going, but I was lazy, it's so easy to just slip him the nipple on my days off, and besides, it's a lovely feeling, once you get past the initial pain. Just like sex, but it's easier to get into the mood even when you're cranky. I once went into a kind of trance and fell asleep in a back office at the bank, before I got used to the strangely hypnotic effect of nursing. At times it feels a little polymorphously perverse, having this tiny boy kneading my breast while he sucks at my nipple. And yet it still feels innocent, a lush, fecund, intimate innocence, Eden as painted by Gauguin.

But enough's enough. I am tired of having gigantic, floppy breasts, tired of having to keep hauling them out. I would like them to be the good china again, the stuff that's admired and not used every day. And I do not want to still be nursing him when he's a year—fine for the perky A, B, and C cups, but I'm a bit further down the alphabet.

Besides, Matthew has become so much of a person that I have other kinds of delight in him. I can make him laugh by blowing raspberries on the back of his neck, and nibbling on his ear; I can have long conversations of ab-ba, da-da, with him; we can slide down the slide at the playground together, and he can ride horsey on my knees. So I keep trying to wean him, sort of. I keep backsliding. I find it hard to let go of any stage once I know it's going to end.

I am also worried that when my milk finally dries up, my breasts will be limp and lifeless, roses two days after full bloom. I collect magazine articles about breast surgery and think about having them made smaller and firmer.

"You'll have to wait until after the second child," says my husband. He does not want to look at the before and after photos. He does not like the thought of breasts being cut.

Glee

I prop Matthew up in his crib and he laughs and laughs, that funny baby laugh that almost sounds like crying. Hunh-hunh. He falls down, I pick him up, we laugh. Pushkin the cat keeps running up, jumping on my lap, rolling on his back, begging for attention. Pushkin has a contagious fungal infection on half his face—like I need this—just as Matthew has developed a fascination for him. Now Matthew really is crying. No, just grizzling.

We go to the playground, where an obese squirrel approaches too boldly and I chase him away. Matthew is fascinated. He also enjoys the pigeons and rats that scamper in and out of the dried leaves, not realizing they are dangerous vermin, to be despised.

I put Matthew in a kiddy swing and push him back

and forth, back and forth, no longer frightened that he will fall out the sides. He does not smile, but furrows his brow and purses his mouth a little. This is his pensive look, which he alternates with his gleeful look. People either call him serious or happy. But more and more often I hear, "Look how happy he is!" He doesn't cry often, but when he does, I feel like wearing a T-shirt that says: REALLY, HE'S NOT USUALLY LIKE THIS.

As we walk back from the playground I see that one tree has gone into unseasonable, post-autumnal bloom. Usually this would make me get all pensive, reflecting on untimely flowering, wasted youth. But I am in my gleeful mood and I just enjoy the unexpected glimpse of spring, pointing it out to Matthew. And I realize that having Matthew has taken all the bitter out of the bittersweet. Maybe having a baby begins to undo all the cynicism and angst you start acquiring in adolescence. You even begin to appreciate your own parents again.

This may be yet another reason why it is hard for me to work.

Transitions

Matthew is sleeping better. Sort of. Last night he became hysterical, and it turned out that he had made a poo—a decidedly dark, firm, odiferous, unbabylike poo—in his diaper. That was at 2:30 A.M., and then he woke again around 4:00 A.M., hysterical again, but with no obvious cause. I resisted the urge to nurse, and eventually he went back to sleep, sucking on his pacifier like a smoker getting in the last few drags before a five-hour flight.

It has been a gradual process, getting Matthew to go to bed at 8:00 P.M. rather than eleven, getting him to sleep (some nights) for six or seven hours at a stretch. The books all say to nurse them on demand, and then they say "if your baby is still waking up six times a night, it's because you haven't put him on a schedule." How are you supposed to know when the magic moment arrives, when infant becomes baby, when the instinctive cry for food becomes an emotional cry for comfort? One day when Matthew was about three months old, we were in a big department store, and we stopped in the toy department. I showed Matthew this little mechanical dog, and then moved on, pushing Matthew in his carriage. Suddenly I heard a distinctive shriek of pain, but it wasn't a shriek of pain: It was a scream of frustration. Matthew wanted that toy dog. It was the first cry I had ever heard from him that was definitely not about hunger or thirst or discomfort—basic animal stuff—but was about the desire for a particular object that momentarily delighted him.

Soon after that Matthew learned how to manipulate me, dropping his toys from his stroller on purpose, giggling as I returned them. I felt as helpless as a Labrador, programmed to retrieve for its master's pleasure. Buy all the educational playthings you like, but you yourself are your child's first cause-and-effect toy.

The Boy Thing

Matthew is up on hands and knees, rocking like a mad thing, getting ready to crawl. "He's a real boy," people keep saying. "Look at that energy!" I seem to remember having had some energy myself, once. (Pause to say da-boom and tickle Matthew.) (Longer pause, as cries of glee turn fretful. We cuddle, I nurse him, we play, I put him in the playpen in front of the TV, oh, bad mother, bad mother.)

My mother also keeps harping on the boy thing. "You can tell he's a boy," she says, apropos the rocking. "You never did that." But I do not think of Matthew as being particularly boyish, or girlish. He is just babyish, my baby, to me still somehow outside classification of gender. There is a great urge to classify. Boys are active, feckless, less connected. For a while, some people actually came up to me and said, "Oh, a boy. Too bad—you know, boys will leave you." I had both old men and young women say this same thing to me, so clearly it's a pervasive bit of folk wisdom. Maybe it's even true, but if so why don't people walk up to a bride and say: "Oh, a husband. Husbands betray you."

"With a boy," one young mother of a son told me, "you're raising someone else's husband." I stared at her in disbelief. "With Jewish mothers," I said, "you wind up marrying somebody else's baby." Still, that's the bad thing about the Jewish mother stereotype: You get to remain emotionally close to your son, but are stigmatized as having somehow stunted his emotional growth. If a mother and her grown daughter have dinner together once a week, people say, "How nice." If it's a mother and her grown son, people suppress a little smirk. We all know what Freud would say about *that*. But as the joke goes, Oedipal, shmedipal. I don't care if he's Greek, Doctor—just as long as he loves his mother. And I'm getting defiant about the whole thing. After all, what good is it being a feminist if you're only intending to raise feminist *daughters*? So I'm aiming for a brave, bright, independent son who will come home for dinner once a week. Even if he has to bring a girlfriend.

The Eternal Now, Reprised

But that is years and years in the future, and I am still in the eternal now of infancy. I am trying to think of a summation for this essay, but it is hard to get perspective in the constant rush of teething biscuit scum on hair, unwashed dishes, and desperate reachings for dangerous objects. It's as if there were no life before baby, no life imaginable up ahead when I will not be required to be of some immediate service. There is simply the all-encompassing moment, nowmommy, nowmommy, nownownow.

On the rug, Matthew is trying to crawl, getting his knees lined up, but keeping one arm too far forward, like Superman. I pick him up and he folds into my embrace, opening his mouth wide in a cheerfully ill-fated attempt to gum my entire head.

Someday he will be a child, a teenager, a man. He will climb trees, drive cars, own a house. His body, that was curled under my heart for so long, will go places I cannot follow. He will be old, and I will no longer be able to comfort him when he cries in the night. But the mother-infant bond, so powerful, will not disappear. It will live on in dreams and the oldest of memories, a mythic age of warm touch and wordless acceptance, a present heaven without past or future, time outside of time, world without end.

III. CHILD OF MINE

REAL ME

SUSAN CHEEVER

For many years, instead of having children I had adventures. I lived in London and on the Riviera. I saw the Sistine Chapel and the Acropolis. I traveled to the Greek islands. I wrote novels. I left my first husband and went out with anyone who asked me. I fell in love with men I worked with. I fell in love with other women's husbands. I got married again. At age thirty-eight, when I decided that I wanted to have a child, I decided it in the spirit of adventure. Having a child was a trip I didn't want to miss. Of course I had no idea then that motherhood was the adventure to end all adventures. I didn't understand that having a child would make all my other experiences seem hollow, frantic, and a little silly. I didn't know that my child would become my whole experience, the standard against which I measured all other feelings and found them wanting.

Back when I was in college, I had learned that the only trip I really needed to take was that trip down the aisle, the trip that would end as the wife of a successful man with whom I would bear successful children. I went to work because I hadn't found a husband in college, but work was just a waiting game. I quit when the right man proposed. When I was a young bride, my gynecologist warned me that I should have children before I was thirty—advice which now seems patronizing and antique.

Sometime during the early years of my first marriage all the rules changed. I had learned to cook and entertain my husband's colleagues. I had ordered monogrammed stationery with my new name to write thank-you notes for wedding presents of silver and china. I happily spent my days as a married woman, spending the money my husband made at work. But all around me the world began falling apart. My heroes were assassinated. My husband and I began to fight more often, and our fights escalated into the battle which would eventually end in divorce. Kids I had gone to college with were desperately dodging what we all thought was an unjust war—or were suddenly, reluctantly in uniform. So I put off having children, in spite of my doctor's advice.

Then two things happened that changed my expectations forever. First, I discovered the joys of work. By accident I ended up with a job as a newspaper reporter; the hectic days and long nights were both fun and rewarding. Second, I discovered sex without the fear of pregnancy—I went on the pill. When I visited friends who had followed their doctors' advice and had children, friends who were still cooking for their husbands and whose days were regulated by school schedules and pediatricians' appointments, I felt as if I had magically escaped a life of servitude.

It took almost twenty years for me to realize I was

missing something. No one talked about the pleasures of parenthood; everyone talked about the perils, the dirty diapers, the loss of spontaneity, the end of sex. While these unfortunate parents scrimped and saved for baby-sitter money and tuition, I spent my money on clothing and ski trips. It was on the way back from one of those ski trips—we were driving through Manchester, Vermont, as I remember it—that I turned to the man I was living with. "You know what?" I said, to my own surprise and his amazement. "Maybe it would be fun to have a child."

This casual attitude persisted through marriage, conception, and pregnancy. Childbirth would be a new experience for someone who craved new experiences. I had serious doubts about taking care of a baby, though. During my first Lamaze class, I decided getting pregnant had been a mistake. After that I played hookey. I remember watching a close friend diaper her new baby when I was about seven months pregnant. She held the little girl as if she were some kind of precious jewel; she even exclaimed over the satisfactory nature of the bowel movement! I promised myself I would get full-time help. I was not about to become a slave to some baby's internal workings. Nor would I ever, ever oooh and ahhh over the contents of a diaper.

Of course, that's just what happened. Sometime during the long night of April twelfth, the night I delivered my Sarah, I also fell hopelessly, madly, mindlessly in love with her. Nothing had prepared me for the tsunami of pure joy that hit me every time I rocked her to sleep, every time I held her in my arms. Her burps were miraculous, her bowel movements adorable. For months after she was born I carried her close to my chest, breathing with her breathing. When I had to leave her, even for a few hours, I felt naked and exposed, as if I had left an important piece of myself behind. When I left Sarah at home to go out, I felt bereft, as if the most important thing in the world were missing. I usually took something of hers with me—and I still do—a small toy in my pocket, a ribbon around my wrist. I had those reminders of her sweet existence. She had a bear called Snuffles.

Sarah was my first child and my parents' first granddaughter, two facts that seemed to provoke stuffed animal–buying orgies on the part of otherwise sensible people. My brother Fred and his wife sent her a stuffed brown bear with a white nose and tummy and a manufacturer's name tag that told us his name was "Snuffles." Snuffles joined the piles of plush bears, dogs, cats, frogs, and clowns in her room. Slowly, as Sarah grew and learned to grab, cuddle, and express preferences, she gravitated toward Snuffles. As soon as she could gesture, she let us know that Snuffles needed to be in her crib at night. She began regularly falling asleep with her tiny hands nestling in his soft fur. Like all first mothers, I had read every baby book from Dr. Spock and Penelope Leach to Margaret Mahler, and I knew that the bear was Sarah's transitional object. I was proud of everything Sarah did, and settling on such an appealing transitional object seemed further evidence of her exceptional intelligence.

Of course she didn't call him Snuffles; she was ten months old and innocent of the silly names provided by manufacturers for their products. She didn't even realize he was a bear. She thought he was a cat and she called him Meow, which she shortened to Me. Me the bear became her most beloved thing, the center of her secure world. "Where's my Me?" she would ask, in her sweet little voice. "Where's Me?"

What the baby books forgot to mention was the devastating effect of too much love. By the time Sarah was two years old, Me was worn and tattered from being caressed, his once gleaming fur had been fondled to a dull, tufted fabric, his eyes were missing and his smile kissed away. After a city-wide hunt, I located another Me—a new Snuffles—and brought him home triumphantly. Sarah was less than pleased. She added the new bear to her menagerie and continued to sleep with the worn-out old one, amending his name to "Real Me" to distinguish him from the imposter.

By the time Sarah turned three, Real Me was a sorry sight. I had changed too. Sarah's love had worn me out and worn me in as it blew my old opinions and preferences to smithereens—to say nothing of my once elegant wardrobe. Coherent outfits became a fond memory as exhaustion drew circles under my eyes and anxiety lined my formerly gleaming skin. As he became more tattered, Real Me seemed to become more necessary—especially after Sarah gave up the bottle which had lulled her to sleep. She couldn't even think about bedtime until Real Me was ensconced on her pillow. When we traveled, Real Me was the first thing I packed. As he crumbled, my anxieties soared. What if he were lost? What if he just came apart at the seams one day after a particularly passionate hug? I was convinced that if that happened Sarah would never sleep again. When I slept I sometimes had nightmares about Real Me. In my dreams he disappeared or disintegrated as I watched helplessly. My psychiatrist asked if I thought my marriage was disintegrating.

But if necessity is the mother of invention, mothers

are inventors from necessity. One day, shopping in a downtown department store, the escalator took me past the toy department. There, displayed as if he were meant for me to see, was a new Snuffles. I bought him with my heart pounding and had him wrapped in plain brown paper. That night while Sarah slept peacefully, I massacred this new Snuffles with a pair of scissors, reducing him to parts—eyes, nose, ears, and swatches of fur. I crept into Sarah's bedroom and stealthily took Real Me from her pillow. With an ear cocked toward the room where she innocently dreamed, I hastily sewed on one new plush leg.

I didn't sleep at all that night. Had I changed the thing my daughter cared about the most, and ruined it forever? Had I failed to respect her feelings for the one object in the household which belonged to her and her alone? Had I tampered with her sense of security? Would she notice and be horrified? The next morning I held my breath. Sarah didn't comment. That night at bedtime, I watched terrified as she stroked the new leg in her sleepy ritual. "Mmmm, soft," she said.

After that, every few weeks, I replaced a tiny part of Real Me with a part from the new Snuffles. I have continued to replace parts of Real Me with dozens of parts from new Snuffles I have bought over the years. An eye, a new mouth, a patch of fur, another plush leg—like the human body, Real Me's body has been continually regenerating itself for the last decade. After a few years, Sarah realized what was happening, but by then my replacement rituals had become as much a part of Real Me as the bear himself, and she accepted the fact that Real Me was a patchwork of old and new.

Real Me sits on my computer as I write this, one-eyed and tattered, his tail all but worn off, his neck a shredded patch of fabric. It's been a few years since I have replaced a part. As he is fondled less, he wears better. Sarah is away this weekend, staying with her father (our marriage *was* disintegrating), going to the movies with friends, shopping. These days Real Me sleeps at the end of her bed in a pile of quilts. She doesn't notice him much, and when she leaves she doesn't take him with her. Her security comes from other things now. For her, his usefulness is over. I still keep him, though. I watched him change from the glossy Snuffles—a bear who was as heartless as he was conventional—to the very special, very worn-out Real Me.

For me, Real Me is a testament to the transformative power of the love between mothers and babies. I'll never again be the self-contained girl who thought it might be fun to have a baby. I'll never be able to leave home so blithely; I never walk out the door without feeling a piece of my heart has been left behind. My daughter's birth and the strain of raising her has irreparably damaged the young body which once brought me so much pleasure. Looking back, however, I would say that I didn't know what pleasure was then. Real Me and I are a pair. A child's love wore him out, a child's love repaired and mended him, a child's love made him old and interesting and precious. Come to think of it, that's just what happened to me.

A FAMILY ROMANCE

LINDLEY SHUTZ

During Katherine's birth, Michael and I were embraced in a strange dance, his breath like a metronome, setting the tempo for my own. As a medical student, he had helped many women deliver their babies. He was practiced in reading the cycles of pain and relief and anticipation in their faces and the squeezing band of their contractions, and he read mine for me, translating them into patterns of breathing that seemed a calm, possible path toward Katherine's delivery. When she was born, he cradled her against his chest and then gave her to me, both of us hovering over her like two walls of a lean-to. At that moment, I felt immense assurance that he was my perfect companion for this new era.

During the ensuing months, we experienced many similar moments of well-being. We also discovered why so many couples divorce. No matter how joyful it is to have finally received that child, the day-to-day demands can be a shock. It is not our child who causes the conflict. Katherine is a marvelous gift, a magnifying glass from God who reveals for us a more complex and wondrous world. We want everything for her. The strain of parenting for Michael and me, the conflict that has evinced rage and suspicion and, sometimes, disappointment in each other, has been the huge discrepancy between our ideas of how we planned to share the responsibilities of parenting and what, in fact, has happened.

To have a child was frightening to me. How could I be a good mother and maintain the creative life I had worked so hard to attain? I grew up in a traditional family. My father was the primary breadwinner, working hard every day of his life to earn the income that would ensure his children a secure home life. My mother was a homemaker who gave us a saturated childhood, abundant in play and exploration. I grew up believing that my parents' time and interest were infinitely everywhere, like air. As an adult, I also discovered the losses inherent in those rigid roles. My father's devotion to work cost us all a closer relationship with him. My mother's dedication to her husband and her children has, at times, left her adrift as an individual. So how could I provide my child with that sense of unending time and attention without sacrificing the talents and interests that I had honed through years of hard work and education? How could Michael redefine his own work goals and his role as a father so that he could have a more vibrant home life and free me up to pursue my work? How could we create a stable home so that our children could feel free to turn their eyes to the world, certain that we were there behind them?

I knew that the answers lay in my husband, Michael. We were partners and equals. No one valued my aspirations more; no one wanted more for me. I felt confident that if ever there was someone I could have a family with, someone who would be as attentive to home as I, so that I could turn my eyes elsewhere without aban-doning the children, it would be Michael. He wanted to be a part of the fabric of his children's lives.

Still, I could not imagine what our family would look like. We had seen enough representations of involved fathers, such as Mr. Mom and Mrs. Doubtfire, to know that men who take on the task of parenting as their right-ful responsibility were viewed as sources of humor, not as genuine models to inspire changes in business and society. And the "parenting" books were no better. A father's responsibilities are addressed in isolated chapters on "changes in your marriage" or "fathering," which are condescending and marginalize his experience with the child. Clearly, although the guides include men in a few key photos and paragraphs, the mother is still con-sidered the primary caretaker and the bridge from the father to the child. What the books seem to suggest is that to actually parent—to take on the thousand myriad details of buying diapers and making doctors' appoint-ments; to learn the nuances of your child's heart and mind as well as you do the complexities of your job; and to know that your child always hides his favorite toy in the laundry chute and that only the red boots actually stay on in the snow—is a choice, a fad or cur-rent custom that the father can put on like a hat. The irony, as anyone who spends time with a child knows, is that it is these thousands of details that make up a child's world. This is where the heart of the parent-child bond is.

In the days shortly before Katherine's birth, I would ask Michael, "What kind of father do you plan to be?"

"What are you asking?" he would say, at first patiently and then defensively, as he sensed there was distrust in the question. What I was asking for was a promise—that he wanted more than society was willing to help him with, that I would not lose myself in the process of trying to be a good mother, that he would not abandon me to this immense task.

During the first months at home, I felt that I was losing myself. I was overwhelmed by the transition from my job to being at home with a baby. When my employer had suggested that I take as much time as I needed for maternity leave, I had welcomed the idea, and Michael and I agreed that in five months we would hire a nanny and I would work part-time while finishing my degree. Of course, I was stunned to learn that maternity leave is not a prolonged vacation. Katherine needed little sleep, and wanted to be walked constantly. Keeping up with this meant that I slept erratically and literally could not pick up a newspaper. As I used Katherine's unpredictable naptime to pay bills or do laundry, I began to understand that to answer all of these needs meant a kind of death of the person I had been. I felt ashamed that I was grieving for my past life and confused by the coexistence of my tremendous love for this marvelous child and my unhappiness at being home to care for her. What I needed was my mate. I waited for Michael to come home, to be my Orpheus, to spirit me back into the world. What I needed was his set of hands to give me respite, to take this child from my arms and tackle these thousandfold tasks, so that I could have the energy to be something more than a housewife and a mother.

The problem, of course, is that, as in the myth, Orpheus has to go under too. He too has to risk the total loss of self so that he and Eurydice can come out together. And in my mind, Michael had changed very little in his life. Many of the choices we made with good intentions had, in fact, removed him from the heart of caretaking. Like many couples, we felt it was impossible for Michael to take paternity leave; so for five months, while I learned to read the pitch of her cries and how to answer them, Michael coped with work and tried to figure out how, exactly, to participate at home. Because Michael needed sleep, I was waking up with her at night. And because Michael's time at home was so limited, I had a difficult time asking him to relieve me of some of the household work so that I could use that time to do something for myself.

One day, my sister sent me an article from *Mothering* magazine. It outlined all of the responsibilities involved in caring for a child and a home, from cooking meals to buying life insurance. The chart was pages long and there were time estimates for the tasks. I viewed it with the same embarrassment I felt toward prenuptial agreements—as though the spirit of my love for my child and my husband were being belittled by their dissection. But I also realized the value of the job description. With a child in our home, "home life" could not be subordinated as it had when we were childless. To keep up with the demands, I was tacitly merging the roles of an entire nineteenth-century house staff (nanny, maid, grocer, cook, accountant, and financial planner) into one persona, the supposedly inexhaustible and ever cheerful mother. Michael did not seem as subject to this melding of roles. When I went out at night, I frequently returned to a kitchen that wasn't cleaned after dinner, a hamper still full of laundry, and a diaper bag with today's remnants in it instead of the fresh supplies that would help me get out the door tomorrow. Task by task, Michael

and I were falling into the gendered roles we had hoped
to re-script. When I grew frustrated, I would reassure
myself that all of this would change when I went back
to work. It only seemed reasonable that once I returned
to being a wage earner, our roles at home would shift
and we would take up the shared parenting we had envisioned so that I could become again the person I
wanted to be.

But when I returned to work I realized that we had
created a division of responsibilities that would not easily be redefined, despite the new demands on my time.
Naively, we thought that with a nanny to cover my
twenty-five hours at work, I would be free to take up
my work where I had left off. We never thought to address how I would accomplish all that I had managed at
home before with only half the time. We did not reas-
sign household chores or the tasks related to Katherine's
care.

I remember one night several weeks after I had returned to work, Michael touched my arm when I was
about to fall asleep, an invitation to make love. I felt
numb and uninterested. At first I thought I was just exhausted, and then I began to realize that the numbness
wasn't fatigue so much as anger and deep disappointment. "What is it?" Michael asked. It was everything.
In order to work part-time, I had delegated many responsibilities I enjoyed for administrative ones that could fit
into a part-time schedule. But most important, I felt unable to devote myself to work and did not foresee a time
when I would.

"What do you mean?" Michael asked. In his mind,
we had found a great nanny, so in theory I was now free
to get back at it. I tried to find an example. "You know
when you took Katherine to the doctor last Monday?"

"Yes," he said. "All during work, I was planning. I scheduled the doctor's appointment for a time that wouldn't interrupt your work. I delegated my responsibilities for the next day in case she wasn't well enough for me to go back to work, and I left work early to buy a humidifier so that I would be home in time to let the sitter go on to her afternoon job. There is a muted tape that runs in my head all day: How long did she cry after we made the transition this morning? Will Helen check her fever if she feels hot? I can't think straight."

We laughed, but we both knew it was only sort of funny. Michael did not need to think about these things because I was thinking them for us. My commitment enabled him to work every day with clarity and focus; I, on the other hand, felt stressed and constantly compromised. While Michael was searching for the best residency (the next step in his training), I was so consumed by the day-to-day details that I had no idea what my priorities were anymore, much less what my next career step might be. When we weighed the changes we had made in our lives to create our family, I felt that I had completely revised my sense of what I wanted by what I could manage. "Co-parenting" seemed to mean that I would be entirely responsible for Katherine and would be free to apply myself to my work only to the extent that we could call in a third party to relieve me. Ruefully, Michael admitted that his profession—his medical training and the future that he was guaranteeing himself and our family—was not up for evaluation. He had really only changed his goals related to working out and having fun. How did we get to this disparity?

As we talked, we saw that what we wanted from each other as parents was ambiguous. Although Michael believed in my work, he was doing little to help it get done. I acknowledged that there was a tape that ran in my head, something right out of a 1950s script, that I should not pressure him: He was working so hard and he would earn more than I, so why should he do more at home?

Because if Michael and I were to define our parenting by the dollars we could earn, we would both lose out. From the very time we began training to support our-selves, we had chosen skills that would, if we deter-mined our roles solely by the income we could generate, lead us into traditional roles as primary and secondary caretakers. But we had not had a child so that Michael could provide for her while I nurtured her heart and mind. We had asked Katherine into the world because we both wanted the pleasures of a child. I wanted Mi-chael to ask himself, not how he compared to other men (who frequently, at the end of their lives, mourn the time they have missed with their children) but to ap-proach parenting as nearly every woman ever has: to measure his work by what he wants for his family. Katherine deserved the commitment of both of her par-ents.

We decided, during those difficult talks, that to "co-parent" meant that Katherine's life had to come first for *both* of us. Over time, we established mutual principles. Although we would rely on the help of child care, we also wanted one of us to be there as much as possible. Both of us felt that we would rather have a less plentiful life of vacations and "things," if achieving those meant less intimate involvement with our children. Both of us decided, too, that time together as a family was more important than high-achieving work lives—at least dur-ing these early years. If we were offered a work opportu-nity, we would take it only after fully measuring its impact on our family and our relationship, asking, "Is it my turn to take this much time away and at what cost?" We also agreed that we would need to stay flexible. No role was permanent.

Trying to be these parents is exceptionally hard. Many times, my parents' approach (the old divide and conquer) seems much neater to me and more reasonable. The simplicity of their arrangement required little conversation and rarely led to dispute. In contrast, Michael and I disagree a lot. Like Harold with his purple crayon, we are using our bold markers to constantly reconfigure our expectations and needs and desires for each other and our family. This means that everything is up for negotiation, and there are times when I feel that all we're doing is skirmishing, skirting, waiting for the other to take the initiative. These are the days when it is as though we are in constant competition, tracking our IOUs. What is difficult about love is that we want to pretend that we do not pull power plays on each other, that we will not use the fact that one of us has earned more or has worked more exhausting hours or has "given up" more lately. At these times, co-parenting feels like this vague virtue called world peace.

We sustain the peace by constantly changing. Because of the unpredictable schedule of Michael's work and my personality (organization happens only in fits of energy), a routine is an ideal I aim for like fitness. Some of our friends seem to have "understandings." They alternate Saturday mornings of solo care to give each other private time. Or he does the morning routine so she can go to work early and she does the evening so he can work late—and then they both read *Goodnight Moon*. For us, no one way seems to work for long. Sometimes, we'll say I'll do the daily things and he'll do the spo-

radic tasks, such as repairs or the lawn; yet, most of the
daily tasks are Sisyphian in their nature (no sooner have
I completed a load of laundry than another is burgeoning
in the hamper) and a lot of sporadic tasks (such as
snowblowing or broken headlights) simply can't wait
until Michael gets home. Most of the time we each just
do what we can, talk about what else needs to happen
and hope that, by each doing a little, the most important
things are getting done.

We also try to respect each others' efforts. Occasionally I do not go crazy and completely denounce his fathering if he chooses to lounge with Katherine on the
floor admiring her toes and reading books instead of
cleaning up the floor after her spaghetti bomb dinner;
usually, he does not suggest that I finish up my work in
that suddenly discovered five minutes between dinner
and bath, as though I can call up the right idea and the
perfect words with more ease than he could do an emergency procedure without all the right equipment. We
have both learned how to turn chores into less onerous
tasks, transforming yardwork into Katherine's first encounter with the wonders of sprinklers and diaper disasters into funny family lore. We have learned to admire
and openly praise the special connections each of us has
with her. And when one of us feels torn about compet-
ing opportunities, we remind each other why we are
here. In this way, Katherine acts again and again as our
magnifying glass: She brings into relief the essentials of
our lives, those things we want for her and ourselves.

There are times that we have to remind ourselves that
our anger and resentment really come, not from each
other, but from the revelation that even as we receive
the gift of children, we also move into the reality of
our adult lives. The sheer tasks of earning money and

nourishing our bodies and caring for a home do not allow the many unbroken moments we had envisioned as family time. Some skirmishes end in a full-out explosion, a moment when one of us feels that we cannot handle the stress anymore and we rage, against each other, against workplaces that do not seem to care for family, against the constant sacrifices we make because we want to. But we also remind each other what all of it is for. We both want to care for our child, to be there when she looks in the mirror and discovers that she is the sparkling person envisioned there. We both need the benefits of our work, despite its demands. And we know that the only way to have all of this—a little of the best of everything—is to keep divvying up the stuff we don't like so that no one of us gets too overwhelmed. There are times that I feel we are still locked in that furious embrace in the birthing room, constantly turning to each other and then pushing away, reminding each other how to breathe through this one, so that our child, begun in our passion, can be borne out of home and into the world, secure that we are there behind her.

BYE BYE BABY
ON MOTHER GUILT AND POVERTY

ABIGAIL STONE

Mother guilt. It comes with the birth, is brought forth from us with the placenta, grows like the piles of laundry, and stays with us forever, like we believe the child will.

Just before my daughter turned one, Stephen left us in Vermont, at my mother's doorstep. He had good reasons. I was difficult. He was young. But Hilly didn't understand any of that. When we moved into a little cabin in the woods behind my mother's old summer place, Hillery stood at the plastic window all spring. She had no hair, but she walked and spoke a lot. She wore clothes we found at the Salvation Army, and while I struggled to get published, we lived on food stamps and money from the state. "What are you doing, Bo Bo?" I would ask, getting buckets to take to the brook by our cabin. "Waiting for Daddy," she would answer. And I would take the buckets outside and follow the path to the brook to fill them for dishes and laundry. When I got back to the little house, there she would be, looking out the plastic, into the trees. She waved. I dragged the buckets in. Rage filled me up, and then dissolved into tears. And while I cried in a wicker chair, Hillery climbed on my lap and comforted me. So you see? I should have been comforting her. I should have gotten a normal job and put aside my longing to become a novelist. Nothing was as important as her grieving heart. But, you know, I thought I could do it. I thought, "one more month and we will make it. Just a little longer and we can have it all."

I took labor classes with Stephen in Kentucky. All the pregnant women lay on the floor with pillows and practiced breathing for those particularly painful moments. Stephen was supposed to time everything and then say "OK, BREATHE" and I was supposed to suck in air from my nose and blow it out my mouth, like a whale spouting water. It was boring and I didn't take it seriously. I couldn't imagine being in pain and we were supposed to be able to imagine that. Some of the other girls in there had their mothers working with them. I felt sorry for them . . . having to lie there and listen to their moms say, "OK, BREATHE!" Stephen was shy so he always whispered the commands and when we got home we never practiced. We made jokes about saying "hee hee hee hee" during the worst part of labor. Later, when I was in labor, Stephen, who had been working all night, was slumped beside my bed in the hospital, asleep on a chair while I groaned, "Help, nurse! It hurts too much," over and over, almost like a technique but not really. The only thing I remembered to do was focus. I kept thinking about taking my child sledding. As soon as it was old enough, I would take the baby sledding through the thick white snow. When Hillery was born, the first thing Stephen said was, "She's a girl!" and the first thing I said was, "I will never do this again."

When I have you, unborn child, I will take care of you.
I promise I will do what is necessary to give you a happy
life. You won't have to grow up poor like I did. And I
will love you most of all. I will always love you . . . child,
we will be so happy. I promise, when you are old enough
to hold onto the sides, we will go sledding together.

When Hillery was born they rushed her out of the delivery room and put her under a bilirubin lamp because she was the beautiful color of a peach. "I'm going to name her Peach," I told my mother over the phone. Stephen was smiling and sitting in the hospital room looking exhausted.

"Wait till you see her," he said to his mother on the phone. But his mother didn't want to see her yet. She was still furious that her son had gotten married so young. My mother was thrilled but she couldn't get to Kentucky for the birth because she had to work. She sent us some money, what she could afford. She helped as much as she could, but she was always on the verge of being broke, too.

"Peaches, maybe," I went on, sitting up in my hospital gown. There was milk leaking out of me and my breasts looked as though they were filled with rocks. We were like that, young ignorant parents who don't know what is going on. The ignorance of seeing the world as easy. When the hospital told us she had jaundice, I cried and expressed milk with a breast pump during the night to give to my peach-colored daughter. "I thought she was that color because she's part Cherokee," I said, when the doctor explained her condition. How young and stupid. But she recovered.

When we took her home, she still had a reddish-orange tone. We had hospital photographs which we handed out to our parents. My mother wept and said, "I wish I could help you, honey. . . . I'll send you money for a crib." How she wanted to help was not monetary. It was to save us from what we were sure to recognize in time. To protect us from the reality of stress, bills, nights walking the apartment floor holding an infant who rejected all formulas. She would help to protect us from our own dismay . . . if she could. All parents would do that, take the pain from their offspring, if it were set up that way.

This isn't to say we were pitiful. We might have been pitiful, but we were really happy for six months. Stephen rode a bicycle to work because he hadn't learned how to drive. Hillery and I sat around the little apartment and, while I wrote, she watched soap operas on TV and waved to me. "Hi Bob," she said.

"Who's Bob?" I asked. All over her crib I had taped up famous paintings from a book Stephen's mother had given me. They were big full-color pictures of Picasso's work, Van Gogh, Rembrandt, Dutch Renaissance painters. She ate the Seurat. I was afraid the ink on the paper would hurt her but nothing came of it. She must have liked all the dots. Or maybe it was the umbrellas and the beach that made her so excited. I found chewed remnants of it near her pillow and when I picked them out of her crib, she squealed and jumped up and down in her pink terrycloth sleeper. Thinking back, I guess she could have *not* liked it, and realized the only way she could get rid of it was to eat it. Maybe that was what later translated into her bulimia bouts . . . of eating and vomiting in secret, her beautiful fingers going down her throat, removing everything, the dots of Seurat in the sink when she was fifteen.

If I had known then what I know now. That is a favorite saying among mothers. We all know, in our hearts, we did some things wrong. We all have some guilt. Because if you choose to stay home with your baby then you often are giving up something else. You might be sacrificing your job you love. Or you might go to work and leave the baby in day care and sacrifice your time at home with it. Or you might live on welfare and sacrifice your dignity.

"What shall we do today?" I said, making scrambled eggs in an iron skillet. The wood cook stove made it seem cozy in our one-room camp. "Shall we have eggs? Eggies? How about that, Bo Bo?" I chattered on. I am told if you don't keep up a stream of constant chatter you are liable to retard their brain cells and render them speechless. The more you yack, the better they will be. "I get toast and you get eggies for breakfast?"

Hillery stood up in her high chair and held a wooden spoon in the air. I had made brownies and she was licking the bowl, covered in chocolate. Then she bent down again, squatting on the wooden seat, and said, "Pee pee in da gwass," which was how I had potty trained her. Our cabin had no running water, electricity, or bathroom. "Pee pee in da gwass . . ." she said again. When I took her outside, the dog came with us. And while she peed quietly by the woodpile, I saw the mailman drive up, through the trees, and stop at our mailbox down by the road.

"Here's the mailman!" I said, and Hillery looked up from where she was bent down, wearing only her jacket, with no pants on. "Daddy is here?" she asked.

"No, the mailman," I said. "I'm going to go check the mail . . . maybe we got some money." When she finished, I picked her up and we ran through the woods to the mailbox. I pulled out the IGA flyer and the threatening letter from some creditor and put Hillery inside my jacket to keep her warm. "Where are your pants?" I said. "Did you leave them by the woodpile?" She didn't answer me. She rubbed her chocolate face into my sweater and sighed. I still have that sweater. If I had only known then that everything I wanted to give her would remain out of reach for so long! It wouldn't be until she was eighteen that the mailman would bring me the acceptance letter I waited for. "Bing bok, bing bok . . . oh bing bok my donnie to me," she sang. Later, when she was fifteen I would remember how we lived together in that cabin, just the two of us and the dog, how simple it was to haul water and light the kerosene lamps and hope for a miracle. When she was fifteen and smoking cigarettes, sixteen and smoking pot, I remembered her face peeking out the plastic window and how she sang "My Bonnie" with me. When she was seventeen and living at a boarding school for kids who couldn't stand living at home, I could not imagine the baby anymore. I could only hear her strained, teenage-childish voice over the phone, saying, "Oh, Mom, why can't you be like the other mothers? Why can't we just be normal?"

Yet we weren't every mother and daughter. We had struggled so far together. In poverty there is an increased intimacy. It is the singular fact that you have no other choice than to be together. Without vacations, without nights out, without babysitters or classes or even, in our case, electricity.

What I want to tell you is something of the way it is. The growing up poor, but only because we didn't recognize another way. The long rays of light cast down on our lives, through the trees. It is the grip of what you have decided, or the inability to decide. That first child, that first step away. When you are no longer on earth for your parents but for your child. When you relinquish all your power to choose what you want, and give it to that small soft human, whose enormous significance obliterates even your desire to *be* loved. Your interest is to love that baby. It overrides the shame of the Medicaid card, the humbling act of buying formula with food stamps. Comfort that child. Give to it your wisdom, hidden in your pool of brain cells, pass on to it what you know. That's sort of it . . . or maybe it's because you get so confused after you have a kid. Maybe all the laundry and the bottles and the lullabies and the Legos give you amnesia and from then on, everything is a big blur.

That photograph of her in the hospital, my orange-peach baby with her fingers splayed, was only the first of thousands. Old blanket chests are full of photographs of Hillery having her first haircut, her first tooth, her first step, her first fit, her first Christmas, her first camping trip. When I look at them my heart leaps, as though I will scream. Where is that child? I want that baby back and she is not here but she is still here. Here is Hillery's first day at day care. She is standing by the fenced-in yard not crying. In her little infant fist she holds the dress of her doll. The photograph shows they are both bald and solemn with large blank eyes. "Here," Hillery had said, when we were shopping for clothes at the Salvation Army store one afternoon. The place smelled of sad, dead people and poverty. We were the only customers in the store. Hillery handed me up a hard rubber dolly which I discovered was an old Madame Alexander doll in beautiful condition. "Here," she said again, pushing it further into my hands.

"You want this?" I said, and she smiled. She was not yet one and could walk and talk, but she had no hair at all. She didn't get any hair until she was three. That day I bought her a red velvet coat with mink trim on the collar for fifty cents. And Hillery got her doll for a quarter. "What's its name?" I wanted to know as we walked back to the car.

"Salvation," she told me.

Who thought of preserving images of the way it was? Here she is standing in front of the apartment building where she sometimes went to visit her daddy when he wasn't busy. She is wearing the red velvet coat and holding Salvation. Where is Hillery who at night asked for nothing? Who listened to the lullabies I sang, or went to sleep without them, never demanding anything? Where are the photographs of Hillery smoking her first cigarette? Her first shot of vodka? When the world broadened beyond the ferns in our yard, and she fell toward her troubled teens, what became of those snapshots?

I left her at that day care for three months, every day. "Bye bye, Baby," I would say, waving to my child. Hairless and solemn, she waited by the fence until I returned. Whenever I drove up, she would be in the yard, alone, waiting. No one even checked when I took her.

One day, when I dropped her off and left, I realized I could not leave her solemn and tearless that way anymore. And I drove back to the day care. And the other children were all inside having "snack" . . . and there was Hillery, sitting by the fence, holding Salvation.

But you see, I didn't see. I ran inside and yelled to a helper, "Do you know where Hillery is?" and the helper said, "Hillery?" and I realized she didn't know my daughter.

I took her home with me. I rocked her in our rocker in the cabin. She was funny. She played funny games with me. She learned to recite poems by Robert Louis Stevenson. Where is the photograph of me rocking her? I see now there are very few of Hillery and me together. I was the photographer, so I am rarely there in the picture. My parenting is a ghost. Hillery, alone in our cabin. Hillery camping alone. Hillery holding her doll, eating her eggies, existing without mother or father. In a way, I admit, that was somewhat true.

Where was I, during all those years of raising my daughter? I recall how I would wake up at five in the morning to read Shakespeare or something requiring real silence, and Hillery would be on the stairs within minutes, watching me light the kerosene lamp. "Go back to bed," I said, every morning, in as severe a voice as I could. I would find her two hours later, sitting on the stairs out of my view, waiting. If I had known then what I know now . . . that the anguish of that memory, that repeated mistake of shutting her out, would haunt me far more than ever a ghost father in Hamlet could haunt . . . well, but you see. We don't always know. We know, and then we are in suspension, wavering in ignorant space, unable to tell what the shapes are that are approaching.

Was that it? What *was* it that did the damage? Was it the single parent? Was it poverty? Was it her mother? Hillery says it was nothing. Just growing up. I see her now, struggling so hard to make her life whole. When she was six months old, she lived each day as breezily as another. Her daddy put her to bed, her mommy took her for walks. Adored and smiled at, her existence was miraculous. But we were too young to sustain our intertwined lives for our daughter. It wasn't his fault. Was it mine? As a child, her tiny frame was darling. At eighteen, she agonizes over being short. Her teeth, which once were so adorable, she has braced and capped and altered. Her pudgy joy turned to diet trauma. Here is a photo of Hilly crawling under the apple trees. Where is my daughter? Some nights I dream she has been stolen. And I call the police and they don't seem to care. They say, "This happens to a lot of them. . . . Most of them leave like this."

Once, I read her the story of the Pied Piper, but she did not like it. I said, "Hilly, it is just a fairy tale about growing up. The big world comes to the tiny village and lures the children away, gets them to leave their parents. The Piper doesn't hurt them, honey. It is not real. It's about how kids grow up. They leave home." But she hid the book and never let me read it to her again.

In my dreams, now, I am struggling to explain to the police my daughter's disappearance while they tell me it is normal. And while I am weeping and yelling, I am comforted too, to know she is with the others, behind the rock, with the pied piper, safe in the crowd.

I promise you, I will protect you. I will not let anyone
harm you. That boy who made you cry all through sixth

grade will be sorry when he grows up and can't have you. I will make the world better for you. I will pray every night to get the chemical companies to stop ruining the world for you . . . to stop the people chopping down the rain forests. . . . Isn't that what your pediatrician told me when I brought you in again and again with strep throat? "Mothers," he said, "that's their job . . . worrying." I promise, Hilly, all the things I have done wrong, I will rectify. When you sat in your room furiously cutting out pictures from magazines and weeping because I threatened to send you to your dad's, and I didn't comfort you, I will fix that. I will fix when I went away for six months and you sat at the window in my sister's house, saying, "Mom, don't leave. . . . Please Mom . . . don't leave me." Ohhh, yes sirree. I will repair all my wrongs, delete all my mistakes. I will make it all right again. You'll see. That check will come. That help will arrive. That father will return. That girl, that foolish girl who thought she could have a baby and give it everything, that woman who thought she knew how to do it, will discover it's only a matter of repairs. So now that you have grown from an infant to a young woman, let me hold you on my old lap of mistakes. Let me for a moment take that baby into my arms and give her back all that she has given me. That sorrowful child who waited for Daddy to come home, for Santa to bring her impossible gifts, for Mommy to get whatever it was she wanted from the mailbox, let me hold her. One more time. That child of my dreams, on a sled, sliding as fast as gravity will pull, toward the bottom of the hill.

THE HAND THAT PUSHES THE STROLLER

ALLISON ABNER

We were standing near Canal Street, just off Sixth Avenue, when we hugged goodbye.

"I love you, All'son," Angela said.

I said it back and remembered she once told me Jamaicans never express their love openly, and that it wasn't until she came to this country that she was able to say it frequently to those in her family. I wasn't sure whether she felt affection for me or actual love, but it didn't matter—what fondness she felt for me I felt for her, and I didn't want to quibble over our individual definitions of love. Before we departed I handed her the fresh bills I pulled from the ATM, and wished her happy holidays. She leaned over and kissed my son Miles in his stroller before I turned and headed for home.

When I was a child, I loved that my mom was a homemaker. Growing up, I learned a great deal about the value of raising kids in the flesh, not from an office, and how something as simple as weekly family chats can save a marriage or keep kids from straying into trouble. What I didn't learn was how to write a book and have a baby at the same time, or basically how to manage work and family life. I couldn't even look to my friends for cheat notes, because they were in the situation I had been in only a year before: single, childless, just getting the concept of adulthood. Once I got pregnant I started taking more interest in people who had kids. But these relationships were new, so I couldn't impose on them endlessly to help me.

I had to come to terms with my feelings about these issues fast, because the deadline for a work project (to which I had committed before I was pregnant) was creeping up on me. Fortunately my husband, Mark, had taken a month of family leave. He took the business of hunting down a babysitter very seriously. In his characteristically zealous style, he packed some pens and paper, threw on his winter gear, and canvassed the neighborhood to get some numbers. Within a couple of hours we had scheduled our first two appointments for the next day so we could see how the women dealt with Miles. We believed, perhaps naively, that we'd know the right person by the way she held our child, and that a lot would depend on how Miles reacted to her.

The first woman we met was black, and maybe she was a little surprised when she saw we were black too. Angela was friendly, easy, but didn't try too hard. Her smile was a little shy, but behind it was a cool confidence many black women have that some mistake for attitude. She had the kind of body that would make any West Indian man follow her for miles: a full, high, round bottom, full hips and breasts, and an arched back. Her thick braids fell into a short pageboy that framed her cocoa-complected face, and her almond eyes were unafraid to make contact.

We got into the interview right away, asking obvious questions about her experience with newborns and her references. She asked about my birth, which like hers was without drugs and with a midwife. I was excited to learn that she too had endured the agony and bliss of natural childbirth, until she explained that at the time of her first birth, she was seventeen and forced to suffer alone without a doctor or the comfort of a family member. The attending midwife spent more time humiliating her for being a "stupid girl" than offering support between her overwhelming contractions. I couldn't imagine having gone through birthing without my husband's and my mother's encouragement.

The three of us had gotten into a conversation groove, so when it was time to go, we had to remember we were still checking each other out. Before leaving we talked about salary. I wanted someone to come in from noon until five or six for five days a week, so I suggested the figure of $200. "OK," she said, seeming a bit disappointed. "I usually get at least $300, but since it's not a full day it'll be all right."

I hated that I didn't have more to offer and felt my BMCG (black middle-class guilt) working on me. Black middle-class baggage is laden with feelings of obligation and duty to "uplift the race" by either dedicating oneself to "the cause" like many admirable people (Myrlie Evers and Angela Davis, to name a couple), or by spreading the wealth in the community. My father, himself a supporter of the Black Panthers, drilled into my head the importance of reaching out to my brothers and sisters, and doing so with the utmost generosity.

Facing Angela now, I felt myself sitting on the wrong

side of the fence. I didn't want to work with a sister for this exact reason: I felt I was betraying my race by paying such piddly wages. Certainly, if Angela had been Latina or Filipino, I would have felt bad. But it's different with another black woman, because slavery, discrimination, and poverty are part of our shared history.

My own grandmother, as a young woman trying to escape from Acadia Parish, Louisiana, took a job as a governess for a Houston family. This eventually enabled her to leave the suffocating apartheid of the South and head up North to make a new life. Her lifelong wish was to attend Vassar, but it became clear that fate would never take her there, nor her daughter. Two generations later, however, it did take me there. It took five generations out of slavery for one female to graduate from college in this land of opportunity. As a black woman I had a direct connection to the obstacles Angela faced as she stepped off the plane from Jamaica.

But I had to get real. Angela needed work and I needed help. As my good friend Sabiyha, who's also black and employs a black babysitter for her daughter, said, "You can't take responsibility for the entire race. You've got to live within your means." During the interview, Angela said that she was going to school to get her GED and needed an income while she did.

So I put my feelings to rest by telling myself that I liked Angela and would pay her what I could. Mark and I talked after the next interview and agreed that there was no comparison. Angela was special. We called her that night and made plans for her to start work on Monday.

The first week Miles, in his baby frankness, spent most of his time staring at Angela with his furrowed brow, studying her face, trying to get a handle on her. Because the living room, study, and kitchen area of our loft is a large, open space, I had the perfect observation point. I would sit at my computer and look across the room at them. I even took a picture of the two of them playing, Miles with his gown hiked up to his diapers and balled fists whacking a rattle, and Angela looking on, smiling. Although this is now one of my favorite pictures, the truth is that I took it to assuage all my "what if" catastrophic thoughts. On the news I kept hearing of babysitters losing their minds and running away with the children, sometimes leaving the country. Miles's soft cheeks, licorice eyes, and gummy smile could make some desperate, wealthy Caribbean couple very happy. How would I ever recover him once he was smuggled away? I found comfort knowing I'd at least have a photo for the five o'clock news.

My fears of kidnapping and other potential harm to Miles meant they had to entertain themselves inside all day. I wanted to get to know Angela before I let her take the most precious thing that had ever happened to me out of my sight to enter New York's land mines of cars, crazy people, and potholes. When I'd see her slumped in the rocker, she and Miles both fast asleep while the O.J. trial whispered in the background, I knew she had to be bored.

Sometimes, when Miles was sleeping, she'd ask me if there was something she could do, dishes, laundry. My BMCG would kick in, and I would tell her no, that I had everything under control, even though I might be on a business call, folding clothes, and have dinner on the stove. I was determined not to let Angela feel taken advantage of. I knew what a slippery slope that could be for some babysitters who start with "light housekeeping" and wind up moving to heavy housekeeping and light babysitting.

After the first couple of days, she started bringing in *Essence* to read when Miles would pass out for the afternoon. I knew she really wanted to go out. But until I felt I could trust her, I couldn't let him go.

For this reason, and because I was truly interested in this woman who came into my house every afternoon, I broke up our days with breast-feeding chats. I learned about her life in Montego Bay, that at nineteen she was a single mother of two with few resources. "What? We were poor, All'son," she would say, as she described manual showers with buckets, washing cloth diapers by hand to get them so white that the neighbors wouldn't talk, living without an in-house toilet or electricity, and eking out a living cleaning at a small hotel. She was the oldest of four and was expected to care for her ailing mother, so she wasn't able to finish high school. Once her two babies came, life only got more complicated. "But I come to this country, and my 'ole life changed."

Indeed it had. She married to receive her green card, began working and making money like she'd never seen at the hotel in Jamaica, had her own apartment in Brooklyn, cable TV, clothes from the Gap, and settled in with a good man. These rewards she savors now, because life had been almost too unbearable to go on.

When she first arrived she cried each day for a year at the pain of leaving her children behind. "I 'ad to leave my kids to be raised by my sister back 'ome so I could make enough money to send for them and have a 'ome for them." She waited five years for the paperwork to go through. Five years of not seeing her daughters, who were six and four at her departure, except once for two weeks. Now reunited for five years, their relationships had never been tighter, and the girls got a chance at life their mother never had.

At the end of the first week, as Angela was putting her $200 cash into her purse, she cocked her head and asked me, "So, All'son, what you think about 'ow things went between us this week?" I thought they had gone well: I was getting work done; I enjoyed Angela's company and hearty laugh; and most important, I was not only satisfied with how she was caring for Miles, I was actually learning from her. Knowing what a novice I was at mothering, Angela was very careful not to undermine my confidence when making suggestions about warming his bottle, how to hold him, or when he was about to reach a new milestone. I said, "I think things went really well. What about you?"

"Me, too," she answered. "I wasn't sure if I would because, you know, All'son, I thought you were a teenager when I first met you, and I wasn't sure if I was gonna like working with you, and, you know, taking orders from a child."

We both had a good laugh. At thirty years old, I still can look like I'm in my teens. Angela and I both liked that she was just a couple years older than me. Without saying, we both felt it evened things out a little.

Over the next several months, as Miles grew, so did my relationship with Angela. She'd come in, we'd catch up, then the conversation would inevitably drift on to slavery and being black. I'd give her books to read by Frederick Douglass, Jamaica Kincaid, Zora Neale Hurston as an alternative to her usual Danielle Steele. We would talk about how reading the words of a black person, especially a woman, opened us, freed our thoughts, and unleashed our deepest emotions hidden in far away, hardened crevices of our hearts.

We'd also talk about the amazing African holdovers that are so prevalent in Jamaican culture: the long sucking of teeth to show disapproval, dishes cooked with goat, balancing buckets on top of the head. I would get these surprising longings to be insulated by a society in which I saw my people in the highest seat of authority as well as the struggling class. Angela would slip into patois, to give me the true flavor of life back home, both good and bad, and I would sit with rapture at the ease with which her tongue danced to a modified Middle-English African-laden melody and then slip right back into "speaky-spoke" (or so-called proper English).

Aside from our morning chats about black life, we often shared our ideas of what we thought was appropriate for child rearing. Angela was honest about how much her attitudes had changed since coming to America. "Back 'ome, if we did anything wrong, we'd get 'it," she would say with outrage. "At school, if you didn't get a right answer, you'd get the cane in front of the 'ole class." The constant humiliation and terror made school and childhood in general difficult for her. Once she came to the States, she learned how to discipline with words and vowed not to hit her girls again.

As I was coming to trust Angela, Mark began working on a story about babysitters for the network news program he works on. When the story aired, there were horrible scenes of babysitter abuse to the children. The next day Angela and I talked about it, and how frightening it was for all mothers. Her own sister, who took care of her two girls in Jamaica, was very rough on them, so she knew what it was like to leave her kids with someone who abused them and have little control over it.

One of the most disturbing aspects of the show to us was that it didn't give a realistic picture of life as a babysitter—the long hours, the boredom, the amount of patience it takes to raise a child, especially someone else's. The irony of the piece was that overwhelmingly it's the caregivers who are mistreated, and that many families who can afford private babysitting are more interested in making money than in their children's wellbeing. I had witnessed the name-calling and disrespect kids I grew up with aimed at their Latina housekeepers, who were raising them. Angela too remembered how degraded and trapped she had felt in previous jobs. Watching the show had made her angry at the mistreatment of the children and angry for being misrepresented in a profession she took seriously.

Around the time this show aired, Angela and Miles had begun to take strolls around the neighborhood. They started making friends at a nearby park they frequented and soon became the talk of the neighborhood babysitters. They were noticed because Miles is the only black baby at the park with a babysitter. "I wish I could push a little black baby in the stroller," lamented one woman, who agreed with Angela that caring for a black baby is a great source of pride. "It makes me feel good to know I'm taking care of a black child and 'elping 'im grow up," explained Angela.

I suppose there's a part of me that was threatened at first by her connection to Miles. When she first started taking him out, I wanted to put a sign on his chest proclaiming him my son, especially after Angela told me someone said he looked like her. But those feelings have given way to clearer thinking, since the more people who love him the better off he is.

I've also gained a greater sense of perspective about

our relationship as black women. In the past I had been haunted by words from a woman I once knew who believed that black women who babysat and pushed white babies in strollers were "setting the race back." She blamed them for taking such traditionally degrading jobs. As horrified as I was at her attitude, I have had to come clean with my own classist attitudes about Angela's job.

I realize that Angela could have taken many other jobs, like waitressing, cleaning, or clerking, but chose this profession. Watching her with Miles—seeing the ways she manages to keep him from crying, her attentiveness in finding new ways to teach or entertain him, and her tenderness that comes from her being such an empathetic person—it's obvious she has a talent for dealing with children. Even in her wildest dreams she aspires to either open a day care center or work as a pediatric nurse's aide in a hospital.

Sabiyha also reminded me recently that, apart from the low wages, babysitting is a great transitional job for women. "It's too bad black American women see it as going backward because it's a great way to get an education, set your own schedule, or make some extra money." I had to admit to myself that I had had a hard time getting past the images of slavery when black women had no choice but to care for—or even *nurse*—other children to the detriment of their own. Even today, it's painful to see women with little education and few options having to spend hours at a job they hate in order to support their families. But, rich or poor, we all grapple with our love/hate relationship to work (love the money, hate the task, or love some parts of the job, hate the rest), and Angela's job is no different.

So Angela and I will continue like this for as long as

it works for both of us. I've been able to maintain a light career at home, as I hope to do until Miles is in school. And Angela has been able to finance her education. Our relationship has reached the point that I invite her to my parties, and she's recently invited me to her house for a visit. But though we've moved beyond simply needing each other to genuinely liking each other, I won't go so far as to say that she's "part of the family." Growing up, I heard many of my peers claim their housekeepers were like members of their family. They never saw the contradiction in that phrase and their housekeepers' having to eat in the kitchen, work six days a week, and being the only one in the house to actually do housework.

However, aside from my mother, there's nobody else we trust to care for Miles except Angela. Miles, who has no concept that Angela shows up every day because she's earning a living, loves Angela. She's the only other consistent adult in his life aside from Mark and me, because we both work and need the extra help. To Miles Angela is family. Maybe life shouldn't be like this, but for now it is.

Angela and I have carved out an unusual and intimate relationship for ourselves. Despite my husband's and my desire to soon leave this city, I dread the idea of having to begin the search for another babysitter all over again. I dread Miles's disappointment and mine that, however qualified, charming, and caring his new babysitter may be, she won't be Angela.

STUDENT MOTHER

ALLEGRA GOODMAN

When my baby was six weeks old, I realized that I was
not going to finish my Ph.D. at Stanford while he slept
on my lap. I wasn't going to get my degree while bouncing him, rocking him, or even by wearing him in a baby
sling. Ezra enjoyed all of these things for about ten minutes, but then his patience ran out. He would cough
politely three times as fair warning, and then begin to
scream. It was time to find a babysitter.

David and I lived in family housing on campus, a
sprawling complex of tiny townhouses arranged in
courtyards around playgrounds. We put our baby in his
stroller and wheeled him over to meet a woman recommended to us by the sympathetic woman at Stanford's
Family Resource Office. "I am Sarwat," our prospective
sitter told us as she stood in the doorway of a house
identical to ours. "I'm sorry, would you please remove
your shoes?" She was from Pakistan, and wore a white
scarf over her hair. Inside, there were imitation oriental

carpets, a low couch, and a neat array of toys. We sat on the couch and she told us about her experience. Three children of her own, now in school, and two little boys whom she'd watched for three years. "I don't know why. Only boys come to me," she said. She picked up Ezra, and he looked up at her, dazzled by the white scarf. She leaned over him and made a sound, "tch, tch, tch," as if she were sucking the last drops of a delicious drink through a straw.

The first day I left Ezra at Sarwat's house I was overcome with nervousness. He was such a tiny baby, only two months old. He couldn't even roll over yet. His white sun hat, the smallest I could find, flopped over his eyes. Sarwat stood at the door of her house with her scarf over her hair. "This is the first time you are leaving him?" she asked me. She sighed. "Today I took my middle son to kindergarten." We wheeled the stroller right into her house, and I left quickly. I walked the short distance to my own courtyard and felt both relieved and at loose ends. I didn't know what to do with my arms, it was so strange to walk without pushing the stroller in front of me. When I got home there was no one to pick up and carry or nurse. I had five hours of time in front of me. Even with my class later that day, I still had the morning free. What should I do first? I didn't know where to begin. I felt I had to use the time, every instant of it. That somehow the clock was running down. But I also felt distracted, much too jumpy to do anything. I paused at the door of our house and stared at the leaves scattered in front of it, the dirt, the lint from the dryer vent. Broom in hand, I ended up sweeping out all that lint and dirt, bagging those leaves, shaking out the doormat. I swept and swept, full of energy and confused emotion, until finally I wore myself out and went inside the house, face streaked with dirt and tears.

And yet I needed that time desperately. The hours from nine in the morning until two in the afternoon were short, and seemed to grow shorter as the term progressed. We didn't consider leaving the baby for any longer than that during the day because he was so young, and because the babysitting cost so much. I later learned that people paid much more than five dollars an hour for babysitters, particularly for nannies who came to the house—a luxury we couldn't afford. My husband and I were both students, and our fellowships weren't designed with child care in mind. During those early months I rushed around campus feeling free, light-headed, and exhausted. I seemed always to run from place to place, and I was surprised to see my classmates sitting and standing around talking. I felt the pressure to get Ezra on time. I felt it physically as milk welled up in me by the end of a three-hour seminar and I had to run out no matter what new question was being raised.

As for Sarwat, David and I quickly saw that she had much more experience with infants than we did, and we began to ask her questions before rushing to call our pediatrician. It was she who pointed out that Ezra had started teething, she who advised us to buy him a winter hat with ear flaps. She could predict by looking at him whether he would sleep that afternoon or whether he would be fussy, and she was almost always right. "He will sleep for you," she would say when I picked him up. "He is very tired." She was a reserved woman. Only occasionally did I glimpse anything of her private life. I saw a quilt she was sewing for a neighborhood quilting class. It was a patchwork quilt in the traditional American log cabin design, but the fabrics and colors she chose were far from American in style and emphasis. Her quilt was pale green with a maroon medallion in the middle. I saw her once, dressed up to go out with her husband. He was a Ph.D. candidate in engineering, big, and rather fierce-looking with his beard. That evening he wore a suit and she wore a tunic, pants, and scarf of peacock blue. I glimpsed the shoe rack on the inside of her coat closet door, and saw that she kept all the family's shoes there. And I realized that she and her husband slept in the living room on that low couch, which she kept folded up during the day. The three children slept in the two tiny bedrooms upstairs. But mainly I knew her through Ezra. She showed me how he turned his head when she spoke his name. She predicted when he would roll over, when he would sit up, when he would crawl. "I think he likes to sit up more in the stroller," she advised me, showing me how to prop him up with blankets. I became used to leaving Ezra with her, and to the sight of her standing in the doorway with him waiting for me to pick him up.

Then, in April of that year, her husband suddenly announced that he was going to defend and graduate in a month. I was shocked. What about me? What about *my* exams in May? I would have to find a new babysitter. Someone completely new, a stranger. Sarwat looked at me sympathetically. She apologized and said she would watch Ezra longer hours so that I could study. But methodically she was packing up boxes of clothes. She put up signs in the neighborhood advertising her crib, her baby swing, and the imitation oriental rugs "in good condition, five years used without shoes." "I am not taking them with me," she explained, "because we have very good carpets in my country." She scrubbed out the apartment—she did not want to be charged by the university for cleaning costs. She washed the windows, and even the stairs. Then, early in May, she and her family left.

When we needed a new babysitter we talked to our neighbors. The student housing complex at Stanford was called Escondido Village, and it was a village, where all the mothers seemed to know each other and information was exchanged at the sandbox. We hadn't realized this when we came as a young couple without children, but magically when we had our baby we discovered that we were part of an extended family full of gossip, advice, and comforting words. The first time I'd taken Ezra out in the stroller and walked slowly on the gravel path around the playground, neighbors I'd never met before began popping out of their houses. "It gets so much easier," they would say—or, "If you feel like you're going to lose your mind, drop him off here for a couple of hours. I'm serious." From these neighbors we heard about a woman who offered child care in the next courtyard. Her name was Concepcion, but everyone called her Tita. She lived in student housing with her daughter, a Stanford medical student, and her daughter's family. She took care of the house and the children. When we wheeled Ezra up to the house we saw all the signs of established student housing residents. Tall geranium plants in front, bicycles and plastic wading pools hanging from the eaves over the patio. Tita's house was identical to ours and to Sarwat's, except that it had three bedrooms. On the walls were huge photographs of the whole family and a print of the Last Supper. The apartment was filled with overstuffed furniture, an oversized television and stereo. We sat with Tita on the couch and she gave Ezra some toys. He was now ten months old. "Smart," Tita said.

"Thank you," we replied, watching proudly as he examined the toys.

"You know how I can tell?" Tita put her hand on Ezra's bald head. "He got no hair."

She was a small, trim woman with sharp eyes and wavy black hair. Among the photos on the wall was a glamour shot of Tita in soft light and makeup, her shoulders framed with marabou feathers, the gold crown on her front tooth sparkling. She'd come to the United States from Mexico as a migrant farm worker, raised four children alone after their father left, remarried, and now was helping her daughter through medical school. Her energy was astounding. She took care of three grandchildren and babysat for three others as well. Did all the cooking, and kept the house immaculate. On weekends she drove all the way to Sacramento to see her family. She picked vegetables free-lance and would come home early Monday with crates of lettuce, cauliflower, tomatoes, or melons. Her table would overflow with produce, a seasonal cornucopia.

As for the children, she managed to keep them all busy, happy, and clean. She bathed them and insisted that we bring a change of clothes for Ezra. Before we picked him up she would change him into clean clothes and, after his hair grew in, she would brush it and spray it with water so it would stay smooth. She did the family laundry and ironing every day and would wash and iron Ezra's clothes as well. His tiny overalls had neat creases. In the summer she would fill up her wading pool first thing in the morning so that the water would heat up in the sun. Then she would vacuum the tiny living room. By the time he was a year old Ezra knew that when he heard a vacuum he should climb on the couch. Somehow she managed to do everything at once, watch the children, cook dinner, iron the clothes. She never waited for a quiet moment, never saved anything for the children's naps. In fact—amazing to us—she didn't believe in making the children nap at all. She only put them down when they told her they wanted to sleep. Ezra would come home from her house exhausted and fall into bed at seven o'clock, actually grateful for the chance to rest.

Ezra loved the constant activity in Tita's house, the Spanish radio station. Tita spoke and read to him in Spanish, and he would use English and Spanish words interchangeably. She taught him to count as he crawled up and down the stairs, how to eat by himself, and how to wash his hands. When Ezra was fourteen months old she became concerned that he wasn't walking. He would take a few steps, but that was all. "I will teach him," she told me. I was surprised. It had never occurred to me that you could or should teach a child to walk. I assumed that children started walking by themselves. The next day, when we came to pick up Ezra neither he nor Tita was home. Tita's daughter told us, "Mom took Ezra to the Inner Quad to practice walking." Sure enough, when we got to the Quad, there was Tita marching our little toddler across the huge courtyard with its Mission arches. She was keeping him late so that he could learn. Magically, after that day he never crawled again.

I was no longer nervous about leaving Ezra with a babysitter. He began staying with Tita longer hours and I began getting more work done. Some of the mothers who sent their children to her told me they felt a little jealous of Tita. The children loved her so much, and she had such a good time with them. I wasn't jealous, somehow. I was relieved to have such a successful babysitter, my second in a row. And I was eager to learn her secrets—the way she got the kids dressed so quickly, the way she cooked dinner while they played on the floor. Where did she find the strength? I was walking through campus with Ezra one evening and I saw Tita playing basketball with some other women. Small and fast, she dribbled the ball down the court and made her shot.

She made it look easy, but it wasn't. She was living with her daughter's family of five in a three-bedroom apartment. Her daughter had terrible hours and worked part time to help make ends meet. Her son-in-law worked as well, and came home exhausted at the end of the day. I never found out what he did, because he didn't speak to me. He never raised his eyes to meet mine. I met him once at a fair in Palo Alto. He was walking with his wife and the children, the two little girls dressed in matching lavender party dresses. They all said hello except for him. He didn't even look at me. It couldn't have been easy for him, living that way with his mother-in-law taking care of the children and the house. And it couldn't have been easy for him that his living room was a day-care center, full of other people's children, their toys, their tiny bits of laundry, and their sniffles.

All students, but especially student parents and their families, feel an urgency about finishing up and moving on. It is a wonderful time, a time of excitement and good fellowship, but also a time of stress, financial and emotional. Student families have to squeeze themselves into their apartments. The lack of space for work, play, and privacy pinches constantly. When Sarwat's husband had announced that he was graduating it was clear that she, as well as he, couldn't wait to move on. In Pakistan they would have a house with a big garden. The children would have their own rooms. It was difficult not only for foreign students, but for American students as well. The American wives of graduate students also earned extra money by providing child care. There was Alison in our courtyard who cared for several children as well as her own, and worked long hours cooking, cleaning, and running after toddlers. She and her husband had squeezed a glossy black piano into their apartment and she would sit down and play when she had a free moment. She was always baking and playing and putting away toys. She gave us a recipe for cinnamon rolls that she'd adapted from her days as a server at Cinnabun. She'd divided the industrial recipe by twelve. There was Monica, an African-American woman who looked after several children along with her own daughter. She hoped one day to manage her own child-care center, and carefully planned the day for her charges: indoor play, snack time, playground, lunch, nap, indoor play, snack. Their husbands were studying physics and chemistry. The hours were long in the lab and at home. In the evenings they, like us, walked along the bike paths pushing strollers and talked about the future, having a bigger place, finishing and getting a job. Every summer after graduating, the big moving trucks would arrive, sweeping away the graduates and their families, swallowing up all the books and toys, the baby swing and wading pool, the cribs and little pink bicycles with training wheels. The rest of us would watch the movers loading their massive trucks and, as our neighbors left, we would feel a mixture of sadness and anticipation. They had done it. They were going to Michigan and buying a house, or New Mexico or Indiana, they had a post doc at Cern. Some day we would be leaving too.

In June, when Tita's daughter graduated, the family bought a house in Modesto where she would start her internship. They packed eagerly. Everyone was thrilled, except for Tita. "I don't like Modesto. Too hot," she said. "And I miss the kids. I miss Esra." She had enjoyed her role as the mainstay of the household, and it wasn't clear if she would be needed in Modesto at all. She did indeed love all the children she cared for. She seemed to dread leaving. Her eyes filled with tears whenever she spoke of it. On her last day watching Ezra she told me, "You take care Esra. He is good boy." We both cried. "You remember Tita," she said to Ezra and gave him a kiss. He wasn't even two, but for weeks afterward he said, "Tita gave me a kiss—mmmuh! Why she went away?" A few months later we went away too, leaving Stanford and the identical townhouses far behind. Ezra stopped asking about Tita, and then he forgot about her.

As I write this I am holding our new baby on my lap. He is sleeping on my legs, his mouth open, his tiny fingers twitching. I've found a babysitter in the neighborhood to start next month. She is Muslim like Sarwat and wears a kerchief over her hair. I tell everyone that this baby is much easier than my first, but I think in fact I am more experienced. When I think about my first two years of motherhood I think of Stanford and the babysitters I had there. It occurs to me that I was an apprentice at Stanford. Not just a student and a mother, but a student mother. My own family was far away when I had my first baby, and Sarwat and Tita were my teachers. I depended on them, paid them, but I was also watching them, trying to learn from and emulate their skill, their pride, and grace.

CONFESSIONS OF A LAZY MOM

KATIE GREENEBAUM

I take my baby on the subway in New York City. I snap her into her spit-up-soiled carrier, sockless, and set off, licking my finger to wipe the banana off her chin. I let her touch the greasy metal pole. I pick up the toys she tosses onto the subway floor and offer them up to her, gift-wrapped in grime. I feed my baby cold formula. And tap water. I let her suck my unwashed finger. I don't use diaper cream. At the health club, I plop her down on a pock-marked carpet littered with runny-nosed toddlers. I stay for a few minutes and watch her stick the fraying plastic toys in her mouth. Then I leave her with the club babysitter, a nice-seeming woman I know nothing about.

It is impossible to say how much I love my Nora. My jaw hurts from smiling at her. My favorite pastime: to kiss her full on the lips then pull back for that adoring drunken gaze. I lie on the floor and let her drool on my hair and gnaw on my chin. I carry her around like an extra limb. I've never had that feeling, the one people tell me about, of wanting to shake her or punish her or give her away.

And yet, I am conscientiously rotting her unborn teeth. Nightly, I give her a bottle in bed, sometimes formula, sometimes juice. I take her out of car seats in moving vehicles, then stick my breast in her mouth as her head bumps against the hard plastic knobs on the door. I don't have a humidifier or a well-stocked medicine chest. I've taken her to dinner at mediocre, smoky restaurants all over Germany, France, and Nashville, Tennessee. In the evenings, when other babies are in bed. I never know when it's naptime until she fusses and reaches up to me with her adorable grasping fists. It is always feeding time; none of these enforced four-hour separations for us. If she seems fussy, I plug her in. I've never washed my nipples in a gentle, circling motion with some sort of hypoallergenic salve or cream.

I am not a painstaking caregiver. But this must be something other than disinterest or neglect. I wanted this baby so passionately, so single-mindedly, that I agreed to quit my job in New York and move with my husband, Josh, to Frankfurt so he could work for a German bank. I had no prospects, only the intention to write, perhaps to teach English, and certainly to have a child. Almost unconsciously, I pursued only pregnant and newly-progenied friends. I paced colicky newborns, swabbed explodo-poops, suffered alongside cracked nipples, watched marriages buckle, wiped postpartum tears. Who could possibly have a more educated desire than my own? Who else, childless like me, would spend her days roaming with this procreative tribe? I began to believe I had left New York for a specific reason: to be someplace where I could own up to the fierceness and primacy of my desire to have children, where I could shed my Phi Beta Kappa past, and with it the assumption that I was hungry for a superwoman type of success, and uncomplicatedly hunker down with diapers and sexless breasts. I left New York to rid my life of potential complications—interesting job, nightlife, demanding friends—so that when I finally became a mother I would have no regrets. I would be leaving nothing behind.

But, as luck would have it, no baby came our way. And, as our months of trying turned into a year, I couldn't help thinking it was those same old bugaboos—my sloppiness, my lack of discipline or rigor—that were threatening to botch the proceedings. Something strenuous and dispassionate invaded our marital bed, very flesh on flesh, like fish slapping on the dock. Afterward, I cycled my legs in the air, or stood on my head, visualizing rushing, clamoring sperm. But I performed these tricks sporadically, with no method to my madness. My doctor handed me basal body temperature charts and a rectal thermometer, sent me in search of the elusive underwater egg. But I couldn't chart my highs and lows. It was too much work. I forgot in the morning, couldn't read the mercury without my contacts anyway. Instead, I cadged leftover ovulation kits from friends. They were easy—just a stick in the urine stream and a wait for that thin blue line. Josh was little help in these haphazard proceedings, believing deeply that any attention paid to the endeavor would botch the magical mystery tour of his squiggly chargers. But it mortified me that I couldn't pay systematic, orderly attention even to this: the great, important thing that was occupying all my thoughts.

I did get pregnant, finally, more than a year later; classically, unthinkingly, on vacation. And while the long wait did make me treasure my condition even more, it didn't make me more cautious or attentive to detail. I wanted to be prepared, of course, so I went to a German prenatal class to learn a few phrases like *"Ich habe mein Fruchtwasser verloren"* (My water broke) and *"Wo ist die Station fuer Neugeborene?"* (Where is the nursery?). But I never worried about the quality of the German hospitals or thought of flying back to the States to have my baby, like some American women I knew. And I was always a little nonplussed when a friend, also pregnant, called with new fears, at first of grave deformities, then, as her pregnancy progressed, of labor, cesareans, colic, mastitis. Ever since my first ultrasound, I had been distinctly unworried, enveloped in an almost cosmic complacency. It just felt right.

Nora was born in one of those huge German monstrosities built without concession to human comfort just after the war. I had no bag packed when my water broke, and I labored on a metal folding chair in the cold, gray hall. Between contractions, I had cause to wonder whether it had been inertia rather than a healthy trust that had kept me from fretting about the fetus or giving up caffeine. Most of the nurses were on holiday, and Josh was sent into a bureaucratic quagmire from which there was no guarantee he would emerge before the baby was born. There was no one to attend me. When I cried out for a painkiller, a nurse with a long needle finally appeared and injected a strong narcotic before measuring my dilation. I was already ten centimeters, it turned out, and Nora's matted hair was making its grand entrance. Nora was born drugged and I was too drugged and Josh too bedraggled to be overly concerned.

On our last night in the hospital, Nora developed jaundice and Josh and I went out for a restaurant meal while our newborn lay naked under the lights. My doctor had recommended that we got out to eat so, cowlike, I expressed milk and went. "How could you leave the hospital with your baby lying naked in an incubator?" my hospital roommate cried out when I returned. I felt naked at that moment, too. "Because they told me to" seemed a weak and pathetic rejoinder. But, really, I wasn't that worried. The jaundice wasn't particularly bad, I had managed to ascertain, and I felt it would be almost arrogant to believe that our case was somehow special. I already believed in Nora, in her strength, her resilience, her commitment to life. And, at 3:00 A.M., when a nurse called me and said, *"Sie will nicht schlafen,"* I padded to the nursery and there she was, the love of my life, her color back to normal, her eyes wide open and alert. It was clear: It was me she wanted. I was the one who knew how to hold her. My heart seized up with love.

Still, as per the books, I tried hard to be careful at the beginning. I burped fairly assiduously, boiled nipples the first few times she had bottles, made lists of questions for the midwife's visits. I changed Nora often and kept her warm. I cared about her outfits. When she threw up on herself I changed her clothes. But I could already feel the laziness creeping in. When Nora got a diaper rash during her first week home, the midwife suggested switching from plastic to cloth diapers. It took our prodigious pee-er about fifteen minutes to desecrate three different ensembles. It took Josh and me the same fifteen minutes to decide to switch back to Pampers, and to take a different, easier tack. When baby acne and painful digestive problems appeared on the scene, I made some vague attempts to change the composition of my breast milk. I cut out broccoli, cabbage, and cut down on caffeine, onions, garlic. But I never went so far as to cut out dairy, which I was craving at a rate of three bowls of cold cereal a day. I always said there was too much conflicting advice out there, which was true. I threw up my hands in the face of the mystery and continued along my half-baked path. Josh followed along, eager to help, unwilling to lead. She'll outgrow it, we decided, and we both willingly paced her and rocked her and bicycled her little legs. And outgrow it, of course, she finally did.

There were many mysteries during the first few months, few of them truly troubling. She spat up constantly but was a prodigious weight gainer. She had an enormous repertoire of barnyard noises, from the black sheep's baa to a dead-on creaking screen door, uncanny enough to make us believe in former lives spent on farms. She preferred the left breast to the right and saved her first social smile for a creepy man neither Josh nor I much liked. She preferred old things to new, which was lucky as everything she had was borrowed, from the threadbare boy's pajamas to her plastic bassinet. She was a sleepy, placid baby, and as the date for moving back to the States grew closer, I guiltily left her in her bouncy chair for hours as I organized boxes and filled out forms. I dragged her with me to countless de-registering agencies and farewell fêtes. Along the way, I was yelled at by many a German Hausfrau about Nora's hat being off or her neck being unsupported or her stroller being too old. Occasionally, my confidence was shaken: It was true that I often left the house aware of a less than fresh diaper and allowed her to fall asleep midway through feeds without switching breasts. But, even in those lonely first months in Germany, I felt a certain confidence taking hold: I am relaxed and healthy and goodnatured, so my baby will be relaxed and good-natured. Skimping on the surface stuff doesn't matter, I'd tell myself, since I'm rich in the deeper loam: the commitment to motherhood, the unconditional love.

It's easy to look around and gather enough evidence to justify or vilify oneself, depending on the mood. On good days, I do feel sort of strong and right-headed: the ur-mother, so clearly a natural with my childbearing hips and breasts, my high threshold for chaos, my big old heart. I look around and see telltale equations in the park: nervous mom/whiny baby, rigid mom/tantrum-y brat. I talk to the mothers in my neighborhood who won't get on the subway, in a taxi, who won't take their babies out in the cold, who wait until the weekends to go anywhere or do anything, who enforce rigid nap schedules, who confess to spending afternoons on the couch crying, feeling so desperate and alone. I think to myself, what could be worse for a baby than having a resentful, unhappy mother? I look at my cheerful and trusting, if runny-nosed, child and think, you lucky girl. I admit to no nature, only nurture, and tell myself that I'm doing the right sort of taking care.

On bad days I think poor Nora's going to grow up like her mother: complacent, undisciplined, and, yes, fat. And then it's not a long leap to the thought that, finally and inevitably, I am turning into my own mother, despite all the preventative steps. I can feel the inexorable pull: I will only be happy when my children are young. I will live life from crisis to crisis, taking care of carpools, dentist appointments, but lacking any long-term vision or plan. More than anything, I will revel in the chaos, grateful for that great big obliterating responsibility that renders tending to my own needs impossible. I will be bereft when my children leave and incapable of proceeding like a responsible adult. Despite my twenties full of promise, I will have no direction, no true career. And when I am older, my own children will worry about my health: physical, emotional, and financial. I will live for my grandchildren and feel cheated every time they are taken away.

My mother, like many, sent a message that was supremely double-edged. But I suppose we are all trying to cull the good from the bad. I know my parents did something right. Four girls and not an adolescent rebellion among us. Despite obstacles—chubbiness, precocity, being the progeny of the school principal, nerdily playing the violin—we grew up well-liked, with self-esteem mainly intact. It was never us-versus-them in our house; and there was something about the quality of attention and love we received that rendered rules and regulations unnecessary. I was the only one of my neighborhood friends who saw home as a warm and welcoming environment, who loved to bring friends home to eat my mom's brownies, never worrying about crumbs on the floor.

But, as I sit here on our couch, sort of typing, sort of watching Nora, sort of watching television, eating absentmindedly, unable to commit to dieting or keeping Nora TV-free, or to finishing this piece I am writing, I realize my mother was guilty of a certain type of neglect: of her self, of taking herself seriously. And I sometimes worry that I am already guilty, too; I have felt lazy and fearful, desirous of a child simply in order to absent myself from the rat race, as justification for a disappointing and meandering personal path. I want to love Nora unadulteratedly, but not as an un-adult. My mother, bereft and inarticulately guilt-ridden, tries to think of ways she has failed us, perhaps to avoid the deeper feeling that we failed her, by growing up, not needing her anymore. She brings out the evidence, and it is all the wrong stuff: photographs of my youngest sister, face covered with chocolate on her first birthday, as if a dirty face said something about the nature of love. She produces memories of perceived lapses. Why didn't we have curfews? Why didn't she make us take French? She hears horror stories from her own friends about their children and turns on us nervously: Did you have abortions in high school? Did you take LSD? These are ridiculous questions. She was my best friend in high school. The one time I tried smoking pot out in the woods before the town fair, I spent my few precious minutes high planning how I was going to tell her. Nothing happened to me really until she knew about it. And *I* was the black sheep of the family, rubbing up against boys on our couch late at night.

I try to grapple with these issues, but, of course, right alongside me while I'm turning inward or paying least attention, Nora is growing up. She is nine months old now, crawling, cruising, cracking herself up. And there are many good signs. She has a healthy mistrust of strangers, but isn't clingy or suspicious. Thank God, she prefers me to all others, but there are many she delights in. She is not a picky eater or plagued by a princess-and-the-pea sensitivity. She can entertain herself. She is becoming independent, which I must try to see as a great, good thing. We had our first fight the other day. She kept flipping over and crawling away when I was changing her diaper. I was stunned by the strength of her torso twist, her determination. Part of me was pleased that she had her mind so firmly set on a goal, in this case the plastic wrapper of a Kleenex pack over by the television, but part of me was alarmed that she had her own ideas. And still another part of me still believed that this mild disobedience was our punishment for not having a changing table, for changing her wherever we happened to be, sofa or kitchen table, for neglecting to teach her a routine.

After the fight was over, and the Pamper firmly in place, my mind wandered back to a visit with my husband's boss and his wife in Germany when both of our babies were four weeks old. Politeness reigned, but it was clear that they were appalled by our casualness, just as we were rendered speechless by their discipline and certainty. There were some things we admired: the gleaming white surfaces, the feeding charts, beautiful nursery walls. But what I remember most was their baby wailing miserably while Birgit calmly baked muffins in the kitchen telling me that it wasn't feeding time yet. Still, it was baby Julius who was well-blanketed in his padded stroller, and Nora exposed in her skimpy papoose on Josh's chest when we set off for a wintry walk. And, as we rounded the first corner, it was I who found myself sitting on a bench in an open field in Offenbach, Germany, breastfeeding my baby in front of my husband's boss. This would simply never happen to Birgit, I remember thinking, who somehow always managed to find herself in the rocker in Julius's nursery when feeding time rolled around.

The other day we got pictures of the smiling nine-month-old Julius in the mail and, as I sat on the floor once again wrestling Nora into her diaper, bribing her with unscheduled bottles and free naked crawls, I couldn't help thinking that Julius's diaper changes probably take two seconds, up on his padded wicker table under his brightly colored mobile. I thought about all of the extra energy I was having to exert in service of my inability to keep an orderly house. The stakes are higher now. Nora can pick pennies off the rug, chew on power cords. She can turn on the microwave that rests on the floor, eat the dust bunnies off the rug, pull her own dirty diapers out of our non-disinfected, open-lidded cans. She can stand up in her crib and bang on the wall knowing that eventually she'll be sprung by me or my softhearted spouse because there are no such things as rigid bedtimes in our house. I have to be much more vigilant than the Birgits of this world, whose houses are baby-proofed, who know just when naptime comes and can schedule their days.

But I am not hugely worried. The truth is, I feel at home taking care of Nora; it's a familiar song, a dress that fits. I will try to teach her about thank-you notes and hospital corners. If I fail, so be it. She will still be loved. The real challenge for me is to remember to take care of myself. I know it is not really the extra work involved in Nora's new mobility that rankles. It is, of course, the fact of her desire to crawl away at all. There is that momentary bitterness I feel when she stares at me blankly like I am a big dumb post in her way, or when she pads away from me toward new, conquerable lands without looking back, that panicky fear that her independence will somehow unmask my own increasing dependence. My worry is not about my housekeeping, or the hot dog and Froot Loop dinners, or even the health of my strong, resilient girl. It is about myself, and the perverse pleasure I feel when she's congested and crying and keeping me up half the night, wanting me to hold her and rock her, that sense of victory when she finally relinquishes that insidious independence and gives in, relaxing that taut, curious neck. It is that seductive, obliterating love I have to watch out for: of a limpid baby, hot head on my shoulder, needing me absolutely, her soft bottom nestled in the crook of my arm.

MAKING IT WORK: MY LIFE AS A CAREER-MINDED MOTHER

KRISTIN VAN OGTROP

The other day something happened that I had been dreading for a long time. I came home from work in the evening and Judy, my son's nanny, handed him to me, as she does every day. My little darling six-month-old Owen gave me a perfunctory smile, patted me on the shoulder with his chubby hand, and then reached back for Judy.

This hurt my feelings a bit. But it wasn't as devastating as I had anticipated. I didn't have to turn away to hide tears or run screaming from the room or quell the urge to fire Judy on the spot. I didn't resent my son or question my own identity as a mother. Judy and I exchanged a smile, then she turned to Owen. "Don't make Mommy jealous," she said.

I am something I never thought I'd be: a full-time working mother. When I was growing up I spent ridiculous amounts of time constructing elaborate plans for my future; if anyone had told me I would be working full-time once I had a child, I would have slit my wrists. My future life as a mother was one of homemade baby food and long afternoons on the front porch swing, not jars of Beech Nut in every color of the rainbow or 3:00 P.M. trips to the office bathroom to furtively change my nursing pads. Then again, I never imagined working full time while raising a child could make me happy. And, for the most part, it does.

The older I get the more I realize I don't make my choices—rather, my choices make me. My decision to go back to work after Owen was born involved maybe eight seconds of deliberation, and was made with my own self-interest in mind. Sure, I can rationalize that our standard of living is higher and therefore my son will be able to have piano lessons, or that he will be a happier person because he will have a more satisfied mother. But the bald truth is that I prefer working to staying at home, and in that way I am selfish. Which is not to say that full-time mothers are inherently unselfish. Many women who opt to stay home with their children are doing so because they didn't like their jobs in the first place. I love my job. As an editor at a monthly magazine, I never work until midnight like some lawyers and investment bankers I know; most mornings I am at home till nine and I rarely stay at the office past six. Still, I could quit, or work part-time. We'd have to move into a rent-controlled apartment and eat Top Ramen noodles with ketchup every night of the week and not buy any new clothes until Owen turned twenty-five, but we could swing it. There are certainly families who get by on less. I don't want to.

The process of choosing to return to work full-time can probably be traced back to Owen's birth. Friends had told me in breathy tones that the moment my son appeared, I'd gaze into his little unblinking eyes and feel an overwhelming, boundless love, beyond anything I'd ever experienced in my life. It just didn't happen. Gazing into his little unblinking eyes, I didn't feel overwhelming love; all I felt was total wonder at the biology experiment my husband and I had successfully completed. And amazement that something so big could fit in my stomach.

As I slogged through the first part of my three-month maternity leave, fuzzy and harried all at once, this much-mythologized bond with my child failed to make its appearance. I didn't *feel* much of anything, come to think of it, except pain from my episiotomy. This was a big shock. I have always considered myself an overly emotional person—what other kind of freak would cry during the NCAA basketball finals and at the end of *Home Alone*? But after Owen's birth I felt inadequate. People would gush, "Can you just not believe how much you love him?" or "Did you ever imagine anything could make you this happy?" and I would nod and smile simply because I was too embarrassed to admit that not only did I love my husband and parents and sisters more, but I was probably happier on a 1991 summer vacation to Cape Cod, during Hurricane Bob.

So I did not exactly spend the night before my return to work weeping and rending my clothing, as friends had warned. True, I was sad, thinking in broad strokes as I tend to that I was going to miss my son's whole childhood and cause him to grow up to be the kind of teenager who intentionally tries to run over squirrels with his car. But I had hired a nanny whom I trusted and I was going back to a new job. I was excited to surround myself with adults, to read the newspaper in its entirety, to use the creative part of my brain to come up with ideas that didn't involve how to write a thank-you note and breastfeed at the same time. And, of course, I was excited to be able to eat lunch and go to the bathroom whenever I wanted.

I made peace with my choice. Not everyone else had, however. My working full-time invites as much unwanted social commentary as my pregnant stomach did. Sometimes I long to be of my mother's generation, and not just because women wore white cotton gloves and drank martinis every day. Being a mother was easier back then because, more often than not, you didn't have a choice. My mother knew it was her job in life to get engaged during her senior year of college, get married the summer after graduation, and get pregnant the very instant my father finished law school. And stay at home with the children, obviously. But everything becomes harder the more choices you have to make, which is why restaurants with six-page menus are so awful.

I can handle the disapproval of women my mother's age, because many of them are so stuck in their own 1950s world that they even refuse to learn how to use an ATM machine. It's the censure of my peers that makes me crazy. Shortly before Owen was born I had a conversation with an old friend in which she asked me if I was having any success in my attempts to work four days a week. "I don't want to work four days a week," I said. "That was never the plan." There was a dumbfounded pause. "Oh," she finally replied. "I must be thinking of someone else." People like this make me feel guilty for wanting to work full-time, as if leaving my child with someone else five days a week constitutes child abuse.

But I guess, in my own way, I'm just as disapproving: I have very conflicted feelings about women who stay home full-time. I've never admitted it out loud, but

I sometimes regard my nonworking mother friends as being on permanent vacation. In my heart of hearts, I know this is not just unfair but untrue. When I think about staying home full-time with my own son, the last word that comes to mind is *vacation*. Instead I imagine being stuck in a crowded elevator with mechanical failure. Yet I still have a terribly condescending attitude toward women whom I perceive as being overly obsessed with their children. Don't they have lives of their own? What's left for them when the kids go off to college?

I'm sure many would disagree, but I imagine life as a full-time, stay-at-home mother would, on balance, be less stressful than mine. Stress comes in all shapes and sizes; I remember reading once that Edith Wharton's husband suffered nervous collapses, and all he did was travel around the world and spend money. I could teach him a thing or two. I recently had a minor revelation—during a particularly tense afternoon—when I realized that I had two options for stress relief: alcoholism or yoga. Unfortunately, alcoholism is at present the most attractive, because drinking is not something you have to work to fit into your schedule.

Part of the reason I am tense is because I suddenly have an additional career to manage, yet—through some cruel twist of fate—I also seem to have tapped into a flaky side of my personality that I never knew existed. Now I sit at my desk at work and know that as I sit there ten things are falling through the cracks, although I can't remember what they are. Sometimes when I'm at the office I even forget about Owen for hours at a time; I'm not sure if this is a good sign or not. Then I look at his pictures on my bulletin board, or listen to his laughter on my voice mail, and I can't wait to go home.

Of course, all is not sweetness and light when I get home. For the most part the child-care and housekeeping division of labor between me and my husband is equal; still, my husband often works later than I do and some nights I feel like I am trying to accomplish everything— cook dinner, do laundry—in the interval between when my son goes to sleep (8:00) and my husband arrives home from work (8:04). The time I spend with my son—during the week, that is—is sometimes so full of struggle (struggling in the morning to get dressed for work, struggling at night to give him a bottle he no longer seems to want) that there seems to be little "quality" about our time together. Owen is tired and cranky half of the time I spend with him at night; if he has bright spots, they are spent with Judy. On darker days I know it is beyond ridiculous to think I can have it all—whatever *that* means. On these bad days I feel one thing is certain: I have chosen my work over my son. This can't be sugar-coated or talked around.

Yet Owen is without question more important to me than any job. This fact alone helps explain why relations between working and non-working (outside the home, I mean!) mothers are often so prickly. My friend Sarah—a stay-at-home mother of two—tells me that all mothers who stay at home think mothers who work have thrown their priorities out the window. How can I insist that Owen is so important when I leave him for forty hours a week with a woman who, all things considered, I barely know? A year ago I wouldn't have left my mailbox key with someone I'd only met twice; now I'm giving her my son? From time to time I come across a working mother who never gets home before her children are in bed, or who spends a lot of her life traveling; I usually twist myself into a little soap-boxy snit and think, "If she's so busy, why did she bother to have kids?" Then I stop, ashamed, because I realize some people must wonder the same thing about me.

I'm sure there are lots of groovy, kneesock-wearing stay-at-home mothers (why I think neo-hippyism and staying at home go together I'll never know) who would laugh scornfully to hear that I consider myself a good mother. But I do. Although it took its time, that mysterious mother-child bond has appeared. In my night-table drawer I keep one of the miniature white socks Owen first wore to remind myself that his foot was once so impossibly small. I can no longer watch movies that involve injury to anyone's son without crying, because I'm imagining my son. (Perhaps this will change if I have a daughter; for now, I'm relatively hardhearted about the fates of fictional girls.) These days—dopey as this may sound—I think twice before jaywalking, because I watch crazy taxis come barreling toward me and think "Don't hit me—I've got Owen to take care of." I feel as if I know and understand my child; hopefully he will one day say the same about me. I do worry, like many working mothers, that he will come to resent the fact that I wasn't there to comfort him most of the times he fell while learning to walk, that I wasn't the one to open the front door when he came home from school, that we never had the effortless, empty moments of just being together that I think my friends who stay home have with their children. I console myself with the thought that I am a better mother than I would otherwise be because I am a fulfilled person, that I will one day provide for Owen a positive image of women in the workplace. Then I wonder if all that is just bullshit rationalization made up for women like me, by women like me.

Everyone brings children into the world for selfish reasons; few embark upon child-rearing thinking the whole experience is going to make them unhappy. My selfish reason for wanting to have kids is that—career or no career—I can't imagine anything lonelier than growing old and not having children to help make sense of my life. I do want to have at least one more, but that decision is not selfish; that is an Owen-based decision. I did not love being pregnant and I did not love having a baby until he was about nine weeks old (and, not coincidentally, sleeping through the night). But I think it would be unfair to deny Owen a sibling. I have two sisters and there aren't a lot of things in life that give me more joy than they do. I hope Owen can have the same experience.

I'm always surprised when I meet people who don't want to have children. Such a disclosure is a real conversation stopper for me, on par with "Last night we boiled the family dog and ate him for dinner." Not having children simply never occurred to me. Which is not to say I was particularly ready for Owen; I don't think I ever would have been ready for a child. Several years ago I came across a Maurice Sendak cartoon that I cut out to explain to anyone who asked why I was afraid of having children. The cartoon features a mother breast-feeding her child; it all begins innocently enough, but with each frame the child devours more of the mother until there is nothing left but a bloated infant sitting on a stool. The mother has been consumed by the child. This, in a nutshell, defined my fears. I never wanted to be "just" someone's mother. I was terrified about losing my own identity.

I think this fact, finally, most clearly explains why I

need to work. There are days when I would trade places with my friend Sarah in a heartbeat, and I would never presume to believe that my solution is the right solution for all women with children. But I need to go away for hours at a time and concentrate on being something other than Owen's mother. For curious reasons that I don't yet understand, my husband—also a full-time magazine editor—does not feel this compulsive *need* to work to establish his identity as something other than Owen's father. This probably has more to do with traditional sex roles than anything else, although the fact that my husband doesn't plan anything beyond dinner and therefore never had any expectations about fatherhood might also play into it. Going to the office all day and then coming home at night to be a parent is a no-brainer for him, not something he has to get all worked up and tortured about. Then again, he's not the one who breastfed Owen for six months. He wasn't in any danger of being devoured whole.

I realize that everything may change as my son grows older. Our time together constantly takes on a new form as Owen becomes more and more aware of the world around him. I recently went on my first business trip and was gone for six days; when I came home I walked straight over to Owen and kissed him all over his precious face, but when I tried to leave the room to wash the taxi and airplane germs from my hands, he immediately started to cry. It was as if he was afraid I was going to leave again. He had never before exhibited any signs of separation anxiety, and I can't deny that this broke my heart. But every work day is not a week-long transcontinental trip. In the fleeting moments when I had apprehensive feelings about returning to work, I had to remind myself that I was not going to Sing Sing for the next eighteen years, but rather to midtown for eight hours a day. Seeing Owen at the end of that day is a beautiful thing. And—at least for now—so is my neat, quiet, babyless office.

THE BUDDY SYSTEM

MEG WOLITZER

By the time I turned thirty, I already had enough friends. Without being fully conscious of it, I had closed myself off to the possibility of new ones entering my life—new people sharing long, giddy lunches, new faces across the table at dinner parties. My expansive circle of friends had been culled, over the years, from various pockets of my life; observing them as a group, one could do a bit of social anthropology and figure out where and how I'd been spending my time on earth. There were friends who go way back to a memorable summer at an arts camp, where we earnestly and ardently acted together in a children's version of *Mourning Becomes Electra*. Others, who date as far back as high school, occupy a distinct place of nostalgia and history. The college friends are the ones with whom big ideas got tossed around like pillows at a slumber party. We read Virginia Woolf for the first time together; we talked freely about sex, our families, the future, and as a result, whenever I speak to these friends now, I still tend to use the dizzy, excited cadences of a student. Then there are the assortment of friends made during the first few years after college: friends who were attempting to be writers, artists, and translators while forced to spend their days as perennial graduate students or waiters or word-processors. In those years, we all lived in walk-up apartments and stayed out late, eating cheap Indian food in tiny restaurants draped to resemble caravans. We were pals, slap-happy, single, responsible for no one but ourselves.

It was during one of those long, aromatic Indian dinners that my friend Lisa announced she was getting married. She was the first among us to do something so permanent, and I was shocked. I attended Lisa's wedding with a surreal feeling of ironic detachment and fascination; the wedding was big, sprawling, fancy. She had signed on for the whole shebang, and I could not relate. Then, the following year, Lisa did something even bigger and more permanent: She had a baby.

When I think back on the way I behaved during those early days of my friend's motherhood, I am ashamed. Lisa brought her infant daughter home from the hospital the morning after Christmas; her apartment was small and overcrowded, and she was terrified of her new set of responsibilities. I have to admit that I did nothing to help, short of bringing over a jumbo jar of macadamia nuts as an offering. I could not comprehend what her life had become; in fact, I did not *want* to comprehend. It seemed almost squalid to me: the mountain of diapers, and the constant shrill crying that was amplified unnecessarily over the Fisher-Price monitor in her two-room apartment, where the Christmas tree stood winking and tilting, totally neglected.

I just didn't get it.

A few years later, I finally got it. Married myself by then, and home alone with my own baby, I found out, as Lisa had found out before me, that most of my friends were irrelevant to the sudden new life I had entered. It was almost as though, in becoming a mother, I had joined an obscure religious sect, complete with rituals and rules and its own arcane vocabulary. Outsiders appeared suddenly peculiar, with their freedom, their laughter, their arms always unencumbered. My son Gabriel was born in late November, while the streets were locked in a deep and seemingly intractable freeze. I would sit in the window of our apartment on the twenty-third floor of our high-rise, jiggling the baby in my lap, looking down like Rapunzel onto the busy crawl of street life that was suddenly unavailable to me, simply because I had taken vows of motherhood.

I tried hard to emerge from my isolation, to keep myself from sinking into the despair that afflicted so many new mothers. This wasn't hormonal, what I had; this wasn't postpartum depression, but, instead, postpartum disorientation. I telephoned Lisa, but we lived in different neighborhoods, and while in the past we used to hop a subway to each other's house on a whim, suddenly arranging a visit was a major event that needed to be carefully orchestrated. Besides, our children were of vastly different ages, and there would be no significant interaction between them. Seeing them together was like seeing two pets of completely different species: a panda bear and a hamster, perhaps.

I understood that my new-mother loneliness was temporary, and that my friendships, which had always been so important to me, would eventually resume, uncompromised. But, in the meantime, motherhood had changed everything. When I talked about my baby to my childless friends, they were curious in an energetically morbid way, like someone wanting to hear details of what it really feels like to shoot heroin. It was difficult for me *not* to talk about the baby, especially since he was always right in front of me, either nursing or crying or dreamily twirling a strand of my hair around his finger. I stopped calling these friends; there was no reciprocity anymore, just my series of predictable monologues that helped them sort out their own musings on whether or not they ever wanted to have children.

Other friends were outwardly bored hearing descriptions of my sleeplessness and debates over whether pacifier use would make for a crippling, lifelong dependency. After a while, these newly-bored friends stopped calling *me*. In retrospect, I really can't blame them, although some of them acted in an extreme manner. One of them actually pretended she'd never known me; at a cocktail party I'd triumphantly managed to attend, baby in tow, I watched as her eyes swept across the room, past me and over to the table of crudités, which apparently offered more satisfaction than a conversation with me and my *enfant terrible*. Spurned in favor of a plate of raw carrots and dip! We used to be close, going out to dinner with our husbands in comfortable foursomes. She and her husband had decided to remain childless, and somehow my decision to plunge ahead and have a child seemed a tacit betrayal of her lifestyle. After sending us a pair of tiny, soft shoes from Baby Gap, I never heard from her again.

Instead of studiously working to keep old friendships alive and vigorous, I began to wander the streets alone, pushing a stroller. Stopping in at little stores with cute names, I bought everything in the entire Fisher-Price *oeuvre*. Eventually I enrolled Gabriel in a class that necessi-

tated that I sit with him in my lap, opening and closing
my hands and singing in a syrupy soprano. I felt ridiculous. I tried to imagine famous women I admired engaging in such inane activity. When Doris Lessing was a
young mother, did she ever take "Mommy and Me"
classes? How about Ingrid Bergman? Bella Abzug? Marie
Curie? But still, there was some perverse pleasure to be
found in this low-pressure environment: Gone was
every overachievement enzyme that had ever coursed
through my body, replaced by simpler desires and
needs. I looked around me at all these women wearing
big, loose sweaters and appearing tired, chanting various
songs that they probably hadn't thought of since childhood. But now, it all tumbled back to us, every song
lyric and nuance, as though it had been only a few
weeks since we ourselves had been small.

One particular afternoon, while singing that classic,
"The Noble Prince of York," and jostling Gabriel rhyth-
mically on my knee, my eye caught the eye of a mother
across the room, her daughter bouncing gleefully on her
knee. ". . . He had ten thousand men," we all sang.
"He marched them up to the top of the hill / and he
marched them down again . . ." This woman and I
smiled at each other (or was it gas?) across the pastel-
colored room. Later, when "class" was over and all that
could be heard was zipping and snapping and the clicking of stroller seat belts, she and I walked out of the
room together, pushing our children before us.

On the street we began to talk, and no, it was not the
smart, witty, and ironic rapport that I have come to expect from my friends. Instead, our exchange was serious,
earnest, slightly dull, yet somehow compelling. Sharon
wanted to talk about all the same things that obsessed
me. Our children were exactly the same age, and we

would discuss our various concerns about their development. On the corner, in the wind, we exchanged telephone numbers. I stuffed hers in my pocket gratefully, knowing I would call her soon. Sharon was nothing like me. She didn't look like me or like any of my friends. She was more staid, more conservatively dressed, somehow more innocent. But she had a baby! And for now, that was good enough for me.

Over time, my friendship with Sharon became something I depended on, even looked forward to with a certain zeal. I could be myself when around her—or at least, I could be a certain version of myself that I had recently discovered. This was the self that constantly had a song buzzing in her head, and that song was "Baby Beluga." This was the self that was aware of the dangers of sleep apnea and knew that you should never feed honey to a baby. I should add that my husband, who works at home, was from the start deeply involved in all the quotidian aspects of parenthood. I'm certain he changed at least as many diapers as I did, and during the hellish first three months known as colic season, every evening he carried our unhappy, gassy baby over his shoulder and waltzed him around the living room to strains of "I Am the Walrus." Yet he did not, as I did, develop a new habit of incessant reading and talking about babies. He would listen politely when I read a detail aloud from a book by Penelope Leach, but his interest did not go beyond that level. He didn't seem to want to bone up on every aspect of baby culture. For him, being a father was merely a new facet to his personality, and with it came a new set of skills and responsibilities. But being a parent didn't overtake him, as it did me.

Perhaps the distinction between our attitudes fell along gender lines, having everything to do with the fact that I had been the one to carry the baby *in utero*, and was now nursing him around the clock. It certainly does seem to me that from the moment a baby is born, no matter how involved and caring the father, the mother is *it*, the center, the axis on which the strange, crowded new household precariously rests. So she must, therefore, become an expert. And all around her, elsewhere in the city, other recent mothers are experiencing this phenomenon too; all these women are staying up long into the night, learning everything they can about baby medical needs and how to choose apparati for getting that baby moving around the streets. I think of these women as being like quietly persistent Talmudic scholars, learning, for the sheer love of learning, this subject that is so powerful and moving.

But every Talmudic scholar enjoys the company of other Talmudic scholars, for a little conversation, textual argument, and a few sips of sweet wine. My new friend Sharon and I would go walking together after our baby class, or on our way home from the park, and as we did we talked in small, intense bursts about our lives and the ways in which they'd changed. Although we were very different, the ways in which our lives had changed were similar. We talked about sleep, remembering it lovingly, actually able to laugh about its absence. We admired each other's babies, and we went to Baby Gap together, where the clerks rang up our impossibly tiny items and placed them in contrastingly gigantic shopping bags. We sat on a bench and ate Dove bars in the middle of the day; this was something I would never have done before. Before, my days were always full and industrious; now they were always full, but sometimes

they were leisurely, too, even indulgent. If I probed
Sharon too deeply, probably certain details would be
revealed that I wouldn't want to see. Her hobbies
weren't mine, neither were her tastes. But what was between us had nothing to do with hobbies or tastes. It
had merely to do with our understandable, shared obses-
sion. For both of us, our babies were everything.

Elsewhere in the world, our babies weren't welcome.
All mothers experience the chill of entering a restaurant
with a carriage in tow, and finding no one to help with
the door, no one to offer assistance. We've all traveled
on trains or flown on airplanes with our babies, experiencing the derision of a dozen businessmen with their
Wall Street Journals stuck like flimsy barricades in front
of their faces. At times, when I think of new mothers as
a group, I feel we've grown invisible to almost everyone
but each other.

When I was with Sharon, this cloak of invisibility
was gone, and I became very much myself in all my
new-mother splendor and exhaustion. Together, she and
I were reduced to a few simple functions and, at the
same time, we were built up to be figures of new power.
Primarily, we breast-fed. Everywhere, all the time. In
the restaurant of Saks Fifth Avenue; on anybody's
couch. We were both very nonchalant and tribal about
the whole business. We did what had to be done; we
nursed and we chatted and we planned for the future.
We never tried to arrange social gatherings that would
involve our husbands; the potential for awkwardness
was great, and there was no use pretending that what
we had was anything other than what we had.

And what we had got us through that first year. It got
us through the first tooth and the first word and the first
frightening bout of skyrocketing baby-fever. After a

while, our world began to widen, incorporating other mothers too, some who reminded me of my "real" friends, and some who didn't. After a while, though, this line of demarcation became blurry, and my notion of "real" friendship began to expand and transform. So what if we only talked about babies? This didn't make our interaction any less essential. I needed *someone* to talk to about babies. I had entered into this entire experience with a certain protective detachment and perhaps a hint of superiority, but that had changed. I admired these women, all of them so different from each other, all of them taking part in this huge experiment, and often feeling inadequate to the task.

I was uncommonly happy when any of my new-mother friends called; I enjoyed hanging out with them on their sofas in the middle of the afternoon, the babies crawling around on the rug at our feet. Time seemed suspended. We hung out easily, barely watching the clock. And as we hung out and chatted, our children got older, stronger, more independent. And so did we. Suddenly, I realized that I had mastered the basics of motherhood. Suddenly, I saw that I didn't need to go over every detail with Sharon or any of the other women. I was reminded of a friend of mine who, years earlier, had realized she was a lesbian, and partook of everything gay or lesbian-related she could find. She joined groups, she marched for miles, she stuffed envelopes, she had lots and lots of sex with women. Then, after a while, she didn't need to remind herself she was a lesbian so often, and even when she wasn't reminding herself, the title stuck. She lives with another woman now. Similarly, I slowly began to understand that I was a mother, and would be one forever, whether I talked about it incessantly or not.

My friend Sharon and I began to see each other less. We didn't need to travel in groups of two or more; in fact, we came to enjoy our time alone with our babies, or even our time alone without our babies. We hired sitters; we let other people take the children to the park for an afternoon of sun. I rarely see Sharon anymore, but when I do, I always feel a nostalgic surge of pleasure. It's not that I miss her exactly; I miss her *inexactly,* the way I miss the first throes of motherhood itself, with all its attendant terrors and wonders. It has been five years since that first winter when we came to depend on each other in such a profound and unspoken way, and in that time we have begun to watch our children hesitantly venture out into the world, where they have begun making friendships as complicated and essential as our own.

MY CHOICE

JANE LEAVY

One day when my daughter was a Tulip, the name given to the oldest children in her florally-arranged preschool, she came home with exciting news.

"This is Being Born Week! Three pregnant moms will be visiting our class to talk about becoming a mother! Please bring in Your Coming Home Story and a picture of yourself as a newborn!"

As the mother of two adopted children, Emma and her older brother, Nick, I was touched by the teacher's upbeat inclusiveness, her perky sensitivity to what are sometimes called "options in family building." After all, coming home is something we all do, no matter who's responsible for the legwork of labor and delivery.

Infused with goodwill, I picked up the phone and called the teacher. "I'm sure you have an adoptive parent to talk to the kids," I said, knowing that one fifth of the children in her class were adopted, including those of the director and assistant director of the school. "But if not, I'm available."

The teacher replied that I was neither welcome nor needed in the Tulip Room. "This is not *family* week," she said, firmly. "This is about biology."

It occurred to me, but only later, the way things do, to question why she was teaching four-year-olds about reproduction. My immediate reaction was stunned disbelief: I'd been banished from the Tulip Room. And in banishing me, the teacher had ensured that my daughter would be an exile among Tulips.

I appealed to the assistant director for help. She demurred, saying she could not intervene without undermining pedagogical autonomy. I demurred, saying no one in a position of authority was going to teach my children that motherhood is defined solely by biology.

I was surprised by my ferocity, as was she. Clearly something fundamental had been mobilized inside. Something I'd been avoiding since the day our first child came home to us: the whole raw complex of nerve endings associated with the word *motherhood*.

The inability to reproduce is a monthly kind of death. Each new moon brings hope, then despair. Oddly, it isn't hope that makes you keep trying, but the opposite. The more you invest in the effort to procreate, the more essential it becomes. Each time my body said no, my heart said, *I can't be going through all this for nothing.* But you can, and we did. Month after month, grief compounded like interest. The embryonic need to reproduce grew—it was the only thing that grew—until it got so big we forgot this wasn't about our gene pool but about becoming parents.

If you're lucky, and I was, a friend will point this out to you. If you're unlucky, she may be pregnant at the time. I hated Diana for having a baby. I hated her more for telling me I should adopt one. And I hated hearing it from her as much as I admire her now for saying it.

The day after our last failed in vitro fertilization cycle, we filled out an application to adopt.

Choice is a loaded word in the modern lexicon of motherhood. But it has a special meaning for me. Accidents don't happen in adoption—it is a concerted decision. And, like most other life choices, it carries special responsibilities and complications, among them the privilege of choosing the gender of your child.

I never doubted I could raise a boy. I liked the idea of being a feminist mom to a macho son. After all, I grew up perfecting Mickey Mantle's swing. Red Barber's muffled voice coming to me through a pillow was my idea of a lullaby. Other girls wore party shoes on the first day of school. I saved my Mary Janes for the first day of the baseball season.

We asked for a boy. A month and a half after filling out the papers, we had a son, a gestation period of exactly six weeks.

The call came late on a Friday afternoon, the last day of a Cape Cod vacation. We were packing up, happily finishing off what was left of the summer rum. A female voice on the other end of the phone said, "There's a little boy waiting for you in Phoenix."

Being a reporter, I took notes on the conversation. I knew I'd never remember anything else she said. After we hung up, we went into town to buy a book, *Name Your Baby*. We chose our son's name by the lake shore: Nicholas *Ariel*, which he hates and I love. He is our airy sprite.

The drive home was a blur; 100 mph all the way down the New Jersey Turnpike. After four years of humiliating fertility treatments, some no more scientific than animal husbandry, we were ready to be parents—which is a whole different thing from being prepared.

On Monday morning, Federal Express delivered a set of baby pictures to my office. I showed them around like any other proud new parent. I just happened to be one who hadn't seen her child. I don't remember thinking that was strange. I remember thinking it was a done deal—I was his.

That afternoon, we plunked down $1,500 in half an hour at a baby store. We bought one of everything, including a mega-stroller solid enough for a presidential motorcade. The saleswoman took one look at us and said, "Adopting, huh?"

On the plane to Phoenix, I tried to read Dr. Spock and quit after two pages, not wanting to know how much I didn't know. That would become apparent soon enough. The first bottle I made Nick spilled all over his fancy new Osh Kosh b' Gosh duds. We were too dumb and too scared to know how to put in a nipple. In the airport lounge where I changed my first diaper, I apologized to my son for my ineptitude and asked silently for his forbearance. I was a rookie, an amateur, newer to this game than he was.

People ask all the time whether I'd feel any differently about Nick and Emma if they were my "own" children. I always reply that I can't conceive of it—which is pointed as well as true. It's impossible to imagine loving them more if they were *of* me. I mean, I love their father and the cat and the dog, and we don't share the same DNA.

There is only one sense in which I feel they are not mine—the proprietary one. I do not possess them. Rather I am possessed by them, an irrevocable transaction that occurred the moment our eyes met. There are pictures in our family album of me waiting for Nick, a supplicant reclining in a hotel bed, waiting for my life to change. Then came the knock on the door. And I was down on all fours with him: engaged. I cannot remember getting there. I cannot visualize moving from the unmade bed to the carpeted floor. But in that instant, my posture in life changed forever—from passive to active, from mine to theirs. Sadness was banished. A joyous new fact of life was *a priori* true.

Once you have a child in your arms, you stop thinking about all that went before: the envy, the fear, the humiliations; post-coital tests, injections, inseminations, failures. It's *all* gone. You no longer worry about what it is to be a mother or how to become one because you're too busy *being* one. Your child supplants your pain.

I quit the *Washington Post* where I was a sportswriter, giving up the job of a tomboy's dreams for an imagined life of playing catch in the late afternoon shadows. Who knew a bum shoulder would force me to the sidelines by the time Nick was a year old?

That spring, I took him to opening day at Memorial Stadium in Baltimore. Nick sat on my lap practicing his new word—Eddie! Eddie!—in honor of the Orioles' star Eddie Murray, while I proudly pointed to the press box where Mommy worked before he came. That it meant nothing to him was irrelevant. He'd put me back in touch with a part of myself that I had locked away in the attic at puberty along with my baseball glove.

And then suddenly he was three and it was time to think about a sibling. That there would be one was a foregone conclusion. Dad's an only child—one of those per household is quite enough. Besides, Nick deserved an ally, someone to share his experience as an adopted child.

Again we had a choice. The adoption agency would have been very happy to find him a brother. Naively, we had believed it was more difficult to adopt boys, assuming that everybody still wants sons. In fact, in adoption circles, it's a commonly held belief that healthy white females are harder to come by. No one can say precisely why that is or even if it is statistically true. But the woman who placed Emma in my arms explained it this way: It's easier to accept a daughter who fails to meet genetic expectations than a son. Since adopted male children are at greater risk for a variety of dysfunctional behaviors, the argument goes, it is also more likely that they will "fail" in their parents' eyes, a risk not everyone is willing to take.

But for me, a woman whose body language was honed on the ballfield, the far greater risk was that I would fail a girl.

The truth is, I was terrified to have a daughter. I'm not talking about the generic panic newborns inspire with their pink fragility and insatiable needs. I'm talking about the abject fear of being the mother of a female child.

Having a daughter meant answering to my own insecurities about womanliness, self-doubts that preceded infertility but were also reshaped and reawakened by it. It meant consciously choosing to confront the diffuse but intensely intimate concept of femininity. It meant resolving for myself the essential question buried deep within my dysfunctional womb: How much is womanhood defined by biology and specifically by the fact of giving birth?

The social worker arrived for our home study on the appointed day, bringing an application and a whole raft of questions about why we wanted a second child, none of which were anything like my own. What if I get a girl who likes to window shop? Or play with makeup? What if I get a girly-girl? I stared at my much-gnawed nails and had a terrible vision: nail polish.

My pen wavered over the little boxes on the application marked F and M. I told myself: *You don't have to do this.* I reviewed the pros and cons of two little boys. All those hand-me-downs. All that testosterone!

While I was deliberating, Nick arrived in the living room carrying a plastic orange jack-o'-lantern with a wounded baby bird inside. One wing was broken, the other beat frantically against the demented, toothless grin. "Can I keep it, Mom?" he said.

The social worker, no fan of Alfred Hitchcock, cowered in the corner while I appraised the situation: My three-year-old adopted son wanted to adopt a wounded bird that had fallen out of the nest, a baby without a mother. There was no way we were going to keep it. But I could not dismiss his identification with it either—not in front of the social worker in charge of our home study.

Nick handed me his new, feathery friend. I hate birds; I have ever since my mother asphyxiated Chirpie the parakeet with Mr. Clean. It required every bit of courage I could muster not to cut and run. In that moment, with the poor, fuzzy thing beating its one good wing against my chest, I realized that if I could overcome my fear of feathered creatures, I could overcome my fear of having a baby girl too.

I handed the bird back to Nick and told him we'd try to find its mother, hoping the social worker would be impressed by my respect for biological mothers, aviary and otherwise. I started to tell her how often I think about the women who bore my children, always on their birthdays, and always with fondness and gratitude. Sometimes I think I can see them, strong, confident women striding through meadows of wildflowers. But she wasn't interested. She didn't like birds any more than I do.

In a panic, she waved the application in my face. My husband nodded reassuringly. I took up my pen and accepted the challenge. In the end, I couldn't face going through life thinking of myself as too scared of my own femininity to raise a little girl. Six months later, Emma was placed in my arms.

By some act of divine intervention, she arrived on August 24, exactly three years to the day after her brother. She was eight days old and very pink except for her eyes, which were wide-open and as blue as my grandmother's on the day she died. I had the feeling she saw everything, or would soon anyway. I decided I'd better quit biting my nails.

I didn't, of course, but that's the only predictable part of the story. I knew things were going to be different right off because I was worried about what to wear. How do you dress to meet your daughter? I chose pink—OK, dusty rose.

The first thing I did was change her into a hooded gown of bold pink and yellow stripes, an act that made her mine. It was an outfit that said girl but not girly-girl. I promised Emma, as I touched her soft, naked baby skin for the first time, that I would never turn her into a doll, all ribbons and bows.

From the beginning, Emma was a lot more accepting of me than I am of myself. To her I am mother, as much a fait accompli as she is to me. Her unquestioning acceptance of who I am began a long overdue process of reconciliation with myself which continues, under her tutelage, to this day.

I came of age in the last generation to believe that you couldn't play ball with the boys and get asked out too. It never occurred to me that you didn't have to choose between them until one evening a year or so ago when Emma appeared in the front hall wearing her brother's Michael Jordan high tops and unadorned red sweats: no cutesy appliqué, thank you very much. Beneath them, she had on pink tights adorned with gray ballerinas assuming the first position (one of many I never managed). Her earlobes were plastered with four pairs of paste-on earrings, her lips with seventeen different shades of gloss, each perfectly applied. On her hands were her father's thirty-year-old boxing gloves.

"Put 'em up," she said to her brother.

For her, the world isn't either/or. For her, there are no internal contradictions. She doesn't see any reason to choose between the lipstick and the sweats. And now, thanks to her, neither do I.

Soon after the boxing match in the front hall word came home in Emma's backpack about "Being Born Week." I remembered the woman from the adoption agency telling us that the need to see a biological relative and the ability to produce one can be a very tempting combination. Emma's birth mother, who was also adopted, was a teenager when she gave birth. Perhaps getting pregnant gave her a way of feeling close to her biological mother. I was determined that the school officials understand that the stakes in the Tulip Room debate were not academic to me at all.

The morning before the visit of the Pregnant Moms, I stormed the assistant director's office, stomping my feet like some four-year-olds I know. Maybe I was trying to prove that adoptive moms can be equally ferocious in defense of their young. Maybe I was trying to protect myself as much as Emma. At any rate, I was loud.

The administration offered a compromise: A mother of newborn *adopted* twins would bring her babies to visit the class. Everybody would be able to see that adopted newborns look exactly like any other newborns and adoptive moms look exactly like any other moms.

"Fine," I said. "As long as she's exquisitely happy."

But that evening, the mother of the twins pulled out, having second thoughts about bringing newborns into a classroom full of runny-nosed four-year-olds, adopted babies being every bit as prone to infection as anyone else.

The next morning, just before circle time, the administration capitulated. The assistant director agreed to talk to the kids. I was not invited to come along.

I waited by the phone for a debriefing. This is what I was told. Right off, the head Tulip explained that most kids go home from the hospital with their parents and some go home to their adoptive parents. Not wanting to muddy the waters any further by also explaining *foster* parents, she said that some adopted children go home with *babysitters* before their adoptive families come to get them.

Then it was time for The Moms. The first to speak decided to explain cesarian section, a subject close to her heart and other parts of her anatomy. She even mentioned that some babies "get nicked on the way out." By the time she shut up, the assistant director was lucky to get in a sentence. She said that adopted kids are special because they are chosen.

Then the children were asked for questions or comments. Emma's hand shot up, her pinky finger glittering with a Barbie Band-Aid she'd put on that morning. She had a cut, she explained, which meant she must have been "nicked on the way out." But that was OK because she went home with our babysitter who took good care of her until her dad and I arrived.

My spy in the Tulip Room related the story to me with a straight face, which is more than I can do at this retelling. She said Emma seemed very pleased with herself at having figured it all out. I was left then, as I am now, marveling at the wondrous ability of my daughter to make sense of the folly of adults, especially those, like me, who try so hard to do the right thing.

A tough lesson was learned that day, but not at all the one I expected. I learned that there will be wounding words and unwanted complications, ambiguity and self-doubt, the nicks and cuts of everyday life. No matter how hard I try, ultimately Emma will have to make sense of them for herself. If she's lucky, she'll have a son or a daughter who'll help her along the way.

My children are my teachers. They have taught me to reject the foolishness of genetic hubris. Because of them, I am a more democratic person. Because they are not *of* me, I do not regard them as tabula rasa on which to inscribe my dreams and expectations. Nick and Emma are the authors of themselves.

Something else: I no longer believe you *become* a mother with a knock on the door, a call in the night, or even seventeen hours of labor. It's an ongoing process. I am always, and still, becoming their mother.

We got out the story I wrote for the Tulip Room the other day. Emma particularly liked the part about coming home on a jet plane and waking her brother up in the middle of the night and going to the beach the next morning with everyone, except the dog who was too loud and not permitted to come.

The picture we sent along with the story was taken on the same beach where we'd picked Nick's name three years before. Emma is lying on her back on a purple blanket, wrapped in a borrowed lime-green afghan, wearing stripes as pink as her cheeks. Her still wrinkled fingers are curled in a fist, except for her pinky, which is pointing at me. I am the unseen person outside the frame, the guiding hand at her side. We are separate, but we are reaching for each other.

BEGINNING

MONA SIMPSON

My parents were young when they had their children. That is probably the greatest crime of which I could accuse them. Yet, at the time, I was proud of their youth: My mother wore fashionable short dresses, they had lived in big cities, in another country. Some other parents I saw were old and I knew I wouldn't have wanted them to be mine, however calm and orderly their kitchen was, however patient their processions of days. We are born, most of us, able to love what we already have.

There were fields near the house where we lived and an enormous sky. I was often let out to play with other children, the way dogs were, also. We ran. Miles every day, shouting to each other, not kind particularly or unkind. The United States Geological Survey was measuring and recording our part of the country in those days and there were also private surveyors. Highways were being built. Farmland was being turned into town, streets were measured out, tar laid, then cement, leading into cul de sacs, where new houses went up, with siding in pale, sherbet colors. Some of the men's tools were left behind, at night and weekends, and we found them. Pipes became tunnels, fields of high corn our hiding spots, the train was four times a day a terrible wonder.

Our elders really had little idea what we did—only that they could call us home, standing on their porches, a cupped hand at their mouths.

I suppose they did worry about what could harm us. I remember dangers being pointed out to me on walks in the lowered, grave, instructional tones their voices took on when they were talking about things that we would not, in the glee of youth, understand. The train was a danger, cars were, and, most mysteriously, strangers. If a parent was talking to a group about these things, when he said "stranger," he would always look at a girl.

Of course, there were also horses that could kick, poles with electric wires, ditch creeks to drown children who didn't yet know how to swim. In an abandoned barn, we played on boards thirty feet above the ground which could have given way under our weight. But they did not. And none of the children on our street died, playing. No one was even seriously harmed.

And this was a street without babysitters, where most mothers had five or more children. I have no recollection of strollers or even one pram. Women set babies down somewhere, often on the lawn, over an old blanket. None of these houses were "child-proofed."

Outside was where we lived, anyway, most of the hours we were awake.

The childhood I was given, like most, had its daily graces and some deprivations I didn't even know existed until years after it was over. It was a house with no books, one early-model cabinet television, and years worth of *National Geographics*. I could no more replicate its virtues for my child than I could bring back to life my own grandparents to be his.

Not that I would wish upon my son the adult lives of my playmates from that dead-end road. Four boys went to Vietnam. One spent years in prison. Another shot himself in the head with a BB gun, five years after returning from Southeast Asia. I remember watching him, years of afternoons, sit for endless hours on the cement square that served as a porch to his house while his mother tried to teach him how to read. He was a large boy, with ears that stuck out and a face that let you know what he wanted. I knew him well; we all did. His name was Dicky.

The girls fared better. They are all alive. Quite a few have their own children.

My son was born when I was thirty-six. And although my Manhattan obstetrician reassured me that I was one of the youngest expecting mothers in her practice, it was of course true that in another time or another place, or even in this time and this place, but in a different culture, such as the one fifteen blocks north of me, on the other side of 125th Street, I could have just as easily been becoming a grandmother.

I wish I could give my son the freedom I had as a child, though even now, I'm not sure of what that consisted. Perhaps it was the land, the sheer size and range of it, the way we could run until we dropped down with our hearts knocking like bells in our chests and the sky carouseling above us. There were few boundaries. I don't remember even being told we couldn't cross the highway or the railroad tracks. But perhaps it had nothing to do with the outdoors. Perhaps it was the luxury of being unnoticed, of being left alone.

There is a particular park near where I live, to which we frequently repair. It hosts old trees, ancient winding sycamores, with their puzzle bark, and low branches perfect to climb or sleep on. The houses near this sanctuary are mostly wooden and suitably expensive and I often drive those streets slowly, imagining what it would be like to live inside a particular one. Even so, it is a small park, a park one could walk the perimeters of in under ten minutes.

And perhaps it is not the crowded mat-floored city parks that curtail my son's freedom, or the cupboard locks and gates throughout our house. Perhaps it is the stories I can't get out of my mind about the Manhattan baby who died from having swallowed a button or of the two-year-old who drowned in his bath after his mother ran to throw the wash in the dryer when the machine beeped.

My parents didn't decide to have me. Each has told me, in his or her own way, how the other didn't want a child "then" and how the pregnancy surprised them. He said she wanted to finish school, get her advanced degree. She says he wanted only boys.

Probably the truth was that too much had already happened: a death, a marriage, a birth. They both probably wanted peace and ease for a while, healing. They didn't get it. They got me.

Even knowing my parents hadn't tried and prayed for a baby, the way a woman we knew had, before her only child was born, I never felt unwanted. For one thing, it wasn't only up to them. I lived with a grandmother, in close proximity to an aunt, uncle, and cousins.

And I was not unwanted by my parents either, once I was there. I was the little girl on the street wearing silly fancy clothes, usually white, and including a bow. Other, more practical mothers made fun of my clothes not quite outside my hearing. I minded a little, but I also felt a breeze of superiority, as if someone had whispered the promise of my better future in my ear.

Even at thirty, if you asked me how many children I wanted, I would have said "four." Despite some vague, inchoate sense that I "wanted children," the implicit "someday" never seemed to move any closer to my present. So the four children I wanted at fifteen still shimmered in the middle-distant future at twenty, twenty-five, and thirty. I never felt that urgent stab of *now*.

Perhaps because of my mother's life, I understood that having a child is the domestic equivalent of a revolution. It is hard to sign up for the complete annihilation of life as you know it. My mother frequently told me that her life would have been very different if she had not had children, and it was plainly obvious that this was true. I don't know any woman of her generation for whom that wasn't the case.

Children were destiny. Whether or not they still are or always should be is a question women of my time will never cease turning around in our conversations and moments at stoplights, waiting, on our way to something unimportant in and of itself, the repeated picking-ups and dropping-offs that are never done.

People make decisions the way they do everything else in their lives. Some people couldn't possibly "decide" to conceive a child, but can carry a child to term once conception has occurred, by accident.

It is a strange moment in our culture when we can speak of "deciding" to have a child, when truly we can no more "decide" to have a child than to decide to be born in the first place or to die. Like many gifts of transformation, our only choice is refusal. We can't choose birth, or love, or pregnancy—we can only decide to continue those steps with the unknown or we can turn the other way.

I remember learning to read, the thrill of how easy it was.

Can I be the only child in America who learned my alphabet out of Campbell's soup? We collected letters on the rim of the bowl. First my name. My grandmother taught and it was so easy, like a blink or a swallow and then you saw it, the whole word. Once I knew a word, on the rim of my bowl, my grandmother would write it in different places. With her fingertip, on the condensation over the night window. "What does it say here?" On the back of a scrap of paper with her pencil no bigger than a pinkie.

The words she taught me? Blue. Yellow. Boat.

With my parents, nothing was like that. It wasn't that I couldn't see the word or get the answer—I saw it, I knew it, but I thought the answer was too obvious. The real solution had to be something hidden, something harder.

I became a good test taker only years later when I stopped looking for secrets in the questions, a problem I inherited from my parents.

A woman I know only slightly once told me that she kept her firstborn in a dresser drawer. I always picture my childhood as being a little like that. My parents didn't seek to express themselves in their parenting. Having kids was something they did too early, definitely on the way to something else. On the way to what? was the question that hung around all our wonderings.

That is not to say I wasn't loved, claimed: I was.

Sometimes I envy their recklessness, the all-at-once of their young lives.

My parents were in "the prime of their lives" and we all knew it. Their lives were what counted in the house. They moved through the world with real stakes—jobs to be gained or lost, money to be made, lives forged. I suppose, looking back, the real suspense was not what it seemed to be—not money—but love. *Can This Marriage Be Saved?*

We were not in the real arena yet. If we won or lost it was still at the kitchen table, they were still noodles on the rim of a soup bowl. We lived on the periphery of the house, even though we took it over when they left, took it apart. We knew the house more than they did: what was inside every drawer, behind every cushion. Grandparents and children, we found each other there in the quiet spots of time.

I know now what I did not know then—we gave them that stature. The reason it mattered so much whether or not the marriage lasted was us.

We were the still-blank slates on which the failures or successes would be recorded, registered. Children: we were the stakes.

As a parent, even of a young child, I often feel the tug of that weight, the easy gravity, that comes with the position. My marriage, my death, my failures or successes, my daily kindnesses or meannesses, all mean more, because they will be felt by a person other than myself as central, determining.

Of course, our parents realized this too and did the best they could, going along. I often wish I could give my son the feeling of running with the same three other kids every day, for long stretches, with no destination, a daily familiarity with animals found in the fields. But we don't live in the country and perhaps even in the country, children's lives are not quite so unstructured anymore.

So I let him stay out in the rain longer than other local children and chase him around our smaller park, getting muddy, hoping that what he gets from this world we live in is enough. And of course it will be, because, though it is only part mine, it will be all his.

LIST OF CONTRIBUTORS

Allison Abner is a journalist who has written on health and teen issues, and has been a producer for TV and radio. She coauthored *Finding Our Way: The Survival Guide for Teen Girls* (1996), and contributed to Rebecca Walker's *To Be Real* and Linda Villarosa's *Body and Soul*. She and her husband, Mark, live with their son, Miles, in New York City.

Sarah Bird is the author of four novels, including *The Mommy Club* (1991) and *Virgin of the Rodeo* (1993). Her articles and essays have been published in the *New York Times Magazine*, *Mademoiselle*, *Glamour*, *Entertainment Weekly*, *MSO*, and *Cosmopolitan*. She and her husband, George, are happy to report that Gabriel, the fully recovered colicaholic, got all the words right on his first spelling test. They live in Austin, Texas.

Susan Cheever is the author of eight books and two children. Her books include a memoir about her father, *John Cheever, Home Before Dark*; *Treetops: A Family Memoir*; and *A Woman's Life: The Story of an Ordinary American and her Extraordinary Generation*. A columnist for *Newsday* and a contributing editor at *Architectural Digest*, she has written articles and personal essays for many publications. She lives in New York

City, except when she teaches at the Bennington Writing Seminars, and is working on another memoir, *Out of the Woods*.

Rita Ciresi is the author of a novel, *Blue Italian*, and a collection of stories, *Mother Rocket*, which won the Flannery O'Connor Award for Short Fiction. Her fiction and poetry have appeared in numerous literary magazines, including *South Carolina Review, California Quarterly, Oregon Review*, and *Prairie Schooner*. She lives near Tampa with her husband and their daughter, Celeste, and teaches creative writing at the University of South Florida.

Marcelle Clements is the author of a collection of pieces, *The Dog Is Us*, and a novel, *Rock Me*, as well as many essays, portraits, and reported articles for national publications. Norton Books will publish her nonfiction work on single women in 1997. She lives in Manhattan with her son, Luc, and is completing a second novel.

Meri Nana-Ama Danquah is a poet, fiction writer, and freelance journalist. She is the author of *Willow Weep for Me: A Memoir of a Black Woman's Journey Through Depression*, which will be published in 1997 by W.W. Norton and Co. She lives in Los Angeles with her daughter.

Janet Maloney Franze lives, loves, teaches (at Virginia Commonwealth University), writes, and wipes up spills in Richmond, Virginia. Her two spillers, Nate and Jenna, live, love, cry, fight, and laugh there with her.

Allegra Goodman's new book is *The Family Markowitz*. Her fiction has appeared in *The New Yorker, Commentary, Prize Stories 1995: The O. Henry Awards*, and in other anthologies.

She is the winner of a Whiting Writer's Award and the author of *Total Immersion*. She lives with her family in Cambridge, Massachusetts, where she is completing her dissertation and a new novel.

Katie Greenebaum's short fiction has been published in *Chelsea* and *Literal Latte*. A former Hoyns Fellow at the University of Virginia, she was the recipient of the Balch prize for the best short story by a graduate student. She lives in Park Slope, Brooklyn, with her husband, Josh May, and their two children, Nora and Jake.

Gail Greiner is a freelance editor and writer. A former book editor at *Self* and associate book editor at *Cosmopolitan*, she is pursuing a Master of Fine Arts degree in writing at Columbia University, and is working on a memoir. She lives in New York with her husband, Michael Stern, their son, Nikolai, and dog, Rosie.

Cathi Hanauer is the author of a novel, *My Sister's Bones*. A contributing editor to *Seventeen* magazine, where she writes the monthly advice column "Relating," Hanauer has published articles and essays in *Elle, Mademoiselle,* and *McCall's*, among other publications. She lives in New York City with her husband, Daniel Jones, and their daughter, Phoebe.

Amy Herrick is the author of a novel, *At the Sign of the Naked Waiter*, and a children's book, *Kimbo's Marble*. Her fiction has appeared in numerous journals and anthologies, including *The Kenyon Review, The Yale Review, TriQuarterly,* and *Prize Stories 1992: The O. Henry Awards*. She lives with her husband and their two sons in Brooklyn, where she is director of The Union Temple Preschool.

Alisa Kwitney is the author of a novel, *Till the Fat Lady*

Sings, as well as an editor and writer for *Vertigo,* an imprint of DC Comics aimed at readers aged nineteen and over. She lives in Manhattan with her husband and their son, Matthew, and their accident-prone cat.

Jane Leavy, a former reporter for the *Washington Post,* is the author of the novel *Squeeze Play.* She is currently finishing a new novel, *Most Wanted.* She lives in Washington, D.C., with her husband and their two children, Nick and Emma.

Amy Ruth Levine is a former staff editor of *The Atlantic Monthly.* Her work has appeared in *Newsday, Boston Magazine,* and *The Atlantic.* She lives in San Diego with her husband, Bill, and their daughter, Sonya Belle.

Ericka Lutz is writing a travel/parenting book which will be published next year. Her nonfiction articles, including the "Travels with Annie" series, have been published in magazines nationwide, and her short fiction has appeared in literary journals. She sees this essay as part of a continuing family dialogue about mothering daughters. Lutz and her husband live in Oakland, California, with their daughter, Anaya (Annie).

Teri Robinson, a former features editor at *Communications Week* and editor-in-chief of *Financial Technology Review,* has written for music, film, and television. She lives in New York City with her husband, Larry Jaffee, and their son, Jake, who, after nearly two years at the breast, weaned himself—without tears—during a trip to London.

Jessica Sabat has been a producer for New York's classical music radio station, WNCN, and a writer for the Arts and Entertainment Cable Network. She continues to work as a full-time mom, part-time writer, and itinerant opera singer in New York City, where she lives with her husband, Robert, and their two children, Nathaniel and Olivia. (Olivia was also born at the Elizabeth Seton Childbearing Center—lightning struck twice.)

Valerie Sayers is the author of five novels—*Brain Fever, The Distance Between Us, Who Do You Love, How I Got Him Back,* and *Due East*—and professor of English at the University of Notre Dame. She lives in South Bend, Indiana, with her husband and their two sons.

Elissa Schappell is a former senior editor at *The Paris Review* and the Hot Type book columnist for *Vanity Fair.* Her fiction and nonfiction have appeared in *Vogue, GQ, Premiere, Bomb, Interview, The Paris Review, SPY,* and other magazines, newspapers, and journals. She lives in New York City with her husband, Ron Spillman, and their daughter, Isadora.

Constance Schraft has published a novel, *Instead of You,* and stories and essays in anthologies and magazines, including *The New Yorker.* She lives in Manhattan with her husband and their two sons, Willie and Miles.

Judith Schwartz is a freelance writer and author of *The Mother Puzzle: A New Generation Reckons with Motherhood.* She has written for publications including the *New York Times,* the *New York Times Book Review, Redbook, Glamour,* and *Cosmopolitan.* She lives with her husband, writer Tony Eprile, and their son, Brendan, in Evanston, Illinois, where she is completing a degree in Counseling Psychology.

Lindley Shutz is a freelance writer and editor. The former associate director of an elementary education foundation run by E. D. Hirsch, she edited and adapted stories for Hirsch's six-book series, *What Your First–Sixth Grader Needs to Know.* She lives with her husband and their two daughters, Katherine and Eleanor, in Cohasset, Massachusetts.

Mona Simpson is the author of *Anywhere But Here, The Lost Father,* and *A Regular Guy.* She is a recipient of the Whiting Writer's Award, a Guggenheim grant, and the Hodder Fellowship at Princeton University. She has taught at Bard College since 1988, where she is now the Sadie Samuelson Levy Professor of Languages and Literature. In 1996, she received a grant from the Lila Wallace-Reader's Digest Foundation and was selected as one of Granta's Best Young American Novelists. She lives with her husband and their son, Gabriel, in New York and Los Angeles.

Celina Spiegel is the coeditor, with Christina Buchmann, of *Out of the Garden: Women Writers on the Bible,* which includes her essay on the Book of Esther, and, with Peter Kupfer, of *Great First Lines: Literature's Most Memorable First Sentences.* She lives in New York City with her husband and their children, Rachel and Jonathan. She is an editor at Riverhead Books.

Abigail Stone writes fiction and songs. She has published a novel, *Recipes from the Dump.* She has three children (two at home and Hillery in college) and lives in Vermont.

Kristin van Ogtrop is a features editor at *Travel & Leisure.* Her articles have appeared in *Vogue, Mademoiselle, Seventeen,* and in the annual *Dictionary of Literary Biography.* She lives with her husband and their son, Owen, in Pelham, New York.

Helen Winternitz has made a habit of going to tough

places and writing about tough subjects. Her books include *East Along the Equator*, about the dictatorship in Zaire, which entailed her arrest by the dictator; *A Season of Stones*, about the strife between Palestinians and Israelis, which entailed her ducking stones and bullets, and *Capitol Games* (coauthored with her husband) about the unarmed war between Clarence Thomas and Anita Hill and their supporters, which entailed many a verbal battle. She and her husband live on the northern shore of Long Island with their son, Paul.

Naomi Wolf is the author of *The Beauty Myth* and *Fire with Fire: The New Female Power and How It Will Change the 21st Century*. Her articles, excerpts, and interviews have appeared in numerous national publications, and she travels the country lecturing on feminism and its impact on women's lives. She lives with her husband and their daughter in Chevy Chase, Maryland.

Meg Wolitzer is a novelist whose books include *Sleepwalking* and *This Is Your Life*, and whose upcoming novel is entitled *Surrender, Dorothy*. She lives in New York City with her husband and their sons, Gabriel and Charlie.

For information about the wonderful
postpartum depression support group
Depression After Delivery,
call 1-800-944-4PPD.
Or write: Depression After Delivery—National,
P.O. Box 1282, Morrisville, PA 19067.